I0817584

The Bottomless Cup

The Bottomless Cup

A Memoir

KEVIN BOEHM

ABRAMS PRESS, NEW YORK

Copyright © 2025 Kevin Boehm

Jacket © 2025 Abrams

Published in 2025 by Abrams Press, an imprint of ABRAMS. All rights reserved. No portion of this book may be reproduced, stored in a retrieval system, or transmitted in any form or by any means, mechanical, electronic, photocopying, recording, or otherwise, without written permission from the publisher.

Library of Congress Control Number: 2025937209

ISBN: 978-1-4197-7524-6
eISBN: 979-8-88707-335-4

Printed and bound in the United States
10 9 8 7 6 5 4 3 2 1

Abrams books are available at special discounts when purchased in quantity for premiums and promotions as well as fundraising or educational use. Special editions can also be created to specification. For details, contact specialsales@abramsbooks.com or the address below.

Abrams Press® is a registered trademark of Harry N. Abrams, Inc.

A small portion of this book describes suicidal ideation, which some may find disturbing. If you or someone you know is suicidal, please contact a medical professional or call your country's suicide prevention hotline. Additional resources are available online.

This book is dedicated to Sofia, Lola, and Luca.
You were always the happy ending to this story.

AUTHOR'S NOTE

MUCH OF THIS STORY UNSPOOLED in the technological Dark Ages before digital record-keeping and photography. I've done my best to re-create menus and menu items from memory, but there may be some inconsequential inaccuracies. The same is true for specific dates and dialogue. Out of respect for their privacy, some people's names have been changed.

CONTENTS

PROLOGUE

IN THE SPRING OF 2018, I stood on a stage at Lincoln Center, delivering a speech I had titled "The Restoration of My Soul."

I explained to the one thousand hospitality colleagues in attendance that I'd struggled to navigate happiness most of my life, and that now, after years wandering the emotional wilderness, I had finally found peace and community. It was the type of symposium where they didn't want you to just identify a problem—they wanted you to share the steps that you used to solve it, so I walked the crowd through how I had changed my life and found my way to true joy and a new me.

It sounded great, landed beautifully, and was complete and total bullshit.

In all honesty, I was a bipolar truth-bender who was struggling to maintain my sanity. It was like the insidious mind game of social media writ large: If I could convince one thousand people that my carefully crafted avatar was real, then I would magically become that person.

"The magic you are looking for, Kevin, is in the work you are avoiding," someone would tell me around this time. This was the absolute truth.

Somebody else told me, "Everybody is responsible, but no one is to blame." This, too, would prove true.

I have Forrest Gumped my way through a lifetime of restaurant adventures, stumbling into opportunities, relationships, and big moments. I have been the hero, the villain, the joker, the teacher, the voice of reason, and the cautionary tale in my half century on Earth. Substances came and went but ambition and adrenaline were always my drugs of choice. I was a master at creating frenzied highs.

Over the past thirty years I've opened forty restaurants, been awarded the highest honor in my profession, served everyone from Mick Jagger to President Obama, created an innovative private wellness club, spoke on marquee stages, cameoed as myself on the hit television show *The Bear*, and even found time to get married and have three children.

I've lived in my car, stood precariously on a ledge, repressed demons, and talked to angels. I've spiraled out of control and been pathologically disciplined. I came from strange stock and upheld the family tradition. I've had moments so exhilarating I felt like I could fly, and times so dark I considered packing it all in.

Ambitious people's lives often look ideal in a snapshot. The white veneers of a fake smile contrasting with a clear blue sky with trophies and an empire towering behind them. I sprinted toward happiness for almost five decades, with a faulty compass as my guide. I believed that if I kept achieving, love, forgiveness, and peace would naturally follow.

As a kid, I liked gamifying everything I did, and one of the only ways I knew to keep score was how I measured up in a competitive work environment. I already knew where I stood with Larry Boehm, my domineering and overbearing father, who told me I was worthless on the daily. I wanted and needed other opinions and positive reinforcement. This would be the type of dopamine rush I would not grow tired of.

I was good at working and turning ideas into reality. As a young boy, I grew tomatoes and sold them door-to-door to my elderly neighbors, delivered *The State Journal-Register* to the surrounding blocks on my beat-up Kmart bike, hawked baseball cards at local shows, shaved roast beef at Hardee's, and worked at my hometown's lone arthouse movie theater. My self-esteem was founded on a hard day's work and having scratch in my pocket.

Selling tomatoes in the driveway of the Little Blue House, 1980

Before I pushed off to college to start a new life, the universe decided to blow it all up. In 1989, just days before my escape from home, a strange childhood became much stranger. More on that later.

Eighteen-year-olds aren't known for balance. They are generally a house of cards, discovering their sexuality, their temperament, intoxicating substances, and living on their own for the first time. I went off so half-cocked and leaning to one side that just driving to the University of Illinois Urbana-Champaign without incident was going to be a trick. I made it to my dorm, but mentally I was weighed down by a paralyzing identity crisis.

Years later, I was successful in every way but the way that counted. I tried to create substitute households and surrogate families through my idealized version of home in the restaurants I helped build. They became my safest places.

The search for happiness has been like a fifty-year treasure hunt. The circuitous route I've taken to get where I am has taken me through magic carpet rides, dark roads, love affairs, wrestling matches, bobcats, booms, and bankruptcy. I wouldn't change one thing.

1
WE GOTTA GET OUT OF THIS PLACE

IT WAS AT THE D&J CAFE in Springfield, Illinois, midway through a Western omelet and my second cup of coffee, that I learned that I wasn't really Kevin Boehm.

That sounds like the first line in a pulpy detective novel. But in this case, your narrator—me—was just eighteen years old and a freshly minted high school graduate. This was August 1989, just four days before I was to push off for college at the University of Illinois Urbana-Champaign. Earlier that week, a phone call had intruded on my leafy, sun-dappled Midwestern summer: it came shrill and sudden one morning on the landline in my family's house. Home alone at that hour, I answered it.

The gravelly voice on the other end was unmistakably that of an older man. It blew in with hurricane force, pushing me away from the receiver:

"Good morning!"

Recovering, I put the receiver back to my ear.

"Good morning?" I said, meekly.

"Is that Kevin Boehm?"

"Yes. Who's this?"

If there's such a thing as a verbal firm handshake, here it was: "Kevin! This is Woody Valentine."

I knew that name. Mr. Valentine was a former employer and longtime friend of my mom's. Before I could say anything, he invited me to breakfast and a round of golf—a gesture of thanks, he said, for my mother's years of dutiful hard work and friendship.

It didn't compute that I should benefit from those sentiments, and I had less than zero interest in hanging with this man who was essentially a stranger. But at eighteen, I lacked the vocabulary and finesse to decline gracefully.

I had met Mr. Valentine a few times. Mom had been his speechwriter and assistant in the late 1960s, scripting his talks and tending to his bookings and billings as a motivational speaker. His signature message was, "Try the impossible—and dare to fail!" At Mom's suggestion, I'd once interviewed him for a school assignment that tasked us with profiling a community leader. And, of course, I never forgot that name: Woody Valentine—suitable for a ventriloquist dummy, or the dust-bowl lothario in a Hollywood Western.

But make no mistake about it: Woody Valentine was as real as they came. And as manly. At seventy, he was roughly a quarter-century older than my parents. I perceived him as ancient, but also stubbornly vital. A former professional boxer and politician, he crisscrossed the country, whipping downtrodden crowds into frenzies of purpose and belief. He projected a commanding presence underscored by a crushing, old-school handshake that mingled God-given brawn and war-vet machismo.

To save money for college, I had taken a summer job in the shoe department in the Montgomery Ward department store where Mom worked. There, I passed the days peddling discount pumps and steel-toe work boots to sensible, middle-class Midwesterners. Occasionally, Mr. Valentine would mosey by on the way to meet Mom for coffee. He never failed to wave to me. He didn't hold a conventional full-time job or have an office, but he did adhere to a uniform of sorts: slacks, dress shirt, and jacket, all neatly pressed, and anchored by freshly shined dress shoes—just buttoned-up enough to launch into one of his rousing addresses on a moment's notice.

Mr. Valentine maintained the boot-camp physique of the Army cadet he'd been a half-century prior and glided through life, thanks to the muscle memory from years of skipping around the ring. His silver hair was thick and slicked back, the same style I favored. Two hundred fights, or thereabouts, had left their mark in a droop in his right eyelid and a crooked nose. He'd attempted a boxing comeback after World War II, but the two toes he'd left on the battlefield cost him precious balance; he was laid out on the canvas after just a few dozen punishing seconds.

Despite an up-by-the-bootstraps backstory, Mr. Valentine wasn't bitter. To the contrary, he radiated a sun-in-your-face

Woody Valentine doing his best James Dean, 1937

American optimism that would have rendered Ronald Reagan morose by comparison. Laughter seemed to ripple just beneath his voice, and he was a born raconteur, with a well-rehearsed, expertly paced story ready for any conversation.

D&J Cafe was a standard-issue family restaurant: freestanding tables; cheap, stackable plastic chairs; black vinyl tablecloths on which streaks and stains vanished as if into a black hole; an extensive laminated menu; and a long counter with coffeepots and milkshake blenders standing at attention along the back bar.

Mr. Valentine struck me as out of sorts and uncharacteristically tentative that morning. As we dug into our pre-golf sustenance, he abandoned his customary attention to pacing and suspense and revealed why he'd summoned me.

"I know from your mom that you have never much cared for your father," he said, his eyes and lips crinkling kindly in their respective corners. Then he sucker punched me: "So perhaps it helps to know that I am actually your dad."

Time froze as the revelation snapped me into a state of shock. Through the sound system, in her countrified breakup song "Jesse," Carly Simon delineated all the things she would no longer do for the title character. I felt a sudden twinge of empathy for Larry Boehm, the man I'd known, painfully, as my father for close to two decades.

Shame, grief, and confusion engulfed me. I felt an urgency to disentangle them (what today we'd call *process*), but not in the presence of Woody, or anyone else.

I shut down, eyes fixed floorward.

"Please take me home," I said, without looking up.

WE DROVE IN SILENCE. THE ride felt exponentially longer than the minute or two it took to get to my neighborhood. The streets and sidewalks I'd known all my life seemed eerie and unfamiliar.

"Here is good," I said, two blocks from my house.

Before he slowed the car to a standstill, I threw open the door and jumped out, staggering until achieving balance, and ran toward Butler Elementary, my former grade school, where I took a seat in the deserted playground.

For two hours, I sifted a young lifetime of received lies from this new reality while waiting for Larry Boehm—an American J. Alfred Prufrock of unfailing habit and ritual—to finish lunch at home and return to his office. I decided to bury this revelation and not tell a soul. It would be years before I even mentioned it to my mom. Then I trudged toward our home on State Street, flanked by other modest houses, mostly populated by elderly folks who only emerged to pluck their morning papers from the lawn or collect their mail.

Woody's claim sheared the witness-protection-level façade of normalcy from my life. The Boehm family presented as conformity personified, from the cobblestone street where we lived, to our standard-issue, pale blue A-frame house, to the boxy, brown 1967 Chevy Impala in the driveway, to my "dad's" job as an underwriter at a small family-owned insurance firm.

Inside that A-frame was another story: Larry Boehm was no Ward Cleaver. He didn't socialize, and a mere three things got his juices going: the television series *M*A*S*H*; berating the rest of us; and a list-making fetish that today would tip even the most casual observer off to the fact that he was an undiagnosed obsessive-compulsive. And yet, Larry took pride in fulfilling the traditional bottom-line responsibilities of the American male: providing for his family and dutifully serving his employer. This burned all the fuel in his tank: He woke at 6 a.m., worked till 5 p.m., rinsed, and repeated.

Superficially, my mother, Dorothy—Dee to my father—was perfectly cast in her role. But if laughter flowed under Woody's voice, a river of tears coursed beneath hers. She had her reasons: A few ill-considered decisions had deposited the whip-smart, vibrant young woman she'd once been onto the loading dock of the Montgomery Ward department store at nearby White Oaks Mall, where most of her colleagues were in their fifties and sixties. In 1978, when she took a job there, following her stint with Mr. Valentine, they resented her for showing them up by working harder than they did. In time, they hated her for leapfrogging them to become operations manager.

The mother I first came to know as a child swayed and sang to Jim Croce and Joni Mitchell, painted watercolor landscapes, and wrote poetry—her soul still overflowing into the outlets of her youth. She was excruciatingly shy and Midwestern beautiful, like *Dick Van Dyke Show*–era Mary Tyler Moore.

I was two years younger than my sister, Missi, three grades behind her in school, and jealous that she elided the angst that nagged at me, maybe because she had a strong bond with Mom while I lacked one with Dad. Whatever the reason, Missi was sweet and straightforward and innately social. She was also what used to be called a tomboy, favoring baseball caps and oversized T-shirts. Like Mom, she was structured, responsible, and creative. We both were blessed with gonzo imaginations and relished funneling them into playacting, like *Escape from the Wild*, an old-timey radio soap opera we created and performed into a cassette recorder, down to a commercial jingle we wrote and produced for the show's fictional cereal sponsor.

Our house, which I've thought of as the Little Blue House since childhood, reflected the family's financial limitations: It was small, as if it had shrunk in the dryer. The sofas sagged when you sat, and stuffing poked out here and there where the fabric had torn. The door from the kitchen to our postage stamp of a backyard stuck, requiring a shoulder to budge it, and the jungle gym

Missi's first day of school, 1973

out there had been improvised from split-open rubber tires. Two rocks marked the resting place of our birds, Cub and Dodger.

Missi and I shared a room and a bed until it was no longer appropriate, then my father converted the attic into two Hobbit-sized bedrooms. Mine had a slanted ceiling so low that I could only stand up straight in the very center, like the seven-and-a-half floor in *Being John Malkovich*. Missi and I bonded over more than close quarters and a shared last name: we also had a common nemesis in Larry, who underestimated Missi simply because of his own insecurities and resentments, and loathed me, for reasons that became more obvious after my breakfast with Woody Valentine.

Oblivious to all of this was our dog Daisy, a beagle/springer spaniel mix. I also had my own personal dog, a stuffed Snoopy, given to me by my maternal grandfather, Avery. That stuffed animal absorbed untold tears as I curled up on my bed and clutched it tightly, sobbing after fights with Larry.

Missi and I had ringside season tickets to the never-ending tussle between Larry and Dee. They seemed never to have heard of the notion of parents presenting a united front. Conflict often ended with Dad indemnifying himself from any consequences that might arise from Mom's permissive decisions. When she okayed Missi and my walking the two blocks to Butler Elementary School in 1978, he declared to my mom, within earshot of us, "If anything happens to the kids, that's on you." Just months later, Missi and I walked home with my frequent companion Chris Blisset, who lived six doors down from us. Chris was impetuous,

I always huddled close to Mom in the occasional family picture.

loud, brash, and aggressive. He was basically Larry's worst nightmare. I loved him.

We were often held in check by Larry's constant worst-case scenarios, and when Chris sprinted across a busy street, we stayed back to let it clear. He was struck by a Ford Torino and sent flying across Ash Street into a light pole. His Snoopy lunchbox landed at our feet, a half-eaten PB&J and pocket change littering the sidewalk.

We thought he was dead. Missi and I led thc police to his mom's house and watched her scream and sprint down State Street. When Larry got home, we sat in shock as he doled out "I told you sos" to Mom and two crying kids.

MY DAD BLENDED RIGHT INTO Springfield's perpetual gray landscape. Mom, as I first knew her, was the sun straining to break through.

But that was an illusion. One of my earliest memories is of happening upon her in our basement, crying.

"Why are you sad, Mommy?" I asked, then ventured the sort of unfiltered guess only an eight-year-old could: "Is it because your life is so boring?"

A TV and pop-culture junkie from earliest childhood, I had seen how fancy city people lived—the jet-setting swells who populated TV shows like *Dallas* and *Hart to Hart*. I'd always thought Mom would have fit in seamlessly at their cocktail parties, posh country clubs, and right in the white-tablecloth restaurants those characters frequented.

"Sometimes I just get sad," she'd said, her tears vanishing like a special effect. "All people get sad, sometimes." She dabbed at the corners of her eyes, smoothed her blouse, and marched upstairs.

I knew that Mom was sad more often than other mothers. I also knew that my father was cruel to her. And I knew that deep down in that reservoir of stifled tears was a talent that, had she zigged a few times when she should have zagged, might have led to a life more rewarding than checking manifests against the cargo trucks that beeped while backing their way up to the Montgomery Ward loading dock.

There was neither a washer nor a dryer in that basement—an anomaly in the 1980s. Missi and I wanted them, but Mom refused, citing a trio of objections: It's too expensive; we kids would waste water by using it too much; and we didn't have the space. (In hindsight, all three reasons were as legitimate as I was.)

Instead, every Sunday for twenty years, my mom would don her finest clothes, make up her face, and mist herself with Shalimar. The routine commenced right around when *60 Minutes* came on; by the time curmudgeon humorist Andy Rooney began his weekly grousing, she had loaded up the laundry and was gone. Four hours later, we would hear her car pull back into the driveway.

One Sunday when I was fifteen, I forgot to toss my favorite Levi's in the hamper. I took off with them in hand to track her down, driving to the three closest laundromats, only to come up empty. When she returned home and I recounted my attempt to find her, she snapped, "Don't do that! If you forget to add something, that's your problem."

In the fall of 2019, I sat beside Mom during a chemo session, holding her hand, just the two of us in a small treatment room at St. John's Hospital in Springfield, just as I'd held her hand as a child when I sat behind her in the family car, discreetly reaching along the passenger-side door.

She was gaunt, a salt-and-pepper wig mimicking the hair that chemo had claimed, but was also strangely brighter and more at ease than usual.

"Well, kid," she said. "If you've got any questions for me, you better ask them now."

I got right to it: "Laundry night . . . that was you and Woody, right?"

I had long since deduced the truth about those evenings, and she confirmed it for me. I didn't ask about another conclusion I'd reached: that her secret life must have offered occasional, fleeting happiness and crushing regret, in equal measure. No wonder she cried.

There's always another layer in my family. Even as the last grains of sand passed through her hourglass, she layered a new revelation over the old ones: Until I was three, she told me, I'd spent weekday afternoons at Woody's house. His wife, Thelma, worked all day, which gave him and Mom a chance to play family, only instead of with a doll, they did it with a flesh-and-blood child—me.

One night, as my language skills blossomed, I started telling Larry Boehm about playing Rock 'Em Sock 'Em Robots at Mr. Valentine's house. My mom abruptly cut me off, along with my double life. After that, Woody had to settle for peering in along the edges of my childhood and adolescence. Both before and after that interview we'd done for school, I'd always felt a twinge of something like déjà vu when I discerned his face in the crowd at cross-country meets and soccer games, an apparition from a past life, keeping tabs on the present.

As with death and dying, there are stages to learning about a forgotten chapter in your life, especially at age fifty: first, it defies belief; then it makes you feel like a bystander to your own existence; and eventually you come to accept it. What choice do you have?

LARRY BOEHM HATED ME PRETTY much from day one. I know from those deathbed dialogues with Mom that she never acknowledged my true paternity to him. But anybody in his position with a basic grasp of reproductive science and awareness of the infrequency of their lovemaking would have known that he couldn't have been my biological father. Still, according to my parents' unspoken pact of deception, and my birth certificate, he was.

This always struck me as unfortunate, for many reasons. Through constant emotional jabs and a few physical ones, he imparted a flawed model of fatherhood, family, and security. Physically, there was the time he hit me in the face outside a JCPenney for having feigned throwing a baseball in the store, and then when he clutched me by the throat for tracking water from my kiddie pool into the living room. But those were isolated incidents. His verbal abuse ran on an endless loop and, in its own way, hurt more. In fourth grade, I retaliated against a school bully. My parents were called in for a meeting, where Larry interrogated me: "What are you doing to make this kid not like you so much?" More generally, he often stifled me by saying, "Nobody wants to hear you talk so much, least of all me." These rejoinders grew more frequent as my natural, gregarious personality flowered, offering him an even greater wealth of opportunities to voice his disdain. And there were daily indignities that didn't require a triggering incident, such as his telling me that I had no common sense, and that I was and always would be a loser.

We didn't dine out much, but MCL Restaurant at White Oaks Mall was our post-church ritual. Although it was just a traditional cafeteria where you carried your dishes from the buffet steam tables to your table on plastic trays, it felt fancy to me, with an Abraham Lincoln–themed dining room, cherry wainscoting, and porters who wore bow ties and crisp white shirts. It was also the first place I ever felt the warm embrace of hospitality.

One Sunday, I accidentally flipped my tray full of food all over my brand-new OshKosh B'gosh overalls. Larry lost his mind. In between *fucks* and *goddamn idiots*, a kind server intervened.

"It's okay, sir. He didn't mean it. It happens all the time. Tell me what you were eating, young man."

Before I knew it, he had helped me clean up, embarrassed Larry into a silent simmer, and replenished my tray. As he walked away, he looked back and winked at me.

I'd found an ally in a restaurant dining room. It wouldn't be my last.

FOR HER PART, MOM HAD instilled in me the belief that idle hands were a moral aberration. She worked fifty hours a week, ran five miles a day, read doorstop-sized books, gardened on weekends, and nurtured both a marriage and a secret love affair. In comparison to her, I wasn't, nor would I ever be, doing enough. Whether working at a job, owning a restaurant, or between gigs, one question always buzzed at a low frequency in my mind: "What's next?"

The dynamic infected me with an emotional tapeworm—starved for love and affection, yet disbelieving of them when they're offered. I wasn't helped by Larry's suspicion of any compliment. "They must be trying to sell me something," he'd sneer whenever somebody outside the family complimented him.

After that breakfast with Woody, I understood that Larry's smacks were intended for him. But it was too late to matter. There are family Kodak pictures from the seventies and eighties in which I now perceive the sadness in the eyes of my young self and Mom's forced smile. I am the keeper of those photos but can't stand to look at them.

MY MOM WAS ONE OF fourteen siblings who grew up on the family's working dairy farm in Roscommon, Michigan. Her clan was a dictatorship, and the strongman at its core was her father, Justice Avery Babcock. Dee joined the farm crew at age six, rousing at 4:30 each morning for three hours of hard labor. She milked cows, baled hay, fed livestock, and cleaned shit out of pens—all before crossing the street to a one-room schoolhouse, where at one point she and her siblings accounted for ten of eighteen students. By the time she was fourteen, she had already felt the full force of Avery's baseball-mitt hand on both her face and backside, and suffered the lifelong trauma of sexual abuse by a distant relative. She didn't share these things with me until she was at death's door, but some vague psychic damage had always shown in her mournful, darting eyes and tentative gait. Except for hand-holding, she also recoiled from intimacy, even the emotional intimacy between parent and child; whenever we hugged, she ended it quickly with a pat on my back.

I guess Mom inherited her artistic bent from her mother, Rosemary, who made beautiful patchwork quilts from fabric squares harvested from hand-me-down dresses and curtains. She made my baby blanket, and my mother took up quilt-making in the last twenty years of her life, donating her work products to Lutheran World Relief Mission Quilts. There are still children around the globe who sleep under quilts that she fashioned.

Mom made most of her teenage decisions with the long view in mind—the overriding goal was to escape Roscommon and Avery. In addition to tending the farm, she worked another job throughout her junior and senior years to save money for college. At her father's insistence, she turned her earnings over to him for safekeeping. When she asked for her nest egg, he revealed that he had given it all to one of her sisters, who, he explained, wasn't "as fortunate" as my mother. My mom had earned valedictorian honors in high school, and been awarded a scholarship at Central Michigan University. She'd planned to use that money for meals and books, and now had to work straight through college. This final indignity hardened her resolve never to return. It also sparked a matrimonial imperative and urgency. She desperately wanted to

Mom, 1964, valedictorian of Gerrish-Higgins High School

pair up with someone who could facilitate her escape, an intention that drove her straight into the scarecrow arms of Larry Boehm. They met in 1964 at the university dining hall when, purely by happenstance, she sat at his table. They were married in less than a year.

Wedding day, 1965, Sylvia clearly not happy about the union

Following college graduation, Larry took a job with the Dow Chemical Company in Detroit, then an internship with Standard Mutual Insurance Company in Springfield. That was when my mother answered an ad seeking a speechwriter for Woody Valentine. When Larry's internship concluded, they moved back to Michigan, which is why I was born in Flint. He then accepted a full-time job with Standard in Springfield, and he and Mom relocated there for good.

Just weeks before Mom died, I asked her by text what the defining moment of her life was. She texted back that it was marrying Larry, a "mistake" she'd recognized within days of tying the knot. Her text read:

> We were coming back from our honeymoon. We were driving in the Houghton Lake, Michigan, area where we were

> going to spend the night. Remember now, that I had never stayed in a motel or cabin before. He started screaming at me because I was unable to pick a suitable one as we were driving. Realization hit as he was screaming. I thought, "Oh my God, I don't know this person. I should never have married him."

She also explained that in her haste to escape her father, she'd married a man just like him. At a time when divorce was frowned upon, this amounted to a life sentence.

Both Larry and Dee would have benefited from therapy, but instead—after the fashion of the time—they chose repression. They didn't sleep in the same bed, and never hugged, kissed, or even held hands, at least not in my presence. Mostly, they fought. Missi and I would crank up the volume of *CBS Radio Mystery Theater* on our clock radio to drown out their arguments.

LARRY BOEHM, SON TO SYLVIA and Arthur, was an only child of German descent, and would have been a perfect movie nerd: He wore thick glasses and, in the summer, sported black socks hiked up to his knees. Arthur was a shipbuilder, softspoken and uncomplicated. In contrast, Sylvia was loud, domineering, and dogmatic. He was the chalkboard; she was the fingernails.

Larry's obsessive-compulsive disorder compounded these flaws. Even the most mundane activities loomed as potentially combustive. One summer, before leaving to visit family in Michigan, Mom, Missi, and I wilted in the car for ninety minutes while he repeatedly checked that all the doors and windows in the house were locked. Ninety minutes, for a grand total of two doors and seven windows. When my mom braved the house to retrieve him, he snapped at her.

His OCD was relentless. He kept a notepad on the dining room table, on which he chronicled our missteps and annoyances. If, say, you left a twist tie off the plastic bag for a loaf of bread, or didn't properly fold a bedsheet, into the ledger it went, rendered in handwriting in block letters like a serial killer's.

I now recognize that my success as a restaurateur owes much to Larry Boehm's terrifying volatility. Out of self-preservation, Missi and I developed a sixth sense for which way his mood was swinging, the same way Floridians know a storm's brewing because they can intuit shifts in barometric pressure that others can't. This is essential in my work: Does a party want you to chat them up, or take their order and beat it? Are they ready for the check, or planning to linger? Do they require a guided tour of the menu, or are they seasoned and self-sufficient foodies? Full credit to Larry Boehm for handing down an emotional divining rod that tells me the answers to these and a million other questions nightly, based only on a feeling.

Larry worked hard, but to little avail or advancement, toiling in a job where others took the credit, or at least that's how he described it. We never had money for dining out or sharp clothing. *Vacation* meant driving across one state line to visit family in Michigan. I didn't fly on an airplane until I was twenty-three. We drank powdered milk and subsisted on concoctions like a Dee Boehm signature dish, Hamburger on Rice—white rice and ground beef, bound together by Campbell's cream of mushroom soup.

These deficiencies, too, seeded the restaurateur I became. Starting at age six, I tried to improve our living situation, or perform a different one. My sister and I often operated a pretend restaurant in our basement rec room, a spartan, garishly lit space with a boiler in the corner. We'd scribble a menu on a reclaimed chalkboard propped against the wall, then one of us would wait on

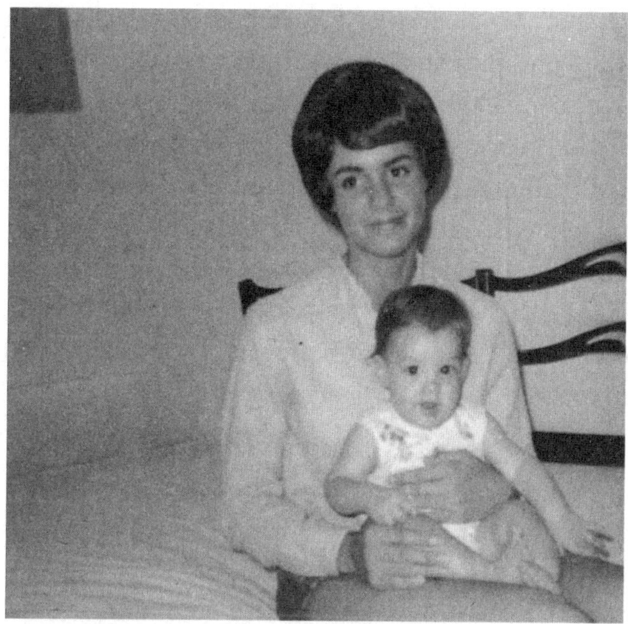

The beginning of a beautiful relationship, 1971

the other. The one house specialty I remember is what she dubbed Apple Fondue: wedges of McIntosh apple arrayed around a cup of water for dipping. When I was just ten, I'd told Mom I wanted to own a restaurant one day. Throughout Illinois, many immigrants had prospered in restaurants, like the Thai family who owned Magic Kitchen in Springfield. So it always struck me as an industry in which anybody, from even the most meager backgrounds, could make it.

I was also transfixed by the magic and mystique emanating from the food presented on television shows, including rare and expensive delicacies that never trickled down to my powdered-milk world. Alexis Carrington from the TV show *Dynasty* was the fictional embodiment of wealth, style, and eccentricity, much the way the nonfictional Kim Kardashian is today. What was it about Beluga caviar that made her shiver with excitement? On

Fantasy Island, Mr. Roarke welcomed guests with champagne and explained to one of them that oysters were an aphrodisiac. I didn't know what that meant, but it sounded as if these gifts from the sea had the power to electrify one's body with pleasure. What the hell was I missing out on! At least the Little Blue House and its small black-and-white Zenith television offered me a window onto exciting worlds and invited me to imagine myself within them.

Outside the house, I was skittish and unconfident. Mom dressed me in off-brand jeans, Salvation Army clothes, and chili-bowl haircuts she did herself, just like on the farm. I was also color-blind, so I failed a color test in kindergarten. I knew other kids

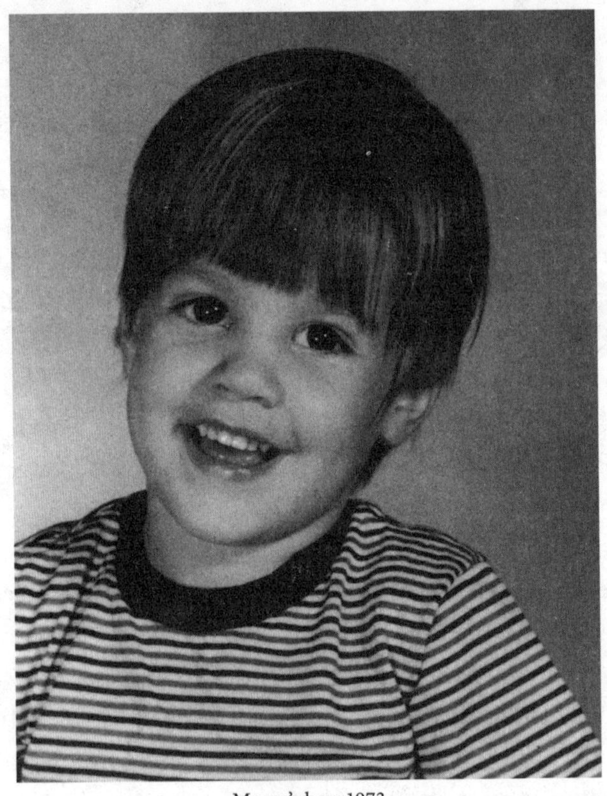

Mama's boy, 1973

ridiculed me for these things. In sixth grade, as a prank, some of them invited me to a costume party that wasn't really a costume party. When a friend tipped me off to the ruse, I thought, *Maybe Larry's right; maybe I am a loser.* In order to afford better haircuts and decent threads, I got my first job, as a paperboy, at age twelve, and the cruel kid chatter subsided.

In my teens, I did what I could to make the house more presentable and cozy for visitors who never materialized: I regularly and compulsively Pledged the furniture, and once bartered my boom box for a pair of used sofas. They weren't much, but at least they

Mom and me, framed by one of her beautiful landscapes, 1978

weren't leeching stuffing. I didn't ask my parents for permission before dragging the old ones out to the curb for trash collection.

This industriousness was counterbalanced by unpredictable periods of sadness and inertia that confused me. Some days I just woke up blue, as I had found Mom that day in the basement. I'd lie in bed for hours, or stare blankly at the TV without retaining what was playing out on the screen. Sometimes it felt like a paralyzing lack of motivation; others, it was as if a pall had been draped over my world, and there was no point in doing anything. Nothing identifiable brought on these bouts. They were as random-seeming and beyond my control as the weather. That's how I came to think of them, as gradations of sunny days, overcast days, stormy days, and dark nights of the soul. I lived in my own meteorological reality, as do most people. However, in the 1970s and '80s it took a Jordan-like leap to go from recognizing your own moodiness to a diagnosis of manic depression. Seeing Timothy Hutton's Oscar-winning turn as a suicidal suburbanite in *Ordinary People* was the first time I considered that my own dark turns might be more than just bad days.

At Southeast High, I was mostly an A student, but a lazy one, coasting through classes without amassing any real knowledge. Only one educator cared enough to call me on it: English teacher Sandy Wands. A towering six feet tall, with a baritone voice, she grabbed me by the arm after I'd turned in a paper that outclassed my earlier work, revealing my untapped potential.

"Quit selectively using your intelligence," she admonished me. "You were blessed to be born smart. Don't waste it."

I received similar encouragement from Beverly Criglar, the no-nonsense mother of my friend Melinda. "I can't wait to see your little movie play out," she would say to me. "Whatever you do, it's going to be fun to watch."

When I was fifteen and school let out for the year, Mom told me that I had to get a real job, defined by her as "someone actually managing you, and you get a real paycheck, with taxes taken out." In her eyes, I had outgrown selling tomatoes and delivering papers. Three weeks into the summer, I still hadn't fulfilled her order. But that didn't keep me from asking her for five dollars.

"I told you to get a job three weeks ago," she snapped. "I did not raise you to be lazy. And, just like God, I only help those who help themselves." Twenty-four hours later, I started working at Hardee's and can count on one hand the days when I haven't had at least a part-time job since.

Mom did most of the essential parenting, including the talks that traditionally take place between father and son. For example, the only sex advice I received from either of them was her admonishing me that, "Once you fire the gun, you can't retrieve the bullet."

My confidence and masculinity began to flourish when I entered high school, and I often found myself keeping the peace in our house. It was so small, with so many hard surfaces, that loud words bounced off the walls like a Super Ball, a cacophony of anger that made my head hurt. It was about this same time that I began to develop more physical courage—when a kid gave me a cheap shot on the soccer field, I took a swing at him with what I now recognize as a genetically lethal right hook.

Missi left for college at Eastern Illinois in 1986. After that, the house never seemed to be inhabited at the same time by the three remaining people. Each of us was on our own schedule; a Venn diagram of our lives would have been three freestanding circles. The only constant companion for all of us was Scooter, the beagle-coonhound mix my parents took in after Daisy passed.

From my sophomore year onward, this helped me discover my innate and probably life-saving knack for independence. I always had a job, including my first food service operation—okay, it was an open-air speakeasy—in a cornfield in Mechanicsburg, Illinois. Those keg parties you see in movies like *Dazed and Confused* created some real work for someone behind the scenes. Some teenage kid, in this case me, had to have a fake ID and the balls to use it, procure a keg, and find an open field sequestered enough to avoid the cops. I ran my little operation on the occasional Saturday at three dollars a cup. This enterprise seeded my restaurateur skill set. I didn't just sell beer, I provided ambience: My car radio blasted local classic rock station Magic 100, wafting the Eagles, Pink Floyd, and Led Zeppelin through the stalks. I developed systems and norms, like changing the colors of the cups I used each week so I could bust scammers who showed up with their own. (I myself got busted once, by the cops, losing me the $35 deposit on a keg. Even at that age, I accepted this as the cost of doing business.)

And I got my first taste of the public's lamentable undervaluing of what people like me do: "What the fuck, dude!" complained Tommy Fink, a classmate of mine who always showed up with his wingman, Mike. "Three dollars for a cup? I could get a whole six-pack for that much." Never mind the trouble and expense it took to procure the keg, the music, the girls I admitted for free—I guess he figured that was all altruism on my part.

This self-sufficiency extended to home life, too: I developed rudimentary cooking skills so that I could prepare my own meals, and kept compulsively busy to distract from the never-ending family turmoil. My phony driver's license was up to snuff at Bob and Norma's Liquors, and I was often a conquering hero when I met my friends, the pony keg in the trunk tipping my Chevy Chevette back on its rear wheels.

I couldn't wait to leave home. I remember sitting with my friend Sherry, telling her that I had to get out of Springfield. "This is a dark place," I said.

She probably thought I was out of my mind, perhaps because I uttered these words on a picture-perfect summer day, and she couldn't perceive the stormy skies clouding my perception.

When senior year wrapped up, I signed everybody's yearbook with "See you back here . . . never!"

I pretty much somnambulated through the four days between breakfast with Woody and pushing off for college. I tried not to think about my true genealogy, but it was impossible to fully suppress it. Somehow, I kept it to myself—I didn't even mention the breakfast to Mom. She was my hero parent, and I didn't want to make her a fallen angel. I needed her too much.

When the moment arrived, I crammed two milk crates with clothes, cards and letters, pictures, and my Snoopy doll.

But who was "I"? I wasn't Kevin Boehm. I wasn't Larry's son. I didn't have any full biological siblings. I probably wasn't only German, Irish, and French. And the one person I counted on for the unvarnished truth had been leading a secret life—had foisted one upon me.

It was time to leave it all behind and figure out who I was, and what I was worth, if I was worth anything. There would be numb times ahead, but this was a moment when I felt everything, as if the act of leaving Springfield uncorked a deluge that would wash me away if I didn't outpace it. Before me, there were seventy-nine miles of corn-stalk-flanked highway. I had eighty minutes to grieve what never was and imagine what might be. I screamed all that emotion out most of the way there, an exorcism that, if nothing else, would enable me to pass for normal when I arrived at the dorm and met my new floor mates.

2
RUNNIN' DOWN A DREAM

I DIDN'T SERIOUSLY CONSIDER BECOMING a restaurateur until my first year at the University of Illinois. Yes, I'd told my mother I wanted to go into restaurants when I was ten, but at that age, I was also counting on being Johnny Carson's go-to sub on *The Tonight Show* and accompanying Olivia Newton-John to the Grammys. I was pretty sure at age eighteen that the American Dream was reserved for the brilliant, and at this point all I knew was that I came from nothing, which made me feel like a nothing.

And, boy, did U of I underscore my nothingness. Two of my housemates were budding successes: One, Mike Hopkins (or Hoppy, as we called him), would go on to become an astronaut; the other would become a published author. They were smart, confident, and wise. They also were relentless in pursuit of their goals, where I didn't even have one. (It's like the comedian Bob Hope once said of a bodybuilder: "He has muscles in places where I don't even have places.") Around my roomies, the voice that told me I was destined for restaurants grew incrementally from a tentative internal whisper to a scream.

Finally, I shared it with one of the guys in the house.

"If you want to open a restaurant," he asked nonchalantly, "why aren't you studying for that?"

"I dunno. I have no mentor. No money. It all just seems out of reach."

He glanced over at Hoppy and deadpanned, "Kevin, Mike thinks he's going to be an astronaut."

Touché, I thought to myself.

Mike probably didn't have a pathologically critical father. Whether or not that alone explained my lack of self-belief, I required a greater reservoir of validation to take such an unconventional leap.

Or that's what I thought. Turned out, I needed the opposite: to be brought so low that restaurants would emerge as the only viable option. My first semester at U of I was a painful lesson in how far behind I truly lagged, not only compared to those two overachievers, and not only academically. Stylistically, I was also bringing up the rear, sporting a hairband mullet while cosmopolitan Chicagoans arrived with heavily moussed, sideburned Luke Perry cuts.

I was, at long last, heeding Ms. Wands's encouragement and trying. Hard. But it was an uphill trudge, and I wasn't sure if I was cut out for it.

I took advantage of the college library for more than just my challenging studies. I naturally wanted to know more about my biological father, and pieced together a dossier, mostly through research in old newspapers. Woody hadn't just been a boxer; he was a bona fide Golden Gloves champion. During his military service, he'd landed in the brig a few times for going AWOL. After his honorable discharge, he occasionally worked the ring as a referee. He'd also been the athletic director at John Brown University in Arkansas, special assistant to two Illinois governors, and head of civil defense for the State of Illinois. He had sold insurance, testified before Congress to advocate for boxing regulations, and trained pugilists. This was all in addition to motivational speaking.

Home for Christmas, January 1990, already plotting my escape

The more I learned, the more I daydreamed about who Kevin Valentine, raised by this high-achieving man of action, might have been. I suspect I wouldn't have become a restaurateur. With nothing to prove, maybe I would have settled into a safe (i.e., dull) but lucrative office-bound profession and raised a family in

Norman Rockwellian bliss. Turns out that alternate reality, at least the Kevin Valentine part, had almost come to pass.

One afternoon in January at U of I, having just turned nineteen years old, I emerged from my last class of the day to find Woody sitting on a bench, nursing a cup of coffee as the sky darkened around him. Establishing a pattern that would endure for years, he had asked my mother about my whereabouts and schedule, then appeared unannounced. We strolled the campus together as he offered me more scraps of my fractured family's story.

When my mother told Woody she was pregnant all those years ago, he had pushed all his chips into the center of the table and asked her to leave Larry and run away with him. He was fifty-one; she was just twenty-four; and they both had families. Missi was only two; Woody's children were wrapping up high school. As Woody told it, his marriage had been slowly, imperceptibly corroding for years, and he was ready to start over with the love of his life, if only my mother would say yes.

He almost got his wish: Mom told Larry she was leaving, but he threatened suicide, activating her Protestant guilt and putting the kibosh on her plans. On December 21, 1970, Woody drove all night through a treacherous snowstorm to be present, or at least in the building, for my birth at McLaren Flint hospital in Flint, Michigan. He lurked in a corridor just off the maternity ward until Larry left for home, then spent twenty minutes at Mom's bedside—their double lives subsuming mine the night I came into the world. After that, Woody was there for her, and me, as much as possible from the sidelines.

ONE SILVER LINING OF GOING to college was that while my new friends and acquaintances contended with homesickness, I luxuriated in freedom from Larry's paranoia and constant surveillance and a break from contemplating my identity. U of I was indeed U "of I"—I could be whoever I wanted to be, with no strings attached. Presumably, the feeling would compound the farther I wandered from the Little Blue House.

This odd jumble of insecurities and sense of self led me to consider finally chucking it all and taking a run at restaurants. The more I considered it, the more it beckoned as the perfect place to harness my social skills. I also thought, instinctually, and perhaps naively, that I had what it took to chart my own course in that world. Most appealing was that it would be my decision.

I hatched a plan to head south in my Chevy Chevette, all the way to southernmost Florida. I imagined myself arriving in sun-drenched paradise and finding employment in a restaurant, any restaurant. I envisioned a training montage in which I progressed through a series of jobs in ever-more-legitimate restaurants, accumulating skills and relationships. In time, I saw myself bringing it all back to the Midwest, but not to Champaign or Springfield. Chicago was the goal—that would be my trip to space.

Why Florida? It would be an extreme and welcome change of scenery and weather, and I wanted to get as far as realistically possible from home. I was drawn to raking in money rather than shelling it out, as I'd been doing since arriving at college. And I was slowly coming to believe that college was a bridge, while restaurants were a destination.

And Florida, protruding like a diving board from the base of the United States, dared me to launch myself headfirst into the unknown. I already had a car and didn't need much money to get there. All that remained was to summon the courage—and maybe a dash of stupidity—to take the plunge.

IN MAY 1990, WHEN MY FIRST year of college ended, I arrived home to an emotional war zone.

I walked into the Little Blue House, duffel bag slung over my shoulder, to discover Larry pacing about in a frenzy, his hair wildly askew.

"I'm sorry to tell you this, Kevin," he said breathlessly. "But your mom has been spending time with an older man."

Here's what happened just before I showed up: Larry had needed to ask my mother a time-sensitive question while she was out walking Scooter and discovered her with Woody. Turned out that for years my mother had been meeting Woody at Washington Park, a few miles from our house. They'd stroll back toward our neighborhood, then separate before they were likely to be espied by neighbors. Larry had grabbed Woody by the collar and cocked his fist. Woody, the former middleweight, calmly and humanely said, "Larry, you don't want to do this."

I couldn't determine if Larry was seeking empathy from me or he thought I might know something about Mom's relationship.

I dropped my duffel bag and put my hand up. "Listen, Dad, I don't want to get involved with this."

Larry told me that he was going to blow things up by tipping off his counterpart in cuckoldry and cold-calling Woody's wife. Sure enough, the phone book was splayed open on our small dining room table to the *V*'s.

I assume he called Thelma but can't say for sure.

Larry pined for emotional justice. He needed me to understand that my mother was not the victim-hero I made her out to be, and that it was he who deserved my sympathy. Of course, he had a point, though he had only himself to blame for not letting her leave in peace when she tried.

I made myself scarce for the rest of the summer, working at the mall, competing in volleyball tournaments, reanimating my keg-party hustle, and enjoying the life of a young single man.

That summer, at Woody's invitation, I had a chance to see him speak to a group of high schoolers whose star athlete classmate had perished in a DUI crash. Woody lectured the group on why drinking and driving was a gamble, not only with their lives but with those of everyone they were connected to.

Watching from offstage, I was impressed and proud of this father I barely knew. He was the opposite of Larry. Just knowing I was the product of him and my mom helped offset years of insecurity and make me believe that I might have the stuff to thrive in the world beyond Springfield.

"According to Newton," Woody said at the crescendo of his presentation, "the force that an object exerts on another object is equal to the mass of the object times its acceleration until—*bam*!" He pounded his fist into the microphone.

The crowd gasped. Young boys held their heads in their hands and girls broke into tears.

As he walked out, the principal said, "Don't you think you were a little hard on them?"

Woody didn't break stride as he simply said, "No."

Come August, as my escape back to college drew close, Mom told me she was leaving Montgomery Ward to take a job as general manager of the T.J. Maxx in Champaign, Illinois, the city where I attended college. She planned to commute the 79 miles each way, and wanted to know if she could crash at the off-campus one-bedroom pad I was renting on the nights when she had to work late.

No matter how much any twenty-year-old loves his mother, the last thing he wants is for her to be his college roommate. I obliged. She only stayed over intermittently, but this intrusion hastened my departure from the University of Illinois. As in a theatrical farce, Mom, Woody, and Larry all took turns showing up, sometimes on the same day.

Between these constant reminders of my family turmoil and my own rudderlessness, I often plummeted to the depths of depression. I didn't connect it to anything diagnosable; to me it was all just circumstantial.

"If it gets any worse, I'll just kill myself," I said once to a U of I classmate. "The only reason I'm still around is I can't afford to buy a gun."

I was half joking, but only half. I hadn't really considered taking my life, at least not seriously enough to have thought about the method or mechanics of it. But I was finding that one of the downsides of maturing, at least for me, was that the innate optimism of youth falls away. My dark times were pitch black. Those inner storms had grown apocalyptic. If fate were to claim me, I honestly wouldn't have minded. I sometimes fantasized about being diagnosed with inoperable cancer, or being crushed by a Mack truck on the highway. Not existing would have been fine.

Something needed to change, and fast. All through the fall term, I sat in classes and daydreamed about restaurants and Florida, sketching out a plan in my comp lit notebook. By the time December rolled around, I had decided to drop out and go for it.

Larry's OCD helped force this decision. The minutes, hours, and days he spent vacillating, reconsidering, and double-checking added up to a squandered life. I would rather throw caution to the wind, make more mistakes, but live. Playing by the rules seemed overrated. Spielberg, Gates, Ellison, Oprah, Geffen—all were college dropouts.

The decision must have seemed rash from the outside looking in. It certainly did to Larry. The last thing he said to me before I left was, "If you do this, you're going to end up a beach bum." (Mom was more supportive, gifting me a calling card so I could stay in touch without taking more of a financial hit.)

The day I left Champaign, Illinois, for good, 1991

I made one investment in my near future, spending most of my little nest egg on a used, dented, tan Suzuki Samurai. I thought it reflected my energy and would be more suited to Florida swelter than the Chevette. I headed south with five hundred dollars cash in my pocket and those crates full of photographs, my Snoopy doll, my clothes, and a basketball.

My plan was to secure two restaurant jobs and save everything I made from one while I lived off the other—work six doubles and sleep on Sundays. Eventually, I thought, I would be able to squirrel away enough money to open my own place.

I had only circled the state of Florida on a map, not a particular city. By the time I reached North Florida, and gas money and meals had just about depleted my meager bankroll, I decided that I'd make Panama City my new home.

I didn't know that midwinter was the low season in that region of Florida because it's colder than the southern part of the state. The only job I could land was an attendant at an amusement park called Emerald Falls, a dinky Six Flags knockoff that sprawled along a vast stretch of Thomas Drive. It paid $4.25 per hour. The daytime crew were the lifers, grizzled and jaded, while the nighttime and weekend team comprised high school and junior college kids.

Among my coworkers there was Jeff, the Putt-Putt cashier, who was in the market for a roommate. When he showed me his apartment, my new reality overtook my fantasy. He lived in a sad little two-bedroom with a stucco ceiling, track lighting, and the subtle bouquet of mold that's omnipresent in Florida. Two weeks after moving in, I walked in on him stealing cash from a shoebox I kept stashed in the closet. Instinct kicked in and I clocked him with my genetically quick right cross. Credit me with a knockdown, but he won the more consequential fight by evicting me.

With very little cash, no place to live, and a week remaining until my next paycheck, I alternatively slept on the beach and in my car, which is a way of saying I was, in the parlance of the time, homeless. I once heard a comedian say that the first time you live in your car, you think, *This is going to make a really good book someday.* The second time you live in your car, you think, *There probably isn't going to be a book.* Fortunately, this only happened once.

For warmth and comfort, I swiped a red-plaid sleeping bag from the back of a flatbed truck and climbed into it when I chose the beach as a bedroom.

After my first night there, I woke up to the cries of a mother warning her kids, "Get away from that!"

I snapped to, ready to be the Good Samaritan, only to be met by a huddle of young boys, gazing down. Turns out she was fearful of *me*.

Another morning, I used the calling card to reach out to my mother from a pay phone outside a nearby Jr. Food Store. I told her things were going well, that she shouldn't worry, and—the only true thing I said—that she wouldn't believe the view that greeted me every morning.

Occasionally, I'd change to a bathing suit and soap and shampoo under the outdoor shower at the beach meant for washing off sand and saltwater.

Eventually, I was able to rent a room at Mrs. White's Boarding House on Middle Beach Road for fifty dollars a week, which included breakfast. Mrs. White owned several cats, to which I was allergic. I woke up most days with puffy eyes and splotchy red welts on my neck; if not for the temperate climate, allowing me to keep the windows open, I would've had to move out.

After paying the rent each week, five dollars remained for living expenses. This called for creativity; in my case, a liberal interpretation of an all-you-can-eat salad bar. One Monday, I ordered the SuperBar from the local Wendy's for $4.28, including tax. After lunch, rather than garbage the Styrofoam plate, I tucked it inside a folded *USA Today* newspaper, which I reused for the lifespan of this ruse. Every day after that, I'd slip in amid the lunchtime crush, ask for a water (no charge), and discreetly pile food on my old plate. The remaining seventy-two cents went into my gas tank. After two weeks' worth of double shifts at Emerald Falls, I had saved enough money to move into a condo with a new roommate, Eric, whom I'd met one Friday night at the Formula K racetrack where we were both hitting on girls. Eric kept a workout bench and weights out back, and seemed to be a stand-up guy.

"Florida Man" headlines weren't yet a running joke in 1991, but an unexpected visitor to my new condo that June was tailor-made for a *Panama City News Herald* front page. A bobcat, kept illegally as a pet by a neighbor, escaped their house and ran into ours. It blurred past me so quickly I couldn't tell what kind of animal it was, then proceeded to treat the house like an obstacle course before running upstairs and finally taking refuge in my housemate's room. I followed it into the dark room and reached for the light switch—and the bobcat pounced on my back, eliciting a high-pitched Mariah Carey scream from me. I finally pried it loose and dashed out of the room, slamming the door in its face. Animal control and the police department came soon after and cornered my furry attacker before whisking him away.

In those days, I thought everything was a sign. Living in my car, scrounging for meals, ferocious animal attacks—these were all just parts of the movie in process, as well as the montage of my summer: I worked as many doubles as they'd give me, pumped iron behind the condo, got the deepest, darkest tan of my life, cruised the strip in my Suzuki Samurai, played beach volleyball, and picked up girls—a *Jersey Shore* season relocated to Florida.

I found calm and patience in the belief that if I could just make it to April, when every business in town staffed up for the coming rush of tourists, I'd be able to land that coveted restaurant job. But when spring arrived and I dropped off I don't know how many applications around town, not a single callback came. I'd lie awake in bed, ceiling-gazing as a waking nightmare played out in my head. I saw myself morphing into one of those amusement park lifers who couldn't remember their long-abandoned dreams. At some point, I got up and started pounding beers. It took about ten Natural Lights to put me down for the night. I wouldn't say I had a drinking problem, but that level of consumption did seem commensurate to that of the amusement parkers with whom I was hanging.

In August, the general manager of the amusement park, a perfectly coiffed guy with a George Michael beard whom we called Johnny Paycheck, told me he was giving me a twenty-five-cent-per-hour raise.

"You're an indispensable part of what we do here," he said, extending his hand.

It felt like an inflection point after which I'd never escape Emerald Falls.

"I have bad news for you," I said, not shaking his hand. "I'm a temporary part of this place."

He stared at me, unsure of what to say.

I thought about it for a moment more.

"In fact, I quit."

I turned and walked away without looking back. He deserved better, but then again, so did I.

IN THE FALL OF 1991 I returned to Champaign to reup for a new term, but was as unmotivated as I'd been the prior year.

Mom reluctantly financed my tuition. She and Larry clearly felt it was throwing good money after bad. But I did well that term, earning solid grades, taking a job at Music Land, a record store at the mall, setting myself up in a little apartment off campus, playing basketball in my downtime, and engaging in my first long-term romantic relationship. I proved to myself and my family that I was capable of academic success and general discipline. But the feeling that college and I were incompatible persisted. And so, after months of plotting my return to Florida, I resolved to head back after finals at the end of the semester.

Training for my rematch with the Sunshine State included penning a work of fiction—my new résumé. Oh, the places I'd been! I invented positions of great responsibility in important-sounding Chicago restaurants. Coining names of all those imaginary businesses while playacting with Missi enabled me to concoct places like Al's California Bar & Grille. According to my résumé, all of them had long since shuttered, denying potential employers the ability to check references.

Before I knew it, I found myself back in Panama City behind the wheel of my car at the intersection of Upas Street and Thomas Drive, deciding to apply at the next restaurant I drove past. The only decision was whether to turn left or right: after a mental coin toss, I chose right, and ended up at the Beach House, a gargantuan restaurant across the street from the Gulf on a manmade lake. It comprised two levels and had soaring thirty-five-foot ceilings and a mezzanine bar, as well as an outdoor deck outfitted with its own bar.

The Beach House was an eatery and watering hole, built to be a fancy oasis among the plentiful oyster bars and airbrush-painting stands. Its unassuming name was something of a Trojan horse, as were the staff uniforms of khaki Duck Head shorts and white polo shirts, and the traditional appetizer-salad-entrée menu format. These trappings made the place approachable to everybody in the knockabout coastal community, but the rest of the experience was elegant, from white linen tablecloths to a hefty leather-bound wine list.

During my impromptu interview with general manager Mike Bell, he asked me to name my favorite grape varietal. As I struggled to improvise a passable answer to a question I didn't understand (*varietal?*), Alice Masker, one of the owners, walked by. Alice was thirtyish with wild curls, a surfeit of energy, a goofy laugh, and hospitality in her genes: her family owned the local institution

Harbor House, and she'd gone in on the Beach House with her siblings and in-laws.

"I like this one, Mike," she said, pinching my cheeks. "Hire him."

And so I got the job without having to rely on my bogus résumé.

The Beach House marked my first, long-delayed taste of restaurant culture. Anything I had read or seen on TV about restaurants had barely scratched the surface of what Tony Bourdain would later dub "the underbelly" of the business.

Being in a restaurant outside of working hours felt like getting backstage at a Broadway show, or onto a movie set. Every day, I got to see the place reconstitute itself, like a Polaroid developing.

I arrived early each morning for training. The five-man cleaning crew would already be there, sweeping, mopping, vacuuming, and wiping, each to their own Sony Walkman–provided rhythm. They flipped inverted chairs from tabletops and tucked them underneath. Deliveries of produce, proteins, dry goods, paper products, and cases of wine arrived in a steady stream at the kitchen door. Most of it came from national wholesalers, but there was fresh red snapper and grouper from Destin Ice, a local seafood market, packed in large Tupperware-like bins. The cooks, a five-man band of haggard kitchen veterans, dragged themselves in reeking of nicotine and alcohol, sometimes not having returned home since the prior night's shift. (Hey, if God didn't want them to do that, he wouldn't have invented cocaine.) As they attacked their work, dicing carrots, onions, and celery; butchering meat and fish; and prepping salads, sides, and such, they shared ribald tales of what they'd gotten into after work and trading filthy jokes that would get them canceled today. Their endless rap sessions flowed naturally from topics as wide-ranging as the Miami Dolphins' current fortune to whose ball sack got sweatiest during service.

They were a pack, and servers weren't allowed. I'd say, "What's up, guys?" and they'd just sneer.

All of this played out amid a cloud of cigarette smoke and the Motörhead that blared from a battered boom box in the corner. Their leader was Chef Bradley, who wore a cowboy mustache and pressed white chef coat and favored a Cleveland Indians baseball cap to a traditional toque.

I wasn't sure which restaurant clique I wanted to be a part of yet. I felt like George Plimpton in *Paper Lion*, an observational fraud, trying to simultaneously glean information and not get caught.

My training included an instruction to do my part to keep one of the cooks, David, sober. We were to deny him alcohol the way Clarice Starling was told to keep paper clips and sharp objects from Hannibal Lecter. He wasn't even allowed a beer at shift drink, the old tradition of a free round for the staff toward the end of service. One night, David asked a new and naive bartender for a bottle of bourbon so he could make a sauce for our apple pie, then drained the bottle before the first seating had made it to dessert. He could barely stand, let alone sauté red snapper or grill grouper. Alice stormed around, holding the bottle aloft, demanding to know who'd fucked up.

The kitchen banter would still be going strong when I changed for service around 3 p.m. to begin playing my part. We straightened up the settings on each table, cut citrus for the bartender, poured salad dressings into ramekins, rolled silver cutlery in white linen napkins, and married (inverted one open bottle on top of another to consolidate) ketchups and Louisiana Hot Sauce.

My dining room coworkers and I were sitcom-ready: There was Trevor, bleached-blond Valley guy and career server who turned and burned—industry-speak for flipping tables as quickly as possible to maximize tips. Woe be unto anybody too slow on the point-of-sale system when Trevor needed access. He knew how to punch in each dish according to its coded number, a veteran trick that saved time. To further accelerate the process, he thought nothing of shoving you out of his way. Lonnie drank before, during, and after each shift, and as aggressively as anyone I've met before or since. If you spotted him crossing the dining room with a lone White Russian on his tray, it was not for a guest. Stephen, all five feet five inches of him, was the most meticulous of the servers and disdained snowbirds. His nickname was Revenue, or "Rev," because that was his primary concern. His running commentary on each service was the best kind of earworm: I can still picture him leaning against the wood paneling, watching a trio of Alabama tourists in tank tops and flip-flops meandering in for dinner, and clairvoyantly describing what would follow as he wearily pushed off for their table: "Three fried seafood platters, Thousand Island dressing, three key lime pies, ten percent for Revenue, thank you for playing." When a party left a stingy tip, he'd mutter, "Thank you. Come again. Next time, ask for Kevin."

The guy I most connected with was Jeff Lane. Jeff had no business being in the Panhandle—he outclassed the entire region. He was ruggedly handsome, with a perpetual five o'clock shadow. He was packaged in crisp button-downs and faded Levi's and drove a baby-blue 1965 Ford Bronco. On the side, he earned extra money building custom furniture for some of the area's better-off citizens. Running against the grain of all that was his cultural clout, with his Leonard Cohen albums and books and poetry by the likes of Sylvia Plath and Pablo Neruda.

Lastly, there was Terri. The Duck Head khaki shorts and white polo didn't do much for the rest of us, but she wore them like they had been tailored for her. She was tan in a Coppertone girl sort of way, strong, outspoken, and wildly sexy.

"Who are you?" she asked on my first day as we rolled silver in the private dining room. Somehow, she made the question sound vaguely accusatory.

"Which version do you want, the long or short?" I joked.

"A name is fine for now," she said, terminating any hint of flirtation. "I'll figure out the rest on my own."

It was just as well. She wouldn't have gotten a true story. Nobody did. I was embarrassed about dropping out of college and overcompensated by making up different backstories on the fly. One had me paying off student loans from U of I. Another had me on a leave of absence from law school. I already felt desperate to advance to restaurant ownership as soon as possible, before my fragile ego shattered. In the meantime, the work kept my mind off things: The rhythm of waiting tables, clearing them, resetting them, and repeating kept my mind focused and off those sudden and persistent storms that only I could discern.

The Beach House's most frequent entertainment was Jay Scott, a well-traveled studio sax player, who had been immortalized on classics from Lynyrd Skynyrd's "What's Your Name" to the disco staple "I Love the Nightlife."

I was smitten with my chosen profession. It was like having a crush on someone from afar, only to discover they were even more dreamy than you'd fantasized. Every day yielded its own highlight reel, and one feature of the restaurant always made the cut: pre-shift.

Alice had left home to make her industry bones in Atlanta, eventually ascending to being a restaurant manager. When she returned to Florida to open a place, she convinced her best friend and colleague James Trahan to come with her. James was a seasoned and serious hospitality professional and introduced me to the tradition of pre-shift, the meeting that immediately precedes welcoming the first guests of the night. This daily ritual is when a manager gathers the troops and briefs them for the service ahead. If there's a special, this is when they'll have a chance to taste it, and to scribble descriptions in their little pocket notepads. Pre-shift is a chance for the manager to discuss any missteps from the night prior and how to avoid repeating them, to alert the team to any anticipated VIPs, to let them know any menu adjustments that may need to be conveyed verbally, and so on.

James gave good pre-shift, in part because he recognized that in a place like the Beach House, one role he played was Professor of Hospitality, dispensing basic service knowledge in digestible bits to a revolving door of blank-slate employees.

Being a good server begins by caring about those in your care. This is the most important part, and fortunately it came to me naturally. You are also a guide, a facilitator, a listener, a problem solver, a technician, a juggler, and a housekeeper. This took education and the nurturing of whatever natural talent you might possess.

To be a proper guide, you have to know what you are selling. How does the crawfish étouffée compare to others? What are the subtle differences among the seven Pinot Noirs on the list? As a facilitator, you punched in orders, fetched them when ready, and delivered them. As an intuitive listener, you picked up on cues that revealed guests' needs without them having to state them; for example, a comment of "God, I'm starving" to their tablemate means get them a basket of bread before they order.

As a problem solver you worked around allergies, aversions, and crying babies. As a technician, you opened wine expertly, held plates without leaving a thumbprint, and cleared four-tops unassisted. You juggled orders, movements, steps, and timing, while housekeeping the tables throughout the meal. Each of these essential skills were taught and reinforced across pre-shifts.

You'd think that all the stuff I did in high school—the keggers and the Hardee's and the movie theater—would have set me up for success in a restaurant. But of the fifteen or so servers, I was the most inept, except for another, also named Kevin, who I was convinced must have been a fellow résumé fabulist. One night, a guest asked Other Kevin for a "Baileys and coffee," a popular order at the time, but apparently unknown to the poor guy—he thought the guest wanted a bay leaf and coffee. He marched to the kitchen, procured a bay leaf, and floated it in the man's coffee. After that, he would forever be known at the Beach House as Bay Leaf Kevin.

I was grateful for this decoy whose incompetence eclipsed my own. If it was only his shortcomings that inspired a nickname, what worries did I have? Well, little did I know that I, too, had been saddled with a mocking moniker: One night, I overheard a server ask the manager if Kevin was working.

"Which one?" asked the manager. "Bay Leaf Kevin or Table Mess Kevin?"

Turns out I was blind to the fact that I failed to keep tables properly maintained. I wasn't crumbing between courses, or clearing salad plates before entrées arrived. The humiliation refueled my resolve to become the best server possible.

IN THE 1990S, IF YOU worked in a restaurant, there was no end to the after-hours drinking, drug use, and partying. If you were in the industry in Panama City Beach at that time, drinking for free was practically a birthright. It began with a shift drink while rolling silver, then we'd descend on any number of bars in the vicinity. A fixture of almost every night was Spinnaker Beach Club, a massive place whose tagline was "Party with 1000's." They held a nightly contest called Bar Wars that awarded a $500 bar credit to whichever restaurant brought the most patrons. We showed up with a formidable and competitive crew every night, and often won.

Those few beers I'd called on as a tranquilizer during my first stint in Florida quickly became several drinks every night. It might cost me the next morning, but I was enjoying myself, and the alcohol kept those thoughts I dreaded at bay when the distraction of service was gone. They also acted as a much-needed ice breaker for me and Terri, enabling us to start to know each other a little.

Over the next few months, I took a second job at Scampi's, a local coastal restaurant, and Terri and I began spending more and more time together outside the Beach House.

There was an undeniable charge between us, and we had much in common: like me, she was a dreamer who wanted to open restaurants. But she wasn't unencumbered like me. Just twenty-seven at the time, she had married young, and had a daughter, Kara, and a son, Jack. She was getting a divorce and had obvious parental responsibilities, so she was careful and disciplined when we were together—never drinking too much or staying out too late. (I'd also made it clear I wasn't in the market for a serious relationship. "I don't know everything about my future," I'd told her. "But I do know that I'm not getting married."

Still, I recognized that I was an oddly perfect distraction for her. My rambunctiousness matched hers and was a welcome break from her ex-husband's seriousness. And my ambition gave her a safe place to discuss her own. She was sure that she could be more than a mom with two kids, and I built on that energy. We would stir each other up, Woody-like, into a frenzy about our respective futures in the industry.

ON MOTHER'S DAY 1991, I experienced a professional rite of passage—my first beat-down.

There are levels of rough service in the restaurant industry: *In the weeds* means a temporary ass-kicking that you can ride out; *extreme weeds* refers to a Sisyphean scenario in which catching up is an impossibility; *completely fucked* is a soul-sucking, ego-bruising death march that takes a physical and financial toll—chafing, sweat-logged shoes, irate guests, and comped meals. You will relive these evenings in your nightmares for life.

This story is about a complete and total fucking.

Along with Valentine's Day and New Year's Eve, Mother's Day is one of the busiest and most dreaded days of service for any American restaurant. Since it's a family occasion, there are often large parties with many guests who don't dine out regularly, so they don't adhere to traditional customer courtesies, like ordering apps and mains at the same time. These holidays are minefields and marathons. They are also exponentially more profitable than most other services, so restaurants suffer through them.

Most Sundays at our restaurant were dead, thanks to hangovers, church, and the siren song of the Gulf. I often wondered why we bothered to open. That Sunday, Mother's Day Sunday, was guaranteed to be an exception, but our general manager, or GM, forgot to schedule extra servers. Once shock melted away, the enormity of the screwup washed over us like a tidal wave. It was all hands on deck as we took to the phones, begging for reinforcements to come in on their day off. When the smoke cleared, we had only cobbled together a skeleton crew of one host, three servers, and two bartenders. I felt like one of those holdouts who foolishly refused to evacuate ahead of a Category 4 hurricane. We were good and fucked; the only question was how badly.

Jay Scott, the entertainment for the afternoon, warmed up, his delirious saxophone riffs mocking our oncoming doom.

There were close to 250 reservations, and I would be tending to roughly a third of them at my sixteen-table station. That's up to sixty-four meals to track at any given time. A normal station in a fine dining setting would be a four-table station.

Regardless of the ultimate outcome, I was determined to leave it all on the field and began triaging the situation. There was a small cooler at my service station that I packed with sixteen pre-poured glasses of water and several rows of wineglasses, filling them with the wines we sold the most of—white Zinfandel, Merlot, and Chardonnay. I pre-made and pre-plated salads, wrapping them individually with plastic wrap, and keeping them cool on a speed rack in the shared fridge adjacent to the kitchen. Finally, I filled carafes with ice water and perched one on each table before anyone had been seated.

The effort paid off: For the first ninety minutes, I cruised. Clear, drop check, place order, "Welcome to Beach House," drop off dishes, clear, take order, "Here's your key lime pie."

Area restaurateur Steve Stevens, who owned Hamilton's, a popular local restaurant, sat at Table 100 with five guests around 7:30 p.m.; by 9, they were getting itchy about their entrees. I dashed to the kitchen to check on them.

"Chef, where the hell is my food for Table 100?"

"I don't even have a chit for Table 100," snapped Billy, waving at the rail where chits summarizing each order hung like clothes on a line.

I scrolled through the point-of-sale system, and cold sweat broke out on me like a rash. I hadn't placed the order.

"Chef Bradley," I asked with considerably more deference, "any chance I can get Table 100 on the fly?" (Restaurant-speak for right away.)

There's an old line in business that was implied (but not given voice) by his non-response: "Poor planning on your part does not constitute an emergency on mine."

I began the shameful return to Steve's table to give them the bad news. As they stormed out, one of the guests huffed, "Thanks for ruining Mother's Day!"

That was the domino that toppled the others. Suddenly, I was engulfed with mounting crises: I got triple-sat, meaning three parties were placed in my care simultaneously; multiple tables clamored for their checks at once; and hot food for three of my tables was hemorrhaging warmth in the kitchen window.

By 11 p.m. I had waited on eighty people; if I were a doctor and they were my patients, I'd have lost twenty of them and the board would be coming for my license. I went home ashamed and mortified for even having pondered a career in hospitality.

But here's the funny thing: On their next visits, many of the guests I served that day asked to be sat in my station. In time, it sunk in that to my great surprise, I had a gift: authentic empathy and my sincere desire—no, longing—to show people a good time added up to more than the sum of its parts. It was like a payoff to all my strengths and weaknesses, treasured memories and traumas.

Cooks will tell you that the extreme focus of a dinner service is the only thing that settles their ADHD overload. The dining room was the same for me. The endorphins produced by a dinner rush was analogous to the one I experienced after a hard workout. It took my mind off everything, and then when my irrational anxiety came rushing back, it was time to drink again.

I SPOKE TO MOM EVERY week without fail. During one call, she shared that Larry had expressed missing me being in the house. I was savvy enough to know that he missed me in theory, not actuality.

He had begun mailing me letters that were part pleasantries and part housekeeping. He was clearly trying, in his way, to thaw things between us. But he also couldn't help from commenting on petty issues like the charges from their calling card that I would occasionally use. Even at this remove, he was still keeping lists.

I didn't write him back, and tried to call Mom at times when I knew he wouldn't be home.

I told Mom about Terri, how she had children and was getting a divorce, and my reluctance to act on my feelings. I paused, waiting for her to confess to her own life experience and perhaps confer upon me her hard-earned wisdom in this area. Instead, she changed the subject.

I didn't share with Mom what made my relationship with Terri irresistible—our mutual mania and our shared ability to turn any evening into a party. Give us twenty bucks and beer on draught, and off we'd go.

Beyond that, there was a clear and undeniable chemistry and simpatico between us, and so Terri was the only person down there I told about Woody. But I held on to my plans to become a Chicago restaurateur. I didn't mind discussing my past, but the future I had in mind was too tenuous to voice.

WHILE THE ROMANTIC PART OF my life was in flux, my professional love had its moment. On New Year's Eve 1992, "it" happened. Up to that point in my life I had loved a lot of things that had not loved me back. The love you have as a young boy toward your father, for one. I also loved baseball with all my heart, but my limited skills doomed it to be unrequited. I loved the idea of college, but couldn't compete academically with guys like Mike.

We were completely booked for New Year's Eve at the Beach House, and I had a ten-table station to myself. The guests were kind, the pace of seating fell just right, and I sold big-dollar wines. I told the right jokes, and my station pulsated like one big party. I loved it, and it loved me back.

All night long, I pretended that I owned the joint. I never once faked a smile, and didn't break a sweat the entire time. I located that elusive Zen mindfulness that grants you perfect attention to each table and the singular relationship between you and those guests. Your station may be straining at the seams, but you can build a true, human connection. The ten-piece band, three-deep bar, and four hundred exuberant guests created a concert-like atmosphere that energized me like nothing ever had.

It was the easiest service I ever worked. I was simultaneously in control of the party and reveling in it. By the time I clocked out, I was sure of what I was going to do with the rest of my life.

To that end, I developed a new, more realistic plan, part of which was to save money to open my own place. My sophisticated method of doing so in 1992 involved envelopes and a hex. When I finished a shift at one of my two jobs, I would place whatever remained after groceries, rent, and gas in an envelope and seal it as I muttered a self-scripted curse: "If you open a sealed envelope, you will never open a restaurant." Periodically, I'd visit the local bank with a stack of crinkled envelopes in hand. Arriving at the teller window, I'd rip them open one by one and deposit the cash in my passbook savings account. The tellers called me Envelope Guy.

THE BEACH HOUSE'S INCONGRUITY TO Panama City was most fully reflected in its guests. It was the most elegant restaurant in town, but that didn't keep NASCAR caps, Crimson Tide tank tops, and spaghetti straps paired with cutoff jeans from walking in the front door.

But one night, a mysterious patron dressed the joint up a bit.

His hair was meticulously slicked back, he wore tortoise shell readers, and his black shoes were immaculately shiny, reflecting the sunset outside.

"I would like to sit in Kevin's section, please."

Yes, it was Woody. His booming voice echoed through the space, which was how I came to know he was there. My first one-top of the evening would not be a quick turn.

"Okay, so what is this all about?" Woody asked when I arrived at his table.

"What's what about? Do you want to hear the specials?"

"Why are you working at a restaurant in Florida?"

"I think this is what I want to do."

"Be a waiter?"

"More than that, Woody. I think I could be something in this industry."

He just nodded, having enough judgment not to be judgmental at this stage of our relationship.

Woody joined me and Terri for a beer after work, and he played a game of darts with her.

She was the first friend to ever meet my dad, or bio-dad, or real dad, or whatever the fuck he was.

"He's amazing," she enthused after he left. "That's a real fucking man. He's got a Sam Elliott thing going on."

I dug the fact that she thought he was cool, but it wasn't surprising. When Woody shifted his charm into fifth gear, he was hard to resist.

IN 1992, THE INEVITABLE FINALLY came to pass as Terri and I started dating.

She had run off for a weekend with her ex, a last-ditch effort at reanimating their relationship. When she returned, she drove directly to my condo and left a note on my door: "Just got back from the Caymans. I really want to see you." I didn't even go into my place, just walked back to the car and went searching for her. I found her at the first bar I tried, a little pub called Zanzibar just down the street from where we worked. Within minutes, we were on the back deck behind the Beach House, kissing for the first time.

A few days later, I took her to dinner in Seaside, one of the towns where she thought she'd like to open a restaurant.

Seaside became best known as the location for *The Truman Show*, director Peter Weir's prescient 1998 film about our increasingly voyeuristic society, starring Jim Carrey at the height of his powers. The town has also been recognized as a hub of New Urbanism. Today, if you drive Highway 30-A, the road Seaside sits on, you will encounter several stunning townships along the twenty-four-mile scenic route: Rosemary Beach, Alys Beach, WaterColor, and historic Grayton Beach.

But if you drove it in 1992, as we did that evening, you would have observed mostly pristine, unspoiled coastland, until you came upon something out of a Wes Anderson wet dream: pastel-colored cottages, expansive porches, white picket fences, a small water tower, the world's quaintest post office, and stunning pavilions that marked beach accesses. Perched near the town square was Josephine's, a small restaurant on the ground floor of a white cottage that was also home to a bed-and-breakfast.

Upon entering the restaurant, and checking in for our reservation, I noticed that the only open table—our table—was next to a nightmare neighbor: a drunken dandy, much too enamored of his own crude jokes, and audible to every guest in the place. As we were sat by maître d' Bruce Albert, the very picture of class, he winked at me.

Terri and I opened our menus. Inside mine was a Post-it that read:

Dear Mr. Boehm,

The guy on your left is an asshole. He will be gone soon. Until then, bear with us.

Love,
Bruce

It was my first master class in another level of hospitality. Bruce was smart, but not stuffy. He was kind, intuitive, and spoke to us like we were old friends. I was dazzled as much by him as I was by the meal.

I made copious mental notes of how Bruce went about his business. A major takeaway was his practice of what I would later learn is called "touching a table," which is restaurant-speak for checking in. Especially impressive was how he adjusted his approach based on each party's vibe. Some only got a look; others got a story.

I admire musical trios. The amount of sound, light, and brute force bands like Cream, Nirvana, the Police, Beastie Boys, and Rush produced seemed impossible relative to their size. Josephine's was run by Bruce and his wife, Judy, in the dining room, and a young Belgian named Olivier Petit, nicknamed Ollie, in the kitchen. They taught me that there is a restaurant equivalent to those bands, and the right three people can bring that same magic and light to a young kid, way over his skis, who's hoping his credit card is approved after the check drops.

Bruce made the strongest impression on me. It was the first time I learned that while there are rules to service, hospitality is a blank canvas. Bruce had clearly established his own style and in turn inspired me to hone my own.

After dinner, Terri and I visited the town square, a manicured little hill tucked behind the post office. There was a stage for musical performances, but that night, a movie screen was set up. We grabbed a patch of ground we could claim for the next few hours. A woman with a custom box around her neck that displayed three wines by the glass approached. She offered us a Chardonnay, we accepted, and we watched *Breakfast at Tiffany's*. It was one of those perfect nights where anything seemed possible. Sitting under the stars, as Holly Golightly paraded larger than life across the screen, I couldn't wait to begin my own adventure. Everything that preceded this moment felt like a coming attraction. It was showtime.

3
STUCK IN THE MIDDLE WITH YOU

AFTER THAT NIGHT, TERRI AND I gave ourselves tacit permission to voice the idea of collaborating on a restaurant. On Sundays, we'd cruise 30-A on Florida's Panhandle, scanning the main thoroughfares for a space into which we might breathe new life.

I considered myself lucky: Terri was athletic, competitive, and a stone-cold knockout. And we were professionally compatible. She was a gifted and intuitive cook, a kitchen Stevie Nicks to my dining room Lindsey Buckingham. She cooked for me at home: straightforward compositions from the Southern songbook, like grouper Pontchartrain, with peaks and valleys of flavor that manifested her passion and palate. Her talents weren't confined to food: She also had a keen eye for art and possessed artistic talent herself, especially for painting, building, and accessorizing her outfits whenever we hit the town.

Our May–September romance was a welcome infusion of fun and adventure, and I was animated by adrenaline and game for anything. On a moment's notice, we'd jump in one of our cars for a day trip. We would hustle off to Apalachicola and eat oysters and stay at the Gibson Inn, or play blackjack in Biloxi. Terri, or *T*, as I took to calling her when we began dating, was as into it as I was, largely because of the new beginning I represented.

We both also were manic, or at least manic-adjacent—we thought nothing of commandeering a rental house's pool at 2 a.m., scattering our clothes across the lawn, and skinny-dipping, or jumping on two beach bikes somebody left in their yard and taking them for a midnight cruise. I had felt emotionally connected to women before, but this one had an electric charge. She was like Tesla's magnifier coil, capable of raising me to a high frequency with just a touch. Our chemistry brought out the lightning storms in both of us. We both drank, liberally, but the romance was as much of a substance as the alcohol. When we were together, I was euphoric and my inner skies were sunny.

For a counterbalance, there was Terri's daughter, Kara, an energetic, blonde-haired three-year-old. Terri was a blunt but loving mother and the bubble of security and affection she provided Kara produced a happy, confident kid. She and I hit it off right away. Terri's other child, Jack, lived with his father, so it was usually just the three of us.

And so, whenever T and I skidded toward rock-star abandon, remembering that little girl bungeed us back. The two of them obviously offered me a surrogate family, but that's not why I was interested in Terri. It was a fringe benefit.

On one of our Sunday scouting outings, we screeched to a halt at the intersection of South County Highway 395 and 30-A. Right on the corner was a FOR LEASE sign. The building it advertised was a cedar structure that was modeled after the nearby residential cottages, but was lifeless and bore a VILLAGE SEAFOOD MARKET sign over its front door. We spontaneously met with the owner, Dennis Franklin, a dockside bruiser with Popeye-like forearms.

There wasn't enough room inside the ramshackle structure to host a coffee klatch, let alone a restaurant. But there was a functional kitchen that the prior tenant had used to boil water for cooking lobsters, crab, and shrimp. Dennis bought into our young-dreamers narrative and offered to lease us the building for $450 per month, at least $1,000 less than it would have cost to rent a more proper space.

With an anemic budget and no construction permits (we never applied for them), we set about making a restaurant. Our plan was to build a deck on the back of the building, with just enough room for twenty-four seats, distributed among six tables, plus twelve seats in the driveway.

For all the dopamine our love affair generated, there were still moments when the darkness came for me, usually in the middle of the night or first thing in the morning. This was about the time that I began a nightly ritual: When I woke up at 2 a.m., which I did without fail, I would move to the couch, and picture myself on a rowboat. Eventually, mentally, I would maneuver myself behind a desolate island thickly packed with trees. Docked in the water behind it was a decrepit old boat of questionable seaworthiness. Upon climbing aboard and entering, however, I discovered—impossibly—a luxurious bedroom. This eased me back into sleep.

The boat was me, inverted. I was shiny and solid on the outside, rickety and waterlogged inside. Every morning, before opening my eyes, I'd contemplate the possible pitfalls of the day ahead, triggering a panic attack, or something close to it. I would break out in a cold sweat, and my heart would spin and whir.

One night, on the couch, I leafed through a quirky little book I owned of poems about adjectives that Terri had gifted me. The page devoted to *Lazy* featured a drawing of a country bumpkin, seemingly without a care in the world, snoozing against a tree. The poem's closing line was, "He loves his Lazy days." That became the inspiration for our restaurant's name, in part because of the magnificent magnolia tree with outstretched branches just beyond where the deck would stand. When silhouetted by sunlight, that tree was a cinematographer's dream, framing our little hidden sanctuary. We changed *Days* to *Daze* to signal that we didn't take ourselves too seriously—an important message in a region whose poet laureate was Jimmy Buffett. Lazy Daze Café's tagline, also born of the illustration that accompanied the poem, was "Hidden in the Shade of Seagrove."

If our restaurant were to be pictured in a sequel to that poetry book, it would have been juxtaposed with *Modest*. This was a time for practicality, not pride or vanity. We installed a Vulcan six-burner stove and a single fryer, just enough of a starter kitchen for Terri. I plumbed our three-compartment industrial kitchen sink myself, using a how-to book for guidance.

We were not building the second coming of Spago. No, this would be the Little Restaurant That Could. To access the bathroom—a lone unisex stall—guests would have to walk outside and around the side of the building. To ease their commute, I built a rickety set of stairs to the bathroom. Thankfully, a group of bemused construction workers took pity on me and corrected and completed my shoddy attempt before somebody broke their neck.

To erect the deck, I sent an SOS to Jeff Lane from the Beach House, and he came to the rescue, thank God. One afternoon, while hammering away at a two-by-four, he told me that the Beach House crew expected to see Terri and me back there within six months. I found the cattiness motivating, and so did she. *Fuck it*, we thought, *we'll show 'em all.*

OTHER THAN THOSE CONSTRUCTION WORKERS' and Jeff's help, it was all DIY. Once the deck was in place, we purchased ten plastic resin tables. We secured them by filling their hollow bases with concrete in the center to give them heft. I laid padding over the drab surface and draped the whole getup with tablecloths to mask the white plastic finish and complete the masquerade. We covered the three open sides of the deck with Visqueen plastic sheeting to deflect drafts in colder months, when a kerosene heater, with an assist from the oven's ambient heat, would warm the dining room.

We also hung a small chalkboard with a blond-wood frame, on which Terri planned to announce each evening's menu, on the dining room's only partition wall, which separated the dining room from the kitchen. Along another side was an antique hutch we'd rescued from a used-furniture shop, in which we housed service items, vinyl albums, and stereo equipment.

In October, when our grand opening was nigh, I pinned five hundred photocopied hand-drawn flyers under windshield-wiper blades on cars all over town. The ad copy wouldn't win me a Clio:

30-A's Newest Restaurant
at the Corner of Hwy 30-A and Hwy 395
Lazy Daze Café!
Delicious food from scratch in one of
the area's most serene settings.

Above that Terri had sketched a simple rendering of our little back deck and the irresistible offer of LIVE MUSIC FRIDAY NIGHT!

We would serve a simple breakfast, then shift to an all-day menu with specials at dinner, usually one meat and one fish. The board would feature our static menu, with the specials presented verbally. For the people sitting on the side of the building, we had handwritten paper menus that we photocopied on the machine of a real estate office at the corner, in exchange for free lunches.

Terri scrawled our inaugural nightly menu on the chalkboard:

Linguine with Shrimp, Roasted Garlic Tomato Cream Sauce
Baked Garlic & Croutons
Chicken & Asparagus Puff pastry with Beurre Blanc

The modest back deck and bucolic environs of Lazy Daze Café

Smoked Ham & Three-Cheese Puff Pastry with Sun-dried Tomato Bearnaise
Sandwich of the Day
Garden Salad with Green Goddess
Grilled Red Snapper with Vegetable Medley

Throughout our first service, Ed Texas, a local musician, strummed seventies classics as I tried to keep up. One lyric in particular spoke to my mood: "Even though we ain't got money / I'm so in love with you, honey." Being a restaurateur was love at first try. For this vagabond, it was the first place that felt like home.

In between sets, a small record player endlessly spun Rickie Lee Jones's *Pop Pop* and two Miles Davis records. The surf's rumble filled the short gaps between tracks.

I wove in and out of the kitchen during service, clearing, marking, running, and resetting as Terri made magic over all six burners. I would occasionally duck under her sautéing to put individual ciabatta loaves in the oven for each table.

At some point, unbeknownst to either of us, the pilot light went out, but gas continued flowing into the oven. When I opened the oven door to warm Table 1's bread, a spark from one of the burners ignited the flowing gas, and I was set ablaze.

Fuck! The oven exploded! Wait . . . what's that stench? Oh, Jesus, my hair's on fire!

I frantically slapped at my head, trying to put it out. Terri screamed, then gathered herself and extinguished me with wet towels. Then she called an ambulance. We cut off service and comped everybody's meals.

Next thing I knew, I had been ambulanced to Destin Hospital, a modest medical center with a handful of treatment rooms. After a couple of hours of mostly waiting, a nurse handed me a barbershop mirror to check the damage.

I recoiled at the sight of myself. I looked like the lesser of Harvey Dent's two faces in *The Dark Knight*. As a banana bag dripped antibacterial liquid onto my face, I wondered if I would be scarred for life.

I wondered the same thing the next day. As I got dressed for work, I studied my face in the mirror, dwelling on my bald head for a good long while. Like the biblical Samson's, my hair had long been a source of strength. The stress of the opening had also robbed me of fifteen pounds, leaving me a gaunt, Matthew McConaughey *Dallas Buyers Club* look. Add to all that a scorched face, and I was far from pleasing to the eye.

My mother always said that life's like a pension—you have to pay into it. She was skeptical of anything that came easily and urged me to be the same. And so, I chose to look at that fire as a test. I winked at myself in the mirror, and left for work.

By the time I arrived at Lazy Daze from the hospital, I'd never been more certain I'd picked the right profession.

Terri was already there.

"How do I look?" I asked her.

"Well, you're not going to win any beauty contests; just keep your head down."

I cracked up. That's restaurant life, the knowledge that my accident could have befallen anybody working alongside me, and that whomever it was wouldn't leave the team in the lurch the next day. And that I could laugh about it. If you want to work in a restaurant, you have to have thick skin, even if it's been torched like a s'more.

WITH ONLY A COUPLE OF years' experience under my belt, my restaurateur tool kit was awfully lacking. I was punctual, so there was that. After Bruce's example, I had developed the ability to touch a table, and to do it intentionally, finding an excuse to check in with a party, even with something innocuous, like asking, "How's the snapper tonight?" I had unlimited enthusiasm, and my work ethic was, like Mom's, world-class-grinder level. Everything else was, at best, embryonic. Thankfully, I knew what I didn't know, so I could fill those gaps a little every day. In the meantime, the rapport between me and Terri propelled us over any speed bumps.

I arrived at the restaurant at 6 a.m., set the dining room, transcribed reservations from the answering machine onto a yellow legal pad, made tea, coffee, and salad dressing, and set up the cold station with romaine, purple cabbage, tomatoes, onions, and croutons.

We would do about twenty covers for breakfast, wash and dry the dishes, scrawl the day's menu on the chalkboard, and run the whole thing back for lunch.

Dishes, change it over to dinner, run it back.

Each daypart gave off its own vibe: Breakfast was mellow, so mellow that we dropped it after a few months. When it comes to pulling levers in a restaurant to see what works, you have to give it a fair shake, but abandon it at the appropriate time if it's never going to work. Lunch dependably drew construction workers, thanks to our unassuming and egalitarian attitude, and dinner was decidedly grown up, with plenty of couples, families, and celebrations.

The kitchen was high-functioning chaos. Without true line refrigeration, Terri's mise-en-place (restaurant-speak for prepped ingredients) was set up in bus tubs filled with ice that constantly melted in the combined heat of the climate and stoves, and the steam from the dishwasher produced shirt-soaking sweat that undid my morning ironing.

Amid it all was my most ardent regular: Kara was always sprawled on the kitchen floor watching a rotating roster of Disney movies: *The Little Mermaid*, *Snow White and the Seven Dwarfs*, and *Pinocchio*. To this day, "Under the Sea" takes me right back. Terri and I kept her endlessly supplied with ice water, apple slices, and the occasional Sprite, and popped the next VHS tape in her combo TV/VCR player whenever we saw credits rolling out of the corner of our eyes. At times, a Disney princess' anthem would mix with, say, Miles's "So What" as the kitchen door swung open, but I was the only one who noticed.

As Terri juggled tasks, I scribbled tickets from my thirty-seat station, made salads and washed dishes when I could make the time, kept the outside heater fueled with kerosene, and flipped records before the needle reached its end and started blaring crackles and hisses.

When all ten tables were going, true bespoke hospitality was out the window and I toggled to raw survival mode.

"Ken-in"—Kara's name for me—"could you change the video?"

"Sure, kiddo."

"Order in, table two, chicken en croûte, pasta."

"We are out of entrée plates, you need to run a rack," shouted Terri.

"Eighty-six halibut."

"Ken-in, I have to go to the bathroom."

There's often tension between the kitchen and dining room teams in restaurants, and in this case, we constituted the entire population of each of those factions. Each shift began friendly, but before we knew it Terri and I were either fighting, grinding, drinking, or gazing lustily at each other in a film noir manner. If any relationship complemented my mania, this was it. And somewhere in between all that, we had to locate the time and presence of mind to shuttle the kids back and forth to their dad's. Kara took to our chaotic world, but when Jack visited, he felt like a fish out of water and was often bored out of his mind.

Terri occasionally emerged from the kitchen to chat up a table, and the room would burst into applause. No matter where we were in our dysfunction, those moments made me the happiest. But even as our relationship deepened, she remained fiercely independent, and her intensity was combustible. The only thing she abhorred more than standing still was being told what to do. T was also frustrated by my emotional immaturity, while her mood swings pissed me off. It was a volatile and intoxicating way of life. It was also addictive.

And things could get petty. I kept lemons for cocktails by the garde manger (salads and cold dishes) section of her kitchen, which annoyed her. I could have easily moved them, but didn't want to give her the satisfaction.

Sometimes, things boiled over in full view and earshot of our guests:

"Why don't you set your service station up closer to the tables?"

"Why don't you concentrate on cooking?"

"Why don't you go fuck yourself?"

That might not sound like foreplay, but trust me, it was.

THE PACE OF PANAMA CITY in its high season spared me long stretches of inactivity that inevitably caused me to wallow in my darker times. But in Seaside, the silence was often absolute. I acclimated to the pace, but not to the whiplash-inducing switch between crazy busy and mind-numbingly slow. To kill time during dead services, I started reading books about restaurants and how to succeed in them. (One product of all that reading was quickly learning to stockpile enough of a bank account to sustain us through the late-winter doldrums and survive the trek to the Valhalla of spring, when the crowds returned.)

After a barren February service, I treated myself to a beer at Salty Dog, a dive bar with wide-planked wood floors, dim lighting at all hours, and a sketchy crowd around whom you instinctively puffed out your chest and exaggerated the swagger in your step, as if arriving in a prison. Greg, the owner, had a glass eye and endless supply of tall tales, including one about the winter slowdown.

"You think this is slow?" he snapped when I tried to commiserate. "Let me tell you a story: The night I opened this place, we had to kick out a woman named Fran. The other customers hung around for more than two hours after that. When we locked up, we saw that Fran never made it across the street; she had passed out right on the white line. In two hours, nobody had run her over. That's slow."

Lazy Daze wasn't bound for the history books, but if you caught us when we were in a groove and it wasn't too hot outside, a caressing breeze was blowing, and you were looking to forget your troubles over some good food and wine, you'd have thought it a very good restaurant.

Terri knew who she was culinarily, and we were able to source pristine product, thanks in part to the local fishermen who appeared at our back door to sell us cobia or Gulf grouper, still dripping with the water they'd been fished from, for cash. It was flagrantly illegal, but this was Florida, where referees rarely blew their whistles.

Lazy Daze was open seven days a week and, for most of its life, was a two-person show. If you wanted to learn everything in the restaurant business in a short amount of time, this was a great way to do it. Open for lunch and dinner, come to work early in the morning, and leave for home in a darkness you can only find in a town without streetlights.

In hindsight, the work was more grueling than glamorous. By the end of each shift the sour alchemy of bleach, dirt, grilled beef fat, vinegar, sweat, and after-service beer left me reeking like a frat house on Sunday morning. I had to roll my windows down on the drive home just to stomach my own stench. For all my troubles, I took home a paltry $1,000 at the end of the month, but it was more rewarding than anything I had ever done. I was really connecting with people. The community liked our vitality and ambition and adopted us with a rooting interest. There was an unspoken understanding that Lazy Daze was for locals, not tourists, and people let us know how much they loved that we weren't serving the obligatory crab claws and oyster po-boys. The Modicas, a septuagenarian couple who looked like Santa and Mrs. Claus, owned the local grocery and were legends in the area; when they chose Lazy Daze as their new canteen, it was a subtle but meaningful seal of approval. Sometimes I'd be chilling in Seaside and a recent guest would tell me how much they loved the restaurant. It was gratifying beyond measure to know that we had created a place where people chose to spend their time and money. T bought me a paisley-print journal with *T loves you* scribbled on the inner cover. One night, I wrote in it: "I know deep down that Lazy Daze will never fill my pockets, but it sure as hell fills my soul." (Lazy Daze also attracted an occasional true celebrity, like Kim Carnes, the raspy-voiced singer best known for her 1981 cover of "Bette Davis Eyes." She and her husband, Dave Ellingson, became very close friends of mine, and we've kept in touch ever since.)

After about six months, we could afford to hire a prep cook. We brought on a guy named Ronnie. He was twenty-one years old, with an ink-black mustache, and built like a lamppost. Ronnie had gone through some hard times, so we let him live rent-free in the guest room at our little house.

Turns out, Ronnie was an archetype: restaurant-smart but incapable of maintaining a healthy life outside of that very specific environment. One evening he asked to borrow my car, and I obliged. Several hours later he called us from the hospital. Ronnie had succumbed to the lures of Panama City's west-side bars, passed out behind the wheel, and drove my car across the center lane head-on into an oncoming mid-seventies Lincoln Continental, collapsing my Samurai like an accordion. He broke his arm and had a concussion, but was going to be okay, and nobody else was seriously injured, thank God. My car and former residence, however, was totaled beyond recognition or repair. I had been through hell in that little tin can. I still have a recurring dream where I'm driving it on the highway, one hand on the wheel, the other holding the soft top to prevent its blowing away—hanging on tight to what little I had.

BY CHRISTMASTIME I'D SOCKED AWAY just enough money to fly home for two days. At age twenty-three it was the first time I'd been on a plane. It didn't matter that it belonged to ValuJet, the fledgling airline that before too long would shutter following a notorious crash, and was essentially a Greyhound bus with wings; to me, it may as well have been the Concorde. I landed on Christmas Eve, excited to see Missi and revisit my family's holiday rituals: Open one gift each that night, sip Mom's homemade eggnog from our fanciest glasses, and attend midnight mass at Trinity Lutheran, the same church where I was baptized and confirmed. We spontaneously decided to go out for dinner but couldn't secure a last-minute reservation at one of Springfield's three passable restaurants. That's when Larry blew up: "Goddammit, Dee, you should have planned this out; now there's nowhere to fucking eat."

Before I knew what had happened, I had slammed Larry against the wall, pinning him by his shoulders. "I listened to this shit for twenty years," I heard myself say. "I won't listen to you talk to her or me like that ever again."

The avenging spirit that had possessed me let Larry drop back to the floor, and he timidly skulked out of the room.

I came back to myself just as Mom shook her head: "I wish you hadn't done that."

As I took a seat on the couch, Larry came back and knelt in front of me. He gently put both his hands on my legs.

"I am sorry," he said, meeting my gaze with sad little eyes. "Work has been stressful, and I'm on edge."

I wanted to ask, "Are you apologizing for the last twenty years or just tonight?"

Instead, I said, "It's fine, Dad. Let's just go to Olive Garden."

At the restaurant, I threw my anger into the unlimited breadsticks and bottomless salad bowl. To be honest, it was pretty effective. Those breadsticks are, in fact, to die for.

Larry pouted, while Mom and I swapped stories about how difficult dealing with the general public in our respective work was.

"The same lady keeps wearing dresses and bringing them back, claiming they have not been worn. It doesn't take Columbo to see the armpit stains," Mom joked.

"I see your dress lady and raise you the two kids from Freeport that dined and dashed on us the other night. Fucking assholes."

Mom's and my rapport aside, it was not a great trip. Dad's dark behavior cast a pall over every attempt at fun. Going home was like a scratch-off ticket that never paid out—initial excitement was always met with disappointment. The two days ahead stretched out before me like one of those elongating shots in a

Spike Lee movie. My grubby life down south had become home. Springfield had become a place I used to live.

THE MORE I LEARNED ABOUT human nature, the more I understood how to make guests happy. Fortunately, for my training purposes, Lazy Daze's shortcomings provided me many opportunities to fail, learn, and recover. Our dining room was often too hot in the summer and too cold in the winter, the menu was limited, and the bathroom was outside. We tried to make up for our modest provisions with warmth and kindness, and most of the time that worked.

But there were exceptions:

"It smells like kerosene in here."

"You need a bathroom inside. It's raining."

"This menu is too small."

"I like my beer colder."

"I hear this album every time we're here. Get some new records, would ya?"

I compiled complaints and suggestions on a mental punch list and methodically addressed them when time allowed.

Ed Texas became our regular weekend entertainment. He was a journeyman musician, but his intros and patter alone were worth the fifty bucks we paid him. He was a sort of hillbilly, Coors Banquet–drinking Mark Twain, a role he continued to play offstage. He also loved probing me with pointed questions into the wee hours, nudging me toward introspection:

"Is this your dream, man?"

"Does that beautiful girl love you as much as you love her?"

"What's next, man? Is there even a next?"

About a year in, my ambitions were beginning to push at the edges of Lazy Daze. I had subscribed to the *New York Times*, and every Friday I devoured its restaurant coverage, especially Ruth

Reichl's reviews. A former *LA Times* writer and editor, Reichl was already making waves in her relatively new post. I can still quote some of her best lines, like the opening grabber of her review of Union Pacific, where chef Rocco DiSpirito was the toast of the town: "The woman at the next table is moaning." And of course I subscribed to *Chicago* magazine, developing a fluency about Chicago's dining scene so I could hit the ground running when I eventually got there. I especially enjoyed Dennis Ray Wheaton's capsule reviews. I was so green that I didn't know many of the ingredients he namechecked in dish descriptions, like juniper and quince, so I looked them up.

Adding adrenaline was an acclaimed restaurant down the street, Criolla's, that represented everything I aspired to. I dined there occasionally (and enviously), sinking into their buttery leather chairs and gazing longingly at original George Rodrigue Blue Dogs on the walls. The maître d' was Duke Bardwell, former Elvis Presley bass player, whose stories of life on the road with the King never failed to delight me, and whose Southern charm helped frame chef Scott Alderson's delicious Southern food.

"How you like that shrimp with the Creole crawfish barbecue, Bubba?" he'd ask me.

Scott had come directly from the kitchen of pioneering California toque Jeremiah Tower at the seminal San Francisco restaurant Stars. At Stars, Scott had worked shoulder to shoulder with such future luminaries as Steve Ells, who'd go on to found Chipotle, and Dominique Crenn, who now owns several restaurants in San Francisco, including one that holds three Michelin stars. I was infatuated with Scott's connection to American culinary history and to the people I'd begun reading about, and he quickly became my first fine-dining mentor.

Scott had come to Seaside to recover from a fraught divorce, seeking quiet contemplation by the Gulf. He was intellectual, excitable, loyal, cocky, stubborn, and looked like Billy Bob Thornton. He was the one person I knew at that point who was as obsessed with all things restaurants as I was, only he had been to the mountaintop.

One day in 1993, while perusing the *New York Times*, I read about the James Beard Foundation Awards, essentially the Oscars of my industry. I understood that standing on my back-deck restaurant of a rural Florida town wearing my cut-off jeans was almost as far away as you could get from wearing a tuxedo at the restaurant Academy Awards. Reading the recap of the night was like reading science fiction; it was exciting but didn't seem real.

I sprinted the mile along the coast to see Scott at Criolla's and showed him the article.

"Dude, did you know there is an Oscar-like ceremony for restaurants?" I said, gasping for air.

"Yeah, babe, it's called the James Beard Awards," he shot back. Scott called everybody *babe*, which usually was fine but felt a little stinging in this context.

Among the group of winners that I read aloud were a few I was familiar with: Charlie Trotter's in Chicago, Chez Panisse in the Bay Area, and Commander's Palace in New Orleans. My dreams at that point topped out at being able to dine at one of those restaurants someday; attending the awards, or winning, never entered my mind.

IF SCOTT REPRESENTED MY BACK-OF-HOUSE North Star, Ollie Petit, the Belgian I had met at Josephine's eighteen months prior, set the bar for me in the dining room through ambition, tone, design, efficiency, and, above all, energy.

After Ollie dined at Lazy Daze Café one night, he told me that he had a little money and wanted me to accompany him to check out the Old Bay Café building, just a couple of miles from Seaside, which was for sale. Compared to my first restaurant, this building was much more ambitious—a two-hundred-seater in a fixer-upper built in the 1800s. On the strength of a humble $35,000 budget and huge cojones, Ollie would turn the space into one of the most iconic restaurants in the Southeast, opened on Super Bowl Sunday 1995: the Red Bar.

Ollie was like my doppelgänger. Well, okay, he stood six foot seven with an enviable Belgian accent that was like a tractor beam for women. In the dining room, he reigned supreme. The son of a respected restaurateur, Ollie was a distinctly European type, with hospitality coursing through his veins, capable of filling any role in a restaurant, including chef (he was a magnificent cook). At the Red Bar he confined himself to the role of cruise director. He sat guests, manned the sound system, ran food, regaled customers with stories, and could upshift to engage in an informed dialogue about the stock market with a wealthy homeowner or downshift to gab vacuously with six boozy dudes from Alabama about girls. It wasn't just the Red Bar; it was the Ollie Petit Show.

But beneath his dining room avatar, he was as manic as I was. It helped me to have a role model. (Today, when interviewing prospective employees, I always ask, "Whose career would you like to emulate?") Criolla's and the Red Bar were the types of places that I could really sink my teeth into. The restaurant business was my purpose, just not the way I was doing it, and nurturing a fledgling restaurant and a fledgling relationship simultaneously was unsustainable. It was becoming increasingly clear to both T and me that it was either the relationship or the restaurant, and neither of us was going to give up the restaurant. This was an especially difficult decision for me because Kara lived with us, providing the semblance of a normal family life that I had always wanted. And, to be honest, I was holding on to the relationship tighter than T was.

ONE EVENING THAT FEBRUARY, AMID a brutal thunderstorm, a familiar and incongruous figure appeared in Lazy Daze's doorway in a tweed trench coat, fedora, and leather boots that smelled of a fresh shine: Woody.

I was surprised at how happy I was to see him and have a chance to show him what I was accomplishing. Still, I had to bust his chops a little:

"You do know we have a phone, Woody. You could have told me you were coming."

He pulled me into a tight clench.

"Nah, I like the element of surprise."

I think Terri, who had hung with me and Woody that night in Panama City, was more excited than I was.

"He's so fucking cool," she said.

For all the roles he'd played, Woody had never worked in a restaurant. But he could commandeer a room like a veteran comedian, and like so many performers, he was sustained by attention. And so, before spending any quality time with me, he had managed to engage the entire dining room in communal conversation, a sort of impromptu Jeffersonian dinner. The highlights, as always, were his stories of combat, both on the front lines and in the ring. He played all the hits, each one eliciting its desired effect:

"It's not about the will to win; it's about the will to prepare to win." (Approving nods.)

"I am not a Republican or a Democrat; I'm an American." (Hoots and hollers.)

"I hit that boy so hard, his ancestors felt it." (Laughter.)

I took Woody for a late dinner at the Red Bar, presenting him as my father to a select few folks.

As ever, even hanging one-on-one with Woody was like getting to see a show without having to buy a ticket. But he was relatively sincere and subdued on this visit. He also brought me a patinaed black-and-white photograph of him in the 1940s, shirtless and wearing boxing trunks, effecting a pugilistic stance. It was the most traditional father-son time we ever shared, but it was fleeting—by the end of the night, he'd gifted the photo to Ollie for the wall of the Red Bar. He said he'd send me a replacement, but never did. A few years later, a drunk swiped the Red Bar's copy. Like most things Woody, all that's left is a memory.

We had coffee the next morning, and then, fifteen hours after arriving, he drifted back out of town. As he always did on the way out, Woody told me he loved me. It would've been dishonest of me to parrot the words back. Sure, he was my biological father, but he hadn't earned the right to more than that. Say what you will about Larry Boehm, but the man never abandoned his family and, as much as his fragile soul permitted, provided for them, even the little boy who he knew wasn't really his son.

THE TIGHT QUARTERS TERRI AND I were trapped in both at work and home intensified the burgeoning tension between us. We lashed out at each other on the daily.

"You need to be more efficient with the dishes," she'd gripe. "I can't fucking run a load while I'm plating. You are holding me up."

"Your problems are not fucking unique, Terri. I am running a fucking full station while being a dishwasher and bartending while trying to make salads. This shit is not easy."

During one particularly cruel argument, I lost it.

"I can't do this anymore. I'm sick of being sad all the time. Take the restaurant. I'm flying home."

I booked a flight, consolidated my belongings into two suitcases, and called a cab.

I arrived at Destin-Fort Walton Beach Airport—a modest facility with just six gates, one security line, and no foodservice—to find I had accidentally booked my flight out of Fort Wayne International Airport in Indiana. This airport's next flight to Chicago was hours away. I took it as a sign that I wasn't supposed to leave and drove back to Seaside and walked into Lazy Daze to see Terri cooking and waiting tables.

"See?" she said, breezing past me to deliver an armful of plated food to a table. "I can do both our jobs."

"Let's see when we get out of this thing how each of us does," I fired back.

"This place doesn't exist without me cooking. But you? You're just a FUCKING SERVER."

That stung as badly as any of Larry's jabs. Actually, it hurt more: unlike most of his putdowns, this one had the force of truth.

SEASIDE WAS FLOWERING INTO A nationally recognized gem. Lady Princess Diana and Prince Charles had visited. *Vogue* and *Time* championed it as the coolest small town in America.

On a weekly basis, I would overhear sunburned couples having dinner, three wines in, hatching a plan to quit their big-city jobs, disappear down to Florida, and open a bar or coffee shop.

As a public service, I sometimes warned them it wasn't as easy as they imagined.

Ollie once overheard me doing that at Lazy Daze when he was dining and scolded me. "What are you doing? They are never quitting their jobs. They are vacation-dreaming. Let them dream. The only difference between us and them is that we were dumb enough to go for it."

Maybe they weren't opening bars or coffee shops, but many were going for the moving-to-Seaside part, and local realtors were reveling in a gold rush. One eager buyer approached our landlord, Dennis, whose attorneys seized on an onerous clause in our lease requiring us to renew it in writing each year, and insisting we'd never given said renewal notice. They gave us eight weeks to leave the property. I panicked, then remembered that when I wrote to explain that we would not be taking an option on our lease to buy the building, I had also casually expressed our intention to renew the lease. It wasn't a signed extension, but was enough to give us leverage. We hired a lawyer and told him we would love to get bought out.

A week later, he called: "Be careful what you wish you for, you might just get it."

Terri's and my prayer had been answered: We'd been offered several thousand dollars—a straight-up payoff for us to fuck off.

If I had learned anything, it was that grit, determination, and just showing up were as crucial to success as raw restaurant IQ. Money might not buy happiness, but it sure lowers the stress level. Suddenly, all the burgeoning tension between me and Terri dissipated, and the pendulum swung back toward something we excelled at: celebration.

Now this—this!—was the Terri I was crazy about.

One night after service, we sat in the dining room and decreed that Lazy Daze was now permanently closed.

"I love you so much, T. Can't believe we survived this."

"We did it. Bigger and better next time! I love you, too. By the way, your skin actually looks really good, Kev. People pay a lot of money for chemical peels like that; you got yours for free."

The day we received the check, Terri and I again sat on Lazy Daze's deck for the last time. We slowly savored a six-pack of

Miller Lite as if it were a prized vintage wine. I had so many ideas for what to do next, I needed that beer just to calm my mind.

I knew peace in that moment, and also something else: An unfamiliar sensation welled up in me—a frightening mix of deliriousness and fear. I was disoriented and overwhelmed almost to the point of tears. Then it hit me: The confusion was because I'd almost never experienced this feeling before.

Happiness.

As soon as it registered, I knew it would be as fleeting as that photo of Woody in the ring. After years of conditioning to the contrary, I didn't know how to maintain it, let alone savor it. That simply wasn't my natural state. It wasn't something I could learn in a how-to book, and nobody had ever shown me how to savor that feeling.

Sure enough, by the time I got in my car, it had left me, already lost amid the stars in the Florida sky. I thought about what my next restaurant might be, and if it might resummon that feeling.

4
INTO THE MYSTIC

ADRENALINE CAN BE A TYPE of anesthesia. When I opened Lazy Daze, the high of owning and operating my own place nullified the pain of sixteen-hour days; vitriolic fights; the crushing, endless workload of a two-person operation; even chafing. It works until it doesn't, and if the meds wear off too soon, you might regain consciousness only to discover that you've been butterflied and are in the midst of open-heart surgery.

Lazy Daze was difficult, cramped, entirely dependent on the two of us, rough, raw, subject to the elements, and had a terrible business model. We didn't know how to properly settle on a restaurant size to maximize profit. If we'd had a bigger space, we could have cleaned up on Friday and Saturday nights, when demand is the highest.

Most restaurateurs are adrenaline junkies who thrive off playing a game of crisis whack-a-mole during service. They're also hooked on restaurants themselves. If you possess the owner-operator gene, you likely harbor a vampiric thirst for the next deal, the next concept, the next opening, the next good run. This is the very definition of the dopamine cycle, or, as *Mad Men*'s Don

Draper once put it, "What is happiness? Happiness is a moment before you need more happiness." This mindset certainly applied to me, deepened by the constants of Larry's criticism and Mom's overachieving.

I think opening a restaurant also must be like giving birth, in that most women I know claim that if you remembered the pain, you'd never have more than one child. I was ready to go again.

Between Christmas and New Year's Eve 1994, Terri and I flew to Chicago. The impetus was to dine at one of those celebrated restaurants I'd been reading about in *Chicago* magazine: Gordon, namesake establishment of Gordon Sinclair. There, we would toast our navigation of hair-immolating fires, scheming landlords, unseasonably cold weather, and our own dysfunction and codependence. In an industry where losses were the most likely outcome of a new venture, we had notched a win. That deserved someone else serving us for a change.

For me, there was another reason that I kept to myself: I sought a spark for my next enterprise.

Part of Gordon's charm was its location, which conferred upon it a speakeasy mystique. Situated in Chicago's then-threatening River North district (today one of the hippest parts of town), where all-night cashiers kept a baseball bat behind the counter, guests—gussied up in observance of the restaurant's dress code—were conspicuous as they exited their cars, limos, and taxis and scurried inside as if trying to evade sniper fire.

Dining at Gordon at that time was an exquisite experience, and a brutal awakening. Sinclair was a former public relations exec whose restaurant success was a mash-up of Studio 54 panache and *Michelin Guide* standards, years before the guide came to the US. Sophistication and good taste personified, Sinclair always hired talented chefs, but it was his style that defined and distinguished the restaurant. From winkingly naughty and gaudy artwork on the walls to Victorian lamps on the tables to elaborate flower arrangements that seemed to explode up out of their vases, all of it set to the soundtrack of a live piano player—it was fine dining with a personality and pulse like I'd never witnessed before.

"Their cheapest wine would be our most expensive at Lazy Daze," I said at the table as I perused the list.

"The appetizers are the prices of our entrees," said Terri.

"I think I have, like, two hundred fifty dollars left on my credit card. It's going to be close," I said, faking a chuckle. "We better keep it to one bottle."

"I feel like we are at the children's table at a wedding."

"This is fancier than any wedding I've been to."

I ordered the cheapest Cabernet on the list. Chef Don Yamauchi's cuisine was a refined yet accessible mingling of French classicism with his father's Japanese roots. We let our server, bubbly as champagne, select our food. (Most memorable was a poached venison with a shiitake-leek cabbage roll that we took in like peyote, closing our eyes to commune intimately with it.)

Gordon Sinclair was a hall-of-fame host, equal parts flamboyant and masculine, reflected in his mostly conservative sartorial sense enlivened with pops of color; for example, a double-breasted blue blazer with a multihued pocket square.

Everything about his restaurant left my past North Stars in the dust: Between the piano player's sets, tinkly jazz fell over the dining room gentle as a first snow; the tablecloths were hospital-corner tight; the silverware, glassware, plates . . . even the napkins were more expensive and elegant than anything I'd used before. And the service was a crazy combination of military precision and good humor: Everybody who touched our table was as suave as Josephine's Bruce. And it all hung together: The food was meant for that room, the waitstaff were so at home it wouldn't have surprised me to learn they lived there, and the guests added that ineffable something that changed nightly. I had never been to California, but I felt that I was experiencing a Midwestern answer to Jeremiah Tower's legendary San Francisco brasserie Stars.

It was as if the industry were one of those old arcade video games in which each level conquered brought you face-to-face with an even more skilled adversary brandishing ever more intimidating weapons and moves. Level 1 had been the Beach House's James Trahan. Level 2 was Bruce. Level 3 was Gordon.

By the time I ate the last sublime morsel of my first course, I was overwhelmed by the realization that my education had only just begun.

Later, on my way to the men's room, I noticed that in addition to artwork, the walls were adorned with hundreds of framed and mounted articles and reviews, many featuring portraits of Gordon himself. I'd never made such a direct connection between a restaurant's name and its proprietor. By the time I headed back to the table, I was almost dizzy. The effect was amplified when I saw that Gordon Sinclair himself was sitting with Terri.

It seemed he'd strolled out of one of those idealized pictures on the wall because the man himself was idealized—an effortlessly charming dandy, with a gift for double entendres and innuendo that would make Sacha Baron Cohen blush. He blocked out the rest of the dining room to grant us perfect attention. I'd never felt so important.

"A small-town Florida restaurant with just you two kids at the helm," he gushed after we told him our story. "I bet people had just as much fun watching the two of you as they do eating the food." (I later found out that Sinclair had a habit of visiting with tables that captured his fancy. I credit his interest in us to the fact that we were the youngest people in the dining room, by at least two generations.)

Over the course of an hour, I pummeled Mr. Sinclair with questions and hung on his every response, imagining how I might apply it to my own restaurant and career.

He toasted our nano-success in Florida, stayed for dessert, and then his new boyfriend joined us all for a postprandial cocktail.

Before pushing off, he invited us to his black-tie New Year's Eve soiree the next night. We accepted, immediately, but when we woke up in the morning, wickedly hungover, we remembered that we didn't have the requisite formal attire, nor anything remotely passable, nor the funds or the time to rent or buy something. We called the restaurant and asked the reservationist to convey our regrets, then just lay there all night, drenched in FOMO before FOMO was a thing.

TERRI AND I HAD DECIDED to stay together as a couple but go our separate ways in business.

Sort of.

This would be my first time making a rough sketch of a restaurant on my own. It started with me writing a prospective name down on my sketchpad: Indigo. It didn't really mean anything. I just thought it sounded cool. As far as concept went, I decided we would be the only wine bar in the surrounding counties. Now, I just needed a location, a food program, a design direction, and a budget.

I would open Indigo Wine Bar, and T would open Affinity, just three miles from Seaside in Blue Mountain Beach. Terri's place would be a clothing and furniture store where she could spread her artistic wings, and I would weave my concept into the same space right next to hers, with no partition or other physical separation. In addition to her creative instincts, she was the perfect model for the clothes she sold and had a gift for reanimating discarded furniture, rescuing it from roadsides and then sanding and finishing it anew.

For me, limitation bred creativity, so Indigo benefited from its minuscule budget, the absence of a hood exhaust system, scant lead time, and the fact that the space was too small to qualify for a full liquor license, only beer and wine. All restaurants have the same core competencies: food, bar, service structure, and so on. The key to creating a successful one is being like a songwriter in search of a melody; from a limited set of notes, the task was to pick the right ones and arrange them as nobody had before. With my antenna up, I quickly identified the right arrangement in two places—one at an existing restaurant, and the other in the pages of a magazine.

To sustain me until I opened Indigo, I took a job at what has since blossomed into a legendary Destin fish house. In addition to the standard Floridian roster of grilled fish, burgers, and fries, the Fisherman served the best sushi in town. I quickly surmised the fact that raw fish doesn't require a hood system, and I had my food concept, just like that.

Within days of that inspiration, in my monthly comb through the pages of *Wine Spectator*, I read about New York City's Soho Kitchen and Bar, which paired casual food with a serious wine program and an eclectic musical selection piped through the speakers. Here was more inspiration. In my mind, we could move seamlessly from Chet Baker in the sunset hours to the Sex Pistols in the witching hours, without missing a beat.

I ordered my business cards:

Indigo

Wine. Sushi. Rock 'n' Roll.

It read like a movie poster.

I had a name, a tagline, and business cards to make me feel important. Now all I needed to do was open a successful restaurant.

LIKE A GENERAL CONTRACTOR, I brought my binder with me everywhere. It housed everything from pilfered restaurant wine lists to manufacturer-provided equipment fact sheets to photocopies of pictures I'd take of, say, sushi bars. Some pages were just silly motivational notes to myself, like: "Smarter every day, nobody outworks you, no beach bums allowed."

One just said "the 1987 Twins." That was a baseball team that won games with chemistry and effort more than talent. I liked the idea of guts over genius. It fit my observation that love of the game can seed a successful restaurateur, and my conviction that no one was going to out-love me.

This time, my ambition was to do something unprecedented in Florida. This led to a boastful sound bite I trotted out for any conversations or interviews about the new venture: "More wines by the glass than anyone in the South!"

Every roadside garage sale, rummage sale, and antique store served as a bargain treasure hunt for the coffee-shop-chic design I envisioned. I found a vintage fire-engine-red meat slicer and bought mismatched chairs and tables. Jeff Lane, who had built our deck at Lazy Daze, came on as my partner, and as part of his equity, he designed and built our twenty-five-foot bar, a formidable cherrywood beauty that immediately became the sun of Indigo's solar system, around which the tables and scene would orbit. Between the two magnificent wine racks on our back bar, we hung a romantic 1920s painting Jeff loaned the restaurant from his collection. It depicted a man with a violin serenading a woman who was up in a tree. We painted the walls antique yellow, then lined them with a collection of paintings and vintage black-and-white photographs that represented a hodgepodge of styles. The front window area would serve as our stage. We programmed live music six nights a week, opened with a small appetizer menu, and served one hundred wines by the glass, long before even the Gordon Sinclairs of the world could conceive of doing the same.

I knew from my research that SoHo Kitchen and Bar in New York City and Hudson Club in Chicago were availing themselves of newly developed tap systems that extended the lifespan of opened wine bottles. We didn't have the thousands of dollars to buy one, so Jeff rigged a small tank of nitrogen with a hose that he affixed to a tap. We'd pump nitrogen into opened bottles, displacing any oxygen and preventing the wine from oxidizing, then quickly cork them.

Our twenty thousand bucks, used carefully, looked more like a hundred thousand. Jeff and I were a mid-nineties version of the Property Brothers. We were design magicians, able to pair the smart-looking bar with mismatched tables draped with indigo tablecloths.

Meanwhile, I continued to earn and learn at that fish house. It showed me a different working culture that offered no shortage of dos and don'ts.

Jacked up on about twelve sweet teas dispersed across each service, I tended to a packed station distributed among four dining rooms (there were no sections). I kept track of them by visualizing a mental map, made my own salads of lettuces, mandarin oranges, and slivered almonds, and sweated right through my Duck Head shorts as I served neon-bright drinks, fresh fish caught from the restaurant's own boats, and traditional sushi.

The restaurant subsisted on tourism, cloyingly sweet margaritas, and cocaine. A longstanding rumor held that the office safe housed two bank bags—one filled with the next day's deposit, one bulging with coke. As the legend went, one day the wrong sack found its way to the bank, where a teller peered inside, quickly retied it, and pushed it back to the restaurant's manager, stammering, "I don't think I can deposit this."

Over the six months I worked there, I came to consider the restaurant both a revelation and a train wreck. Like any successful restaurant, they had established a way of doing things that worked for them. But I fatigued on their lack of professionalism and embrace of drug culture, especially because of the contrast with all the serious restaurants I was reading about. I could have stayed a bit longer and learned more, but if I didn't punch out on that final night, I was going to blow a gasket. I didn't want to play other people's songs anymore; it was time for original compositions only.

RESTAURANT MOVE-IN WEEKS AND PREP days energized me like the first intoxicating weeks of a new love affair. I didn't need days off or even sit-down meals.

We parked the meat slicer, slick as a Corvette, in the corner for making beef carpaccio. To keep pace with the dining room, we pre-plated charcuterie trays and held them alongside the bottles of white wine in a 1950s Frigidaire Cyclamatic. We also stocked four beach coolers with ice and bottled beer and stashed them behind the bar.

Our team was tight. Jeff and I manned the bar on one side, while Glenn Fullin and Scott Randolph rolled sushi where the bar L-turned in front of the windows. The pair were a culinary Abbott and Costello. Glenn was a talented working chef on 30-A, and when I casually mentioned to him that I was looking for a sushi chef, he volunteered his services and called his buddy Scott in South Florida to come travel north. Scott was six foot four, sandy haired, and easy as a Sunday morning. Glenn was five foot six, hairy as Robin Williams, Boston as they come, and could be

My Indigo partner, Jeff Lane, and me, bartending in 1996

ultra-charming or ultra-grumpy, depending on the current state of the Red Sox.

Both were true-blue professionals. We navigated being friends and coworkers without a hitch. Glenn and I would spitball for hours about sports and music. One minute we'd gush over the physical prowess of the Red Sox's Jim Rice; the next we would analyze every track on Van Morrison's *Astral Weeks*. He was intellectual and Southie tough. I liked him as much as I respected him. Hanging with Scott required little effort. He didn't feel the need to fill every pocket of silence with small talk. Going for a beer with him was almost meditative in a sense. He took life a lot less seriously than I did, which was a good counterbalance for me.

I had an unusual financial arrangement with the chefs: At the end of each month, we generated a bifurcated P&L, with allocated expenses, separating the wine bar from the sushi bar, as two distinct businesses. We accounted for expenses, then we split the sushi bar profit with them fifty-fifty, and kept the entirety of the wine-bar profit for myself and Jeff.

As in any good spousal relationship, the chefs and I respected one another's physical and professional boundaries and benefited from a like-minded fastidiousness and an appreciation for accuracy.

For live music, we cobbled together a motley lineup: Voluptuous fiftysomething Phyllis Hasty, whose bright red lipstick popped like an editor's pencil marks above her form-hugging black dresses, purred torch songs on Mondays and Tuesdays. The Buffaloes, a ragtag bunch of twentysomething stoners, punk-band T-shirts hanging loosely over their sinewy torsos, rocked Wednesdays and Thursdays. Melissa Baxter trilled her Lilith Fair–like repertoire on Fridays. And Saturdays were reserved for one of the most talented musicians I've ever encountered: guitarist-singer Kenny Oliverio, who treated patrons to an irony-free romp through seventies rock 'n' roll.

We opened without fanfare on a Wednesday; by Saturday night the bar was three deep.

One of life's great adrenaline rushes is commanding a full bar and watching the congregation swell as the opening chords of whatever song you tee up—"Mary Jane's Last Dance" was among my favorites—receives a collective cheer. You look at the clock, it's 2 a.m., and those next forty-five minutes until last call fly by like the view from an express-train window. Those early, riotous nights were a drunken carnival that kept my anxiety fully at bay.

I would naturally transform into a hospitality assassin—pouring, clearing, washing, and schmoozing like my life depended on it.

THERE WAS A SEDUCTIVE, HAZY stillness to mornings and afternoons around the little seaside town, a pleasing calm in which we ran errands and readied the restaurant for service. Glenn and Scott would stroll to the fish markets together around 10 a.m. to procure the most pristine catch. I would pick up the prior night's earnings from Indigo and drive through the sparsely trafficked streets to deposit them at the bank. On the way back to the restaurant, I'd hit the local Winn-Dixie supermarket to buy lemons and limes for the kitchen and bar. Meanwhile, Jeff laundered our napkins and bar rags at his house and brought them into the restaurant neatly folded when he reported for duty.

The routine, and the meditation it invited, was an essential corrective to the nights of service, and what came after.

In the afternoon, as we prepped our respective stations, we took turns playing our favorite music on the turntable or CD player. There was a *High Fidelity* Championship Vinyl level of snobbery to what we each considered to be our superior taste. An unstated goal was to out-obscure each other while layering in the essentials of any respectable catalog, so standards like Hendrix's version of "All Along the Watchtower" and Van Morrison's "Into the Mystic" might alternate with, say, a deep track from Hüsker Dü or the Replacements.

I had developed a work ethic, biorhythm, and temporal sixth sense that kept me in on track to be ready when we opened the doors every night. Now I just needed the commensurate knowledge. To that end, I'd created a syllabus for completing my metamorphosis from server-caterpillar to restaurateur-butterfly. During downtimes at the wine bar, I'd devour Kevin Zraly's *Windows on the World Complete Wine Course* and Hugh Johnson's *The Story of*

Standing in front of some of the one hundred wines by the glass we served at Indigo

Wine. These took my ability to schmooze about wine to another level. It was one thing to serve one hundred wines by the glass, quite another to know the nuances of what you were pouring. My homeschooling in all things oenophilic worked so well that I was appointed coordinator of the Seaside Wine Festival, a respected local institution.

My bible, though, was the more business-focused *Restaurants That Work: Case Studies of the Best in the Industry*. With its help, I started to figure out simple formulas: 30 percent cost of goods sold, 30 percent labor, 4 percent occupancy, and 16 percent everything else meant 20 percent profit. I was not able to achieve these lofty benchmarks, yet, but they were something to strive for.

This was my first stab at a financial model that would evolve and change over thirty years. It's excruciatingly difficult to turn a profit in restaurants. All the traditional models are not only tricky to navigate; they are also batshit crazy. Like most of my contemporaries, I will defensively point out that I didn't invent this system, I just inherited it.

The strata of income tiers under a restaurant's roof defies logic. After the executive chef, the servers usually make the most money, even though they are hourly employees, and several management-level positions are paid a weekly salary. In forty-three of the fifty states, servers are paid a tipped minimum wage that, when combined with their tips, must equal a state's minimum wage. At the time of this writing, Boka Restaurant Group servers earn an average of approximately $43 per hour. Cooks, who usually do the most physically taxing and stressful work and put in the longest days and nights, get paid anywhere between $18 and $24 per hour. Often they are willing to accept this in exchange for the possibility of becoming the next Stephanie Izard or Daniel Boulud or Marcus Samuelsson.

As I put all of this down, American restaurants themselves, on a national average, make a 5 percent profit. In 1995, profitability averages and standards were much higher. In the three decades since, the cost of a restaurant meal has not kept pace with inflation.

Imagine that a restaurant in 2025 has 100 pennies to spend. Typically, in the US, rent will take 10 of them, cost of goods sold will take 25, labor will take 40, and 20 will go to covering all the miscellaneous costs required to operate. You are left with just five measly pennies to save for a rainy day, and that's if you are respecting all those guidelines and doing as much business, day in and day out, as you have projected.

Several factors might impose themselves on that model. Fine dining usually makes less money than casual. The old adage is "Feed the Masses—Eat with the Classes, Feed the Classes—Eat with the Masses." If you sell a lot of booze, profits go up because the cost of liquor is lower than food, the inherent lack of spoilage, and it takes less labor to put out drinks than plated dishes. If you have servers in North Carolina or Texas, where there's a tipped minimum wage, you pay them $2.13 per hour as opposed to $11 per hour in Chicago, where there's no longer a tipped minimum wage. If you open in New York City, your rent is going to be astronomical, but you also have an almost unlimited upside on what you might gross in sales. If you relish a challenge, you could open in California, a state with no tipped minimum wage, high rents and taxes, and onerous labor laws.

Liquor taxes, labor laws, minimum wages, and property taxes differ among cities and states, making growth outside of your backyard a risky proposition unless you have an A-team of lawyers and accountants who specialize in this sort of thing.

And then there is the most potentially threatening and unpredictable factor of all: the government.

You can decide to build a restaurant, borrow from the bank, put up your house as collateral, all based on the current system. But the next thing you know, the new mayor and city council have decided that tipped minimum wage should be abolished, and suddenly you are paying everyone in the front of house $5 more per hour, and now your shiny new restaurant that turned a 5 percent profit barely breaks even.

All of these norms raise valid ideological, racial, systemic, and sustainability arguments. But without a nuanced and holistic approach to tweaking or overhauling the system, one constituency will always lose. If you abolish tipping, servers will make less. If you get rid of tipped minimum wage, the added labor burden keeps cooks from getting a raise at their next review and makes a perilous business even more so. Any of these cost-adding changes makes restaurants more expensive to consumers.

It's risky, maddening, and tedious. It also plays right into the emotional ebb and flow so many of us in the business are drawn to because it's so fucking rewarding when you beat the odds and open a profitable restaurant.

All of these things were true in 1995, but I didn't know any of them yet. I was just hoping there was some money left in the bank at the end of the month.

WITHIN ABOUT FOUR MONTHS OF our opening, the *Northwest Florida Daily News* reviewed Indigo, my first turn under a professional critic's microscope. We didn't know it was coming until we opened that morning's edition, because we didn't know what the critic looked like. Thankfully, she bestowed four stars—the paper's highest rating—on us.

Our little four-man band celebrated. This was the family I had been searching for. We were open and honest, held each other to a high standard, and respected one another's individual talents. We were all doing multiple jobs, but there was never a discussion of who stood where. We all just naturally gravitated to our lanes of expertise and stayed in them.

I was host, cook, sommelier, bartender, and DJ between musician sets early on, and my duties expanded to bouncer late at night. I had also kept Bruce's hospitality moves in my head all these years and relished opportunities to improvise and create in order to adjust situational temperatures up or down, like the night we hosted a twenty-fifth anniversary party for an older couple from Atlanta.

The focal point of the evening, and of the menu we'd devised, was to be a 1961 Lafite, an expensive wine so fabled that the invitation featured a sketch of the bottle. The afternoon of the party, the husband brought the wine to be decanted for a couple of hours, cradling the bottle as if it were a newborn baby. As I engaged my wine knife, tears pooled in the man's eyes. He explained that his recently deceased father had given him and his wife the bottle two and a half decades prior as a wedding gift.

As I dislodged the cork, it began to crumble. I lifted the open bottle to my nose, and immediately recognized a dreaded musty scent.

"I hate to be the one to tell you this," I said, "but this bottle is corked."

He gasped and looked at me as if I'd just told him a loved one had passed, and his tears of happiness turned to ones of shock and sadness.

"What if we replace it with something else from my list?" I asked.

"These guys are way too sophisticated to think that a '97 Silver Oak is a Lafite." He bristled, insulting me, my restaurant, and my wine list.

Then inspiration struck. I called my pal Bob, a local wine collector, and gave him the lowdown. An unabashed romantic, Bob sold me a '66 Lafite for a mere $100, roughly 10 percent of its market value at the time.

"It's not a '61," he said, "but '66 is still very good."

I told our guest of honor my plan to pass this wine off for his, and his eyes dried up.

"That might work," he said.

I procured the bottle from Bob, decanted the '66, discarded the bottle, rinsed out the '61, and proudly displayed it alongside the decanter.

Two hours later, the couple's guests were rhapsodizing over the finest wine that had ever graced their palates. The man performed a twenty-minute soliloquy about his father that brought the house down. After, he approached me with an ounce of our imposter wine in his glass, kissed me on both cheeks, and whispered in my ear, "You, young man, are a beautiful liar; my father would have loved this."

It's important to be an honest broker in my profession, but sometimes a victimless lie is the only way to make a guest happy.

THE WINE BAR WAS FUN, and not by accident. The trick was not to let guests see what went on behind the curtain to make it so.

For example, I began each day by asking myself the same questions: *How do I convert those I serve today into regulars? What do I have that no one else does? And how do I make those things "sticky,"* meaning memorable to our guests but without clubbing them over the head with them?

If, say, you were a young couple on a date, I would give you two copies of the Proust Questionnaire, inviting you to fill it in and compare your answers, which would accelerate your intimacy.

Or, if you were a wine nerd, I would present our reserve list from a collection we had on consignment and invite you to scribble the name of an expensive wine you wanted to sample on our chalkboard, with your name beside it. If two more brave souls added their names, we'd open any bottle. When a second guest wrote their name beside a bottle, excitement built.

"Come on, let's open this '76 Ridge Zinfandel, who's got the balls??"

When the wine on offer was epic, we didn't have to egg people on; the abundant cork dorks did our bidding for us: "Come on, Phil, this is why you work hard all year. You deserve a glass of a second growth!"

I might have two actual chess games going on over the bar on any given night. One was usually with Klaus, a journeyman server and 30-A's version of Bobby Fischer, who would always grab the back of the bottle while I was pouring to try to get an extra ounce.

By September 1996, Indigo had found its rhythm and insinuated itself into the community, and I had become a real local, medium-famous on 30-A. At the supermarket, owner Mr. Modica and his son Charley hollered "Mr. Boehm!" when I walked in, and I never paid for a meal at the Red Bar or service chairs at the beach.

My fellow locals brought a panoply of personalities to Indigo: There were fishermen and boat captains, artists and architects, real estate developers and retirees, strippers and sommeliers. I remember many of them vividly. There were Nikki and Paul, proprietors of Grayton Corner Cafe, a restaurant that announced itself with a sign that read: HOURS MAY VARY DUE TO QUALITY OF SURF.

The town's requisite man of mystery was Eric Bloom, owner of Bloom's Café, who we all were pretty sure was going by a pseudonym, and whose true identity and background I never solved. Ridiculously tall, with wavy red hair and a perpetual three-day beard, he always wore shorts with no shirt and either bare feet or sandals, even when cooking at his restaurant. He only opened the joint on weekends, if then, and cooked and served whatever he felt like—take it or leave it. Rumors abounded that he was a former CIA operative or chemical warfare specialist. Both seemed plausible.

One night, Eric gave me an ancient coin, rescued from a shipwreck.

"Kevin, I know this specific coin and all its markings," he said. "If you are ever in trouble, mail me the coin and I will be there in twenty-four hours." As I was writing this book, I heard via my Florida network that Eric had died. I never got to find out if he would have heeded the call of the coin.

Indigo was a sixteen-seat bar. From 9 p.m. to 2 a.m., it was my holding cell. When I had been a server at Beach House, Scampi's, or the cocaine fish shack, I could periodically scream in a walk-in cooler, steal a respite by the host stand, or bitch to a coworker at the server station. But you couldn't leave your bar post for a moment, and whenever you were making a drink or uncorking a wine bottle or popping the cap off a beer, three people were already waving you down to place another order. When it was slamming and rhythmic, and stick-and-move bartending, that was heaven. It was the nights where the vacuum sucked you into conversations you didn't want to have that slowly, insidiously smothered your soul. You could have some of the best conversations of your life between 6 p.m. and 9 p.m., but late-night in mid-nineties Walton County, Florida, you were forced to absorb and volley with so much nonsensical bullshit that you could only wash it all down with alcohol. My sweet spot was between the slow periods and the go-for-broke hours.

A few regulars had their own de facto stools. Barstool number 1 belonged to Julie Wilson, Indigo's very own Penny Lane, the nomadic groupie in *Almost Famous*. She came in every night, functioned as

Greg Barnhill rocking the crowd, Indigo Wine Bar, 1996

our most ardent ambassador, showered Jeff and me with kind words, nursed three glasses of wine over six hours, and lit the place up with a one-hundred-watt smile. She was our most devoted fan, mascot, publicist, and a steady contributor to our bottom line. Barstools 5 and 6 were the unofficial domain of Eric Bloom and his drinking buddy John, who would come in to drink wine before heading off to one of their homes for their Scotch-appreciation rituals. And there was Dana Toups, who opted to stand, a self-proclaimed 265 pounds of twisted steel and sex appeal, spouting Tulane football stories to anybody who'd listen.

AT HOME, THE PEACE THAT came with excising Lazy Daze from our lives was proving short-lived. Terri and I were coming apart at the seams. No action or fact of life was too small to set one or both of us off, like a customer leaving a glass sweaty with condensation on one of the antique tables at her shop, or her dresses stinking of smoke from the bar. We might have endured all of that, but she worked during the day, and I worked at night—so we were denied even the compensation of great sex.

The last thing Terri wanted when she wasn't parenting or working was more work and more parenting, and I often required both. I could keep my restaurant running and balance customers and the dishes, but my car needed constant repairs, and I mismanaged my bankbook. Often, when I returned home at night, there'd be a message on the answering machine about an overdue credit card or car payment. Terri had divorced a full-fledged adult, and now it must have felt like she'd demoted herself from the penthouse to the frat house.

Terri's scathing responses to all of this (e.g., "Clean up your shit. I'm not your fucking mom!") left me reeling. I always felt like I was struggling to catch up, and would have happily done so to appease her, but I didn't know how to accelerate my maturation. If

I'd possessed more experience and awareness, I would have seen the writing on the wall and done all I could to turn things around. I still loved Terri, and I loved Kara as if she were my own daughter. I had internalized the notion that we were a family. But on one of those tranquil mornings, Terri let me know, in a very businesslike fashion, that she was going to relocate Affinity from the wine bar space to Grayton Beach, and that she would be moving on from me.

She then, parentally, informed me that I would need to find a new place to live, in case I hadn't put that together myself.

My anguish was that ugly kind of anguish that you can spot from one hundred feet away. *From now on*, I thought, *I will take a cue from my boxing dad, Woody. Stick and move, baby. Stick and move.*

Of course, none of this kept me from calling Terri every few nights around 2 a.m., after downing two bottles of wine, begging her to take me back.

FINDING A SUMMER RENTAL ON 30-A was a fool's errand, so I took up couch surfing. Most nights I washed up at one of my employee's pads at the Brickyard, the nickname for a short strip of about twenty-five trailer-sized redbrick houses, mostly populated by construction workers and restaurant people. When nothing presented itself for the night or I was the last person remaining at Indigo, I crashed on its Burgundy-splotched yellow couch. Finally, I found a place to rent, at the home of a steady customer of the wine bar who was only in town one or two days a week.

It was around this time that I realized there were rules to the human connection I strove to establish with guests. If my smile turned upside down, or my shoulders slumped, or God forbid I answered a "How you doing?" with anything other than "Great!" it would be met with some variation on the sarcastic, "Well, aren't you a barrel of laughs."

Moral of the story: No patron is interested in a sad bartender, server, or owner. We are there to help them escape whatever might be on their minds. Does that make the relationship insincere or the guest selfish? For a moment I might have felt that way, but quickly realized that part of our job was to compartmentalize whatever might be going on with us to fully focus on the guest. I learned to hide my heartbreak behind a passable poker face. No matter how low I might be during a given service, I served up food, drinks, and colorful anecdotes with a wink and a smile. Of course, grief doesn't have a shelf life. At some point, it will impose itself on you. If anything, its powers only redouble while it's bottled up. I didn't know that yet, so once I figured out how to get the cork in, I kept that bottle on the shelf for a good long while.

One night, Ollie, who was dealing with a breakup of his own, called to invite me down to Red Bar post-close. After letting me in, he relocked the door, turned to me, and said, with baroque gravity, "Tonight, we drink."

He whipped up a pasta. I made margaritas. (The objective was inebriation, not sublime food-and-drink pairing.) Ollie wasn't much of a drinker, especially for a restaurant professional, but we killed pitcher after pitcher until we shambled out the door at 5 a.m. First light was just beginning to turn the night sky a pale blue.

I'm ashamed of this, but it's the truth: That morning, I tried to drive home to my temporary spot in Point Washington, a little town across the bay. I almost made it. About five hundred feet from the house, passing over a small wooden bridge, I fishtailed and skidded. Two tires lifted off the bridge, leaving my Grand Am listing to one side. I climbed out and walked the rest of the way home to sleep it off.

A few hours later, freshly showered, caffeinated, and groomed, I returned to the bridge to reclaim my car. It was gone.

Tucking my tail between my legs, I collected my car from the Walton Police Department. (Turns out, they'd been called when a driver couldn't get around it.)

For a few months, I wore heartbreak on my face like a tattoo. Barely able to get out of bed, I'd drag myself to work, bloated and bleary eyed, grind till 2 a.m., then drink myself to sleep, often crashing on the yellow sofa.

Occasionally the wine bar phone would ring and Kara would be on the other end of the line. "Ken-in, what are you doing?"

Her voice shattered me every time. The poker face came in handy: "Just missing you, kiddo."

I spent the better part of three months marinating in maudlin music (belated apologies to the patrons who endured Sarah McLachlan's *Fumbling Towards Ecstasy* on an endless loop), still lobbying Terri for another chance. I knew we weren't right for each other, but that didn't matter. I was heartbroken and couldn't bear it—I needed her back, to be distracted by all-consuming services, or to dull the pain with alcohol.

In time, I'd realize that I hadn't thought about her for hours, or a day, and then not at all. Increasingly, I could concentrate on the good things in my life: Indigo's space had doubled, there was room for growth, and a beautiful woman named Julie had been smiling at me from across the bar.

Julie was a rich girl from Birmingham. She had similar father issues to mine (up to a point), was sophisticated and smart and funny as hell. She also had a flair for flirtation. One night she wrote me a note and slid it across the bar:

"What do you say I help you clean up tonight and then you come home with me?"

"That's the most extraordinary idea I've ever heard," I wrote below her note, then slid it back her way.

Nothing with us was complicated, rushed, or fraught. She was living on her own for the first time and just wanted to have fun. Her planning for the future didn't extend beyond "What are we doing tonight?"

One morning I walked into Indigo and there was an envelope from T waiting for me on the bar. Word had reached her that I was hanging with Julie. She waxed on about how much easier it must be to date someone with less responsibility and children than her.

"I still love you, and we all miss you," she wrote.

At the bottom of the letter was a sketch of her and Kara—she still knew how to hurt me.

I wanted so badly to be in love, and to have a supportive partner. Terri and I tried to get back together, igniting an on-again-off-again stretch. But after months of back and forth, we finally and permanently euthanized our relationship at the end of the summer. For all the ugliness our relationship brought out in us, I will always look back fondly on my time with Terri. Lazy Daze never would have happened without her. And she was always game for anything. We did a lot of cliff-diving together. It was and remains the wildest relationship of my life. She was the Bonnie to my Clyde. I'm just thankful we called it off before our game of chicken culminated in a tragic end.

A HUMAN BRIGADOON, WOODY SKIPPED through the front door of Indigo one night, a year after he'd materialized at Lazy Daze. He'd begun making an annual tour, visiting old war buddies, and had added me to his rounds, even though we were the opposite of comrades in arms: I had been alone in the foxhole all those years and my ruminating on the situation had driven us further apart, not closer. The same could be said for the fact that we never spoke on the phone; he kept tabs on me via Mom and showed up unannounced, on his terms, same as ever.

Woody took every opportunity to engage with strangers as a new audience for his stories. This time, Jeff got forty-five minutes of The Woody Show as I worked around them. Twenty-four hours later, for the I-don't-know-what time, this phantom of my life vanished into the ether once more.

The most surreal pop-in came on the quietest of Mondays, as I cleaned up after service. Robert Davis, the pioneer developer of Seaside, came into Indigo around midnight, accompanied by a cosmopolitan stranger with an Australian accent, a welcome departure from the usual beer-swilling late-night crowd. Davis had never visited one of my places before, so I was jittery. He was the sort of metropolitan swell you didn't see much around town, balding, with a thatch of salt-and-pepper hair, a beard to match, and designer spectacles. He had inherited land on 30-A from his grandfather many years prior. As a condition of the will, he was required to do something impactful with it. Davis, a Harvard graduate, had collaborated with two German architects to design a utopian community, one that became an iconic tourist destination for the elite of the Southeast, and tangentially but not technically my home base. (I lived in an adjoining township.) As they sat down at my small bar, the Aussie commented on my music of choice, Chet Baker's haunting "Let's Get Lost."

"Just imagine: someone playing Chet Baker in the Panhandle with this type of wine selection," he said. "This place makes no sense. I love it!"

Robert told stories of the early days of Seaside and his vision for it. The charming stranger told much more elaborate tales, including one about his time in the Philippines with Mel Gibson and Sigourney Weaver.

I was out of my league, so I just poured wine, DJ'd, and nodded my head in agreement at what I thought were the right cues. It was at this point that I asked the stranger his name.

"I'm Peter Weir," he said, extending his hand.

At the time, Weir was one of the most sought-after movie directors in the world. He'd made *Gallipoli*, *The Year of Living Dangerously* (the reason he was with Sigourney Weaver and Mel Gibson in the Philippines), and *Dead Poets Society*, the Robin Williams vehicle that had earned Weir an Oscar nomination.

"I think your cute little town could be the right location for something I'm looking to film," he said.

As Peter left that evening, he thanked me for the time, and told me that if he returned, he would find me again.

Not long after that night, news broke that Jim Carrey, the rubber-faced contortionist comedian and actor, who was one of the biggest movie stars on the planet, would be spending a few months in town filming *The Truman Show*. That was the mystery movie Weir had told me about. The entire population of Seaside was giddy. When the production arrived, it was like a circus coming to town, and everybody, it seemed, scrambled to be an extra, or stand just out of the frame during exterior shooting days and watch the movie magic.

Weir kept his promise and suggested that Indigo occasionally cater the dailies. I saw to it personally, delivering our food to the set and keeping the buffet neat and tidy. As far as he still had to go, Table Mess Kevin had come a long way.

On my first day, Carrey walked up to me, grabbed a piece of sushi, and, in cartoonish Ace Ventura glory, said "Ohhhhh, got some sushi today," really snapping the word *sushi*. He took a savage bite, looked me in the eye, and said: "That's gooooood sushi."

I occasionally had the opportunity to shoot the shit with Carrey. He was always friendly and kind, but his energy was erratic and unpredictable. One day he'd treat us to a private improvisational stand-up set; others he disappeared inward. I felt a kinship with him, and learned years later that he, too, carried psychic souvenirs from his childhood. Unlike me, he revered his father, but based on interviews, he seems to have never lost the pain of watching his dad lose his job, become unhoused, and ultimately lose his appetite for life. Years later I would read a quote from Jim about his dad that effectively summed up many of my own choices: "You can fail at what you don't want, so you might as well take a chance on something you love."

Seaside was thriving but I was starting to feel like I had outgrown it. I felt an irresistible pull to be in a city that was at the forefront of innovative dining. As the new millennium approached, American cuisine and service were reaching their all-time zenith up to that point. In cities like New York, Los Angeles, Boston, and Chicago, chefs and restaurants were closing the gap between this country's historically inferior offerings and those of the most acclaimed European restaurants.

As I was pondering my next move, Jeff and I were approached with a six-figure offer for Indigo. We accepted. As part of the deal, I would stay on for six months to orient the new owners. Chefs Scott and Glenn took this as an opportunity to stake their own collective claim. Both gave us three-months' notice, and began collaborating on a new place, Basmati's. Indigo had been my second at-bat with a chef collaboration, this time sans romantic entanglement. It helped me develop an understanding of the importance of that relationship. Scott would go on to be the corporate executive chef for American Airlines, then TGI Fridays. Occasionally, I'd see him on the Food Network. But it was Glenn who broke my heart. Just weeks before opening Basmati's, Glenn—just twenty-seven at the time—suffered a major heart attack and died. I was the last to see him alive.

At the end of my final six months, I was back down to clothes, a box of pictures, and my Snoopy doll, but this time I also had my journals, a small box of press clippings about my budding career, and a relatively hefty bank account for a twenty-six-year-old.

I THREW MYSELF A GOING-AWAY party. It paled beside the six-year tornado that had preceded it. We played records, ate pizza, and told wine-bar stories. I was still broken, but less broke, and while I still felt an antipathy toward the world, I liked myself a little more than before. I was held together with bubble gum and Scotch tape, but moving on felt like moving forward.

Half the guests fell asleep at my house. I didn't wake them in the morning. I tiptoed over and around them and showed up at Terri's shop to cry with Kara and give T a long goodbye hug.

I ran into Al, a local restaurateur, as I walked into breakfast staple Wheelhouse for my final 30-A breakfast.

"Did you make enough money from your sale of that crazy-ass joint to buy me a cup of coffee?" asked Al, loud enough that the whole restaurant could hear.

"Yup, about a hundred thousand of them."

I left my last dining room on 30-A with a roaring laugh.

I called Mom with my first-ever cell phone and told her that her son might be paying her a visit, this time with his pockets a little fuller.

"You made it out alive!" she joked.

"By the skin of my teeth, Mama. The bobcat almost got me."

I made a stop in Chicago to get a bead on the real estate and construction costs. Sticker shock quickly ensued. Then I drove to Springfield to pay Mom that visit and check out the town with fresh eyes. The truth is I was allergic to the idea of failing publicly, and doubted life would afford me a second chance in Chicago. Maybe, I figured, Springfield was ready for something different, and maybe it'd be better to be a prince there than a Chicago also-ran, at least for the time being.

My second day in town, I found a lawyer and incorporated INDIGO INVESTMENTS, INC. I was given momentary pause by the continued existence of D&J Cafe. The entire town had been transformed in the years since my breakfast with Woody, but the café abided—a shrine to my own distinctly screwed-up family history.

I slept on the couch at my parents' house. The next morning, a rustling in the dark woke me. Larry was hunched over the dining room table, stealing a look at my corporation paperwork. Hearing me sit up, he shot me a look of disdain.

"Presidents of corporations don't sleep past six a.m.," he said.

I didn't engage. Just rolled over and promised myself I'd never spend another night in that house.

5
TURN THE PAGE

"IT SOUNDS LIKE YOU'RE BIPOLAR."

This was in the office of a therapist named Sharon, whom I found in the Yellow Pages, a hefty phone book of business listings that was common pre-Internet. I was baffled that Indigo's success hadn't naturally produced sunshiny days of the soul. I had sold my restaurant for six figures, returned home flush for the first time, and walked with a strut that had eluded me in adolescence. Surely even Larry must've admitted to himself that I wasn't a complete loser. Things were going well; my mind just hadn't caught up, like the lag between something occurring and being reported.

I expected the therapy session with Sharon would produce an immediate result, like popping an Advil for a headache. Her office was in a drab building along a drab stretch of downtown Springfield. The building was populated by businesses that time forgot; most hadn't been redecorated since the 1970s. The good doctor and I simply didn't relate. My strong sense was that she'd been monotonously dispensing one-size-fits-all diagnoses and guidance since earning her license. And her stoic assessment of me only intensified my reaction.

"No!" I snapped. "That's not what I am." This was our first session and she clearly didn't understand me. What was she even talking about? "I am not bipolar."

Why couldn't she determine that I was merely confused?

Fuck you, Sharon, you don't know me, I thought to myself.

One night during my first week back, I met some friends for a late-night beer at J's on the Curve, a dive bar with cigarette smoke thick as London fog and harrowingly perched on a hard turn between two of Springfield's busiest thoroughfares. Tommy and Mike, my high school classmates whom I hadn't seen since the eighties, materialized through the mist, clutched my arm, and spun me around.

"Kevin fucking Boehm!" Tommy bellowed. "I heard some shit about you. Let me ask you a question: Do you manage these restaurants, or are you like Dave Thomas?"

"I guess when you put it that way I'd be Dave Thomas," I said, happy to be compared to the affable, gray-haired founder of Wendy's who was a household name at the time, thanks to his turn as a television pitchman for his hamburger chain.

"Good! Then you can afford to buy us some shots."

Springfield hadn't changed much.

I was another story: The last time I lived in Springfield, I was a stick figure in boxy jeans and T-shirts that concealed my wiry frame, like David Byrne's big suit, and sported a $5 haircut and ripped Chuck Taylors. Eight years later, I still had a massive chip firmly in place on my shoulder, a phantom parrot to my itinerant inner pirate. Only now, I looked every bit the fancy kid I'd daydreamed about being: blazers, designer jeans, Bachrach suits, starched Arrow shirts, slicked-back hair, and a vintage silver watch. I always unbuttoned my shirt just enough to make it clear I wasn't a banker . . . Okay, maybe one button more than that.

Once a week, clad in my flashiest suit, I'd brave Springfield's best fine dining restaurants, like Maldaner's, an institution that dated back to the Lincoln administration and still remained a watering hole and feeding trough for state senators. Sebastian's Hideout, the new kid on the block, glowed like a spaceship; it was sleek, well-lit, and served standard-issue contemporary American food. Café Brio was where local wannabe hipsters congregated for appropriated Mexican street food. And Gumbo Ya Ya, true to its name, was a Cajun joint housed in a revolving space at the top of the Hilton.

Other nights were for chasing fun. I still had a handful of friends in town, including one of my U of I chums who was clerking for the Illinois Supreme Court. We would find a casual dinner, drink until 3 a.m., then wash up at Steak & Shake—home of Springfield's best grub, a grease-laden patty melt with a crunchy iceberg side salad drenched in Thousand Island dressing.

By day, I would set up office at the Starbucks inside the city's lone Barnes & Noble and plot my restaurateur reincarnation. I kept my to-do list and critical paperwork in my old baseball-card binder. On its cover, I had Sharpied: "Project 3, Indigo Springfield. Best or Bust."

Action item #1 was "Find a partner," and I already had a lead.

On one of Mom's days off, when Larry was at work, I asked her: "Mom, how would you like to quit your job at T.J. Maxx and be my business partner? I think it's time to tell retail to go pound sand after twenty years."

"Why on earth would you want me?" she asked, her voice—as it did at awkward times—hitting a jolly, fluttering Julia Child high note.

"Easy! You can help make my crazy ideas a reality. You're wicked smart, and you make anything you touch more beautiful."

Her voice sailed even higher: "Well, I'm not so sure about all that."

"I'm sure enough for both of us."

She had worked in retail since the mall opened in 1978, and yearned to earn a living without having to answer to anyone. The ripe quince didn't fall too far from the tree. Her restaurant learning curve would be steep, but she was hardwired for entrepreneurship. As for self-managing, nobody could possibly push Mom harder than she pushed herself. Her quasi-pathological fear of failure drove her to pursue absolute perfection in everything, perhaps because men in her life had always been quick to pounce on any vulnerability.

Finally, she acquiesced.

I'd never created a formal budget before, because it would have made it impossible to maintain my denial over how little money I'd had to spend on prior projects. But this time, there was proper funding, and more things to buy, so I had to get serious and write it all out. In Springfield, my opening budget was $55,000, about what we spend on barstools these days (that's not a joke), but at the time, it seemed like a lot of money. Only $8,000 of that would be spent on the kitchen, which would have to get by with a leased dishwasher, a Vulcan six-burner stove, a used grill, a convection oven, and one fryer, limiting how much food could be pumped out at any time.

We'd pour the lion's share of the money into décor, and we stretched those dollars as if we were competing on a penny-pinching game show. I formulated broad ideas and Mom executed with all the style and ingenuity of Martha Stewart—if Martha were forced to operate on just her gardener's salary. With no money for a designer, I sketched out the dining room on a white poster board from Walgreens. It only took a few minutes, because I had been imagining this since Lazy Daze Café.

We bought a 1920s bar from Punky's Palace antiques, and I purchased 130 threadbare 1940s chairs. The little apartment I'd rented after Larry's early-morning quip became a furniture workshop: With windows flung open for ventilation, and an oscillating fan whirring nonstop to disperse the toxic fumes, we refinished the bar and stripped and reupholstered the chairs with indigo fabric. We painted the walls of the restaurant mocha with burnt sienna accents, and I bookended the bar with two living room sections on either side.

Our long days together gave me an opportunity to get to know Mom all over again, this time much more deeply, as a fellow adult. Our conversations ranged from existential to political. Grown-up me adored her as much as child me had.

"If you could go anywhere, Mom, where would it be?"

"I'd like to see the Holy Land. I think Bethlehem would blow my mind."

"Well, let's figure out how to get you there once we get this place humming!"

To help Mom identify and improve in all aspects of management, I retrofitted fifteen cards from a Bicycle card deck, gluing a piece of paper naming a necessary skill, decorated with a clip-art image, to each one. The idea was to continue using it as a management tool and award managers cards as they mastered each aspect. The cards were:

- Attention to Detail
- Financial Management
- Spirit and Punctuality
- Touching a Table
- Pre-shift
- Food Knowledge
- Wine Knowledge
- Cocktails and Beer
- Conflict Resolution
- Discipline of Staff

- Hiring
- Relationship Building
- Front Door
- Expediting
- Technical Service Skills

The final step was asking Mom, a gifted painter, to fashion an imitation of the famous George Rodrigue's Blue Dogs that I'd envied on the walls of Criolla's years prior. She painted one that hewed so tightly to perfection, I doubt Rodrigue himself would have known the difference.

"That's perfect, Mom. Now I need seventeen of them."

We perused a book of the artist's images to select which ones to imitate.

"The Blue Dog in the poppy field," I said, stopping on a page. "I love this one."

"I love that one, too. I bet you I can do that one exact," she said with uncharacteristic brio.

Mom had always been under the thumb of someone. She didn't locate confidence in many things, so the Blue Dogs were a booster for her. As her renditions proliferated, anyone and everyone who laid eyes on them made a point of telling her how much they loved them, something that would continue to happen after the restaurant launched. It was the first time since high school that she'd received attention for her talent.

We built massive frames and sewed canvases together to obscure the three twenty-foot window bays. On these, Mom would paint gargantuan Blue Dog murals. Larry was uncharacteristically gracious, helpful even. He assisted me in building those frames, and helped me install our massive bar. It was a welcome improvement over our usual dynamic, and a stinging glimpse of how things could have been.

Years later, Rodrigue called me, curious because so many people had come to his gallery reporting they'd spotted originals on our wall, including the biggest Blue Dog murals they had ever seen. I sensed a cease-and-desist letter in my future, but after I told him the full story, he gave us his blessing, just so long as we weren't passing them off as his or selling them. Sometimes, people's generosity outstrips your imagination. I remain surprised and heartened by that random act today.

Action item #2 (undertaken simultaneously), "Find a chef," was proving more challenging.

Two candidates engaged with me for a heartbeat, then dropped out. Both offered the same reasons: They didn't agree with my menu ideas, such as a sushi program in a city they considered pedestrian, and they were scared off by my boundless ambition and manic energy, sure that they couldn't match it or meet my expectations.

Desperate, I called Scott Alderson. He had just finished a stage—an unpaid kitchen stint undertaken for learning purposes—at Charlie Trotter's, a landmark Chicago restaurant that had just been named the best in the world by *Wine Spectator.*

After we briefly caught up, I worked up the nerve to ask if he would come to Springfield and anchor the kitchen for a spell. When I did, there was a long, disquieting pause before he hemmed and hawed, rattling off a litany of reasons he couldn't do it: He had just returned to Florida. He needed a break after Trotter's. Springfield winters are cold.

My heart sank. This was an emergency, and I'd already broken the glass.

Then he revealed that—thank God—he'd been toying with me. As we were talking, he'd been chucking clothes into a duffel bag. At the end of the call, he said, "I'm already driving toward you. See you in fourteen hours." The one caveat was that he would only stay on for a few weeks. He was happy to help a friend, but not to relocate.

The next day, Indigo was on the launchpad. As I sat on one of our new leather couches, I whispered to myself, over and over, "This is an actual restaurant. This is a real restaurant." I had experienced fleeting moments of pride, but nothing like this. Indigo 1.0 had started with a pen and paper and a meager amount of money in a black space in a three-unit strip mall. But even though this was in a strip mall, this was no strip mall restaurant. Once inside, you were transported somewhere, like Dorothy escaping drab, black-and-white Kansas for vibrant, Technicolor Oz, without having to endure a tornado.

Moments later, Scott appeared in the restaurant's doorway, red-eyed from his marathon drive.

"What. The. Fuck?" he exclaimed. "I had no idea I was walking into this. It's beautiful."

Seeing the kitchen brought him back down to Earth. "Well, I can tell you're a dining-room guy," he groused.

Scott asked me to leave him alone for a few hours so he could work on a menu. I had drafted a list of dishes to illustrate my vision—a highlight reel of late-nineties food trends. Tuna tartare, goat cheese and beet salad, fish au poivre—they were all there. Fortunately, Scott treated it as an outline, imposing his own worldly palate and panache. He sketched the plating of the dishes in his notebook, diagramed the components, roughed out recipes for each one, catalogued which ingredients he thought might be tough to source in Springfield, wrote down and circled estimated raw cost, and ranked them by approximate product mix hierarchy, a guesstimate of what percentage of sales each offering would represent.

"Hey, babe," Scott said, "I need meetings with every purveyor in town."

I sat at the bar and worked on the beverage lists and wrote a mock schedule. Then we caucused, hashed out a plan for the week, wolfed down two tough sirloins at LongHorn around the corner, and got some sleep. We were seven days out.

Proust asks when or where were you happiest. My answer up to that point in my young life was that night in Springfield, adrenalized, prideful, and hopeful, my brain firing on all cylinders, energized by the possibilities. I couldn't wait to take Indigo out for a spin, and see how fast and far she could go.

Scott's time cooking in California was well represented on my first real restaurant's menu. Among the items were: panéed chicken with red pepper–fennel coulis with salad niçoise; seared tuna with ginger cabbage stir-fry over a Mandarin soy ponzu; and filet mignon with a Creole crawfish BBQ. I told everyone in town that would listen to come see us. I even did a radio spot that ended with my narration in full exaggerated announcer voice: "Indigo Restaurant, bringing the WORLD to Springfield."

I received a respectable number of résumés for front of house (FOH) and dining room positions. I decided to hire mostly young, inexperienced, or no-experience servers and bartenders I could shape to my specs, rather than the veterans who would need to have bad habits trained out of them. (It also seemed easier to sell the dream to exuberant youths than to jaded veterans.) My inexperienced Beach House incarnation would have fit right in. I hedged my bets by also hiring Sebastian and Danny, two cagey vets who could be counted on to maintain tempo and order, when they weren't taking extended smoke breaks.

Scott, on the other hand, only received five applications for cooking positions, despite our description of his pedigree in the classified ads. Some of the people who applied were named like a Springsteen-song cast of characters, the others like rappers:

Coolio, Psycho, J-Dog, and Ray-Ray. The fifth member, Chris, must have felt crippling name envy.

Scott hired them all. For the next week, he put these local ham-and-eggers through a crash course in elevated contemporary cuisine and shored up their rudimentary skills. They spent their days doing everything from honing their knife cuts to learning the proper way to grill a soft-shell crab to assembling maki rolls. It was grueling and not for everybody: One afternoon, Scott dispatched one of the cooks to fetch a mint sprig from the cooler, and the guy never came back.

Less than one week after interviewing our first prospective employee, we'd assembled this crew—like others I'd cobbled together, this one was more tenacious than talented—and were ready to take our project out for a test drive.

Chef Scott Alderson and me, opening night of Indigo, 1998

The afternoon preceding our first service the mailman dropped off a small stack of bills.

"When are you guys going to open?"

"Tonight!"

"Really?" He seemed confused, looking up at our raw industrial ceiling. "You know you can put a drop ceiling in here for almost nothing."

"I know. We want the ceiling exposed. We like it that way."

"Well," he said, "it's different, I guess."

Our first review was in. We were different, and by my standards that was a good thing.

A few hours later, I pulled the string on a tiny blue neon sign above the front door that now signaled OPEN.

INDIGO WAS MY FIRST REAL opportunity to conduct nightly preshift meetings with the front of the house, and that first night I seized it, sharing what wisdom I'd accumulated by that point in my career.

I told them about bobcats and fires, Scott Alderson's generosity, and how everything inside the restaurant had a story behind it. I told them about the importance for me of returning home, and how my mother figured into the love behind this place. We all joined hands, and I talked about how we should support each other and hold each other accountable at the same time.

"There is one way to do many of the things in this restaurant. When you don't know the answer, or come across something we haven't discussed, just be nice. Guests will forgive us for so much if we are nice."

I wrapped the whole thing up with this bow: "We don't live in Springfield; we live in Indigo, Illinois."

There was a formality to this Indigo that I hadn't been associated with before. There was a host stand, a ticket system, tip-outs, and a training guide with defined service steps. I had so many new ways to fail. The pressure was both smothering and intoxicating, like a shot of Malört.

The reservation book was an old accountant's ledger I'd picked up at an antique store. The menu was printed on bright white eight-and-a-half-by-eleven-inch paper, thick stock with black script in Times New Roman. At the top of the menu, this story greeted customers:

> Welcome to Indigo. The origins of my journey began in 1992 on a back deck in Seaside, Florida, and on a small hill in Blue Mountain Beach, Florida. Indigo and Lazy Daze Cafe were my first two restaurants, and they were hand crafted, personal, and built on the idea that fine dining can also be fun. I am so pleased to bring these same ideas to Indigo Springfield. Please let us know anything we can do to make your stay with us more enjoyable.
>
> Kevin Boehm

We bought bread from a local bakery and served it as a complimentary welcome nosh to guests, with olive oil, balsamic vinegar, olives, and hummus.

On our first night, I was able to lure Kim Carnes to be the musical talent. We served 150 dinners without too many missteps, and to me it felt like the top of the mountain. Hell, I think even Larry had a good time. He was three Seven and Sevens in by the time Kim sang "Bette Davis Eyes."

As I scanned the room for glasses that needed clearing and napkins that needed refolding, my eye caught on an ebullient Dee Boehm, basking in the attention being lavished on her paintings and enjoying something that she'd helped create, not to mention the sight of her son, all grown up, thriving, and in his element.

I was more effective on the service floor than behind the bar simply because the freedom to move made me happier. (I hadn't yet developed the ability to identify the few perfect spots to observe the dining room without calling attention to myself or becoming an obstacle; that would take time.) I enjoyed popping up one moment at the host stand, then disappearing and reemerging by Table 35 so I could explain the black-and-blue tuna dish to a bewildered older couple who'd only ever eaten tuna from a can.

The hardest nights really tested me, and I didn't want it any other way. Finding yourself in the weeds and enjoying the adrenaline hit is the restaurant version of storm chasing. You know the phrase dinner rush? For me it contained a double meaning: the onslaught of customers at peak service hours and the dizzying feeling that managing that churn could bring. For me, the sweet spot was feeling like it could go off the rails at any moment, but you are the hero who never allowed it to. The kind of service where I'm sweating, but my poker face (and black suit/black shirt combo) prevents anybody from noticing.

For example, Indigo experienced occasional twenty-minute drags on reservations all night long. That's not enough time for people to become apoplectic, but still gave me an opportunity to flex my hospitality muscles. One of my moves was to welcome a waiting party into the inner circle by bringing them a plate of food, silverware, and napkins and setting them up at the bar. "Chef's been tinkering with this dish," I'd say. "We haven't put it on the menu yet. Mind doing me a favor and tasting it and letting me know what you think?"

I always overbooked by two tables, to make up for the inevitable last-minute cancelations and no-shows. (This was years before reservation apps made it possible to charge those offenders.) On sweet-spot nights they'd all show up, but I was covered: I kept extra-small two tops in dry storage and would add them as needed, precariously set wherever we could fit them on the night. Those parties knew they weren't getting prime real estate, so I'd start them with complimentary champagne and treat them to dessert, to make them feel like we were in this together.

One of our servers, Cassie, was very pregnant, and I would occasionally cover for her during the last turn of the night, which gave me a chance to keep my server capabilities honed.

A conservative older customer, unmoved by Scott's menu, might say, "I don't understand this chicken dish. Lose the panée and the red pepper crap. I just want chicken."

I generally tried to placate customers without compromising what we did, but when they clearly had made up their minds, I saved time and gave in. There was always a table that didn't get us, but we didn't care. We could grill chicken with the best of them and put mashed potatoes on the side.

I would write little notes on Post-its to give servers the scouting report on a table:

"He's a pussycat, but she's tough. Let her lead the conversation."

"Don't pretend to know more than you do. Bill knows a lot about wine."

"Loves the expensive Napa Cabs."

"Does not like chit-chat, keep it all business."

Sometimes I would just write something to crack them up:

"Five bucks if you can make this couple smile."

Indigo was also the place where I was introduced to employee archetypes whose stylistic and temperamental soulmates I'd encounter again and again in other cities and restaurants.

David was the charming/shady one, and also the biggest liar. (His résumé said he'd graduated from Oxford, which may have been true. He was brilliant, just unethical.) I think he ultimately made us more money than he stole, but who knows. He loved working his tables, but he loved alcohol and ill-gotten gains even more. He also called me boss in a smarmy way that annoyed me.

One night I returned to the restaurant at 2 a.m., well after closing, to find David there. Turned out he had jammed a scrap of cardboard in the side door to keep it from closing all the way and locking, then let himself back in after everybody else had left.

"What are you doing, David?"

"Just helping clean up," he lied.

"I think you cleaned up at dinner; if I remember right, you made three hundred dollars. Go on, get out of here."

"Sure thing, boss."

Tracy Wells was the star pupil. She hung on every word out of my or Scott's mouth, studied food and wine in her off time, lived and breathed Indigo, and outworked everyone. Danny was the bar vet: battered, bruised, and nicotine stained, but capable of rocking out cocktails when we got slammed. Rachel was the unflappable one who could manage, say, an eighteen-person birthday party without betraying a hint of stress. Jason was turn 'em and burn 'em, a starting pitcher who could eat up innings. Nicole was young and eager, new to the profession and prone to rookie mistakes, but so nice that everyone forgave the occasional misstep. And Sebastian was the salesman who relished pitching expensive wine to men and himself to women.

The whole crew were likable, excitable, loud, and beautiful, and the politicians, who traveled in packs, adored them.

But not everyone loved the restaurant those first few weeks. We were still doing what I call "the shake out." I had become a firm believer in not acting on the whims of first-weekers who want to mold you into their ideal restaurant. It took months of operating interactively with guests in the dining room to further hone your concept, and believe in it enough to find your

My Indigo Restaurant family in 1999, celebrating after a successful catering gig

people—those patrons who love what and who you are and will sustain you for years to come. This still happens today. When we opened Momotaro in Chicago years later, some of our inaugural diners sought dragon rolls and aioli-drenched maki rolls. Neither fit our vision. Fortunately, at that point we had the confidence to know it sometimes takes a few months to find a new restaurant's core clientele. In this case, that meant savvy eaters looking for a Japanese fish program with pristine cuts that might be "sauced" with nothing more than a scant brushstroke of nikiri, a soy mixture of shoyu, mirin, sake, and dashi.

At Indigo there were customers who demanded the tuna well done, or the music lover who felt we should only play instrumental tunes, or those who editorialized that the Blue Dogs looked odd and out of place. To them all, I was polite but unapologetic, and my message was unspoken but clear: These were intentional choices, and if you don't like what we offer, that makes me sad, but there are plenty of other restaurants in town.

The mistakes that were execution based, however, destroyed me. One week after opening, I received this letter:

> Dear Mr. Boehm,
>
> Springfield needs a restaurant that offers the promise that yours does. The decor, wine list and the way the menu reads are a major boon for this town. The food however, is an empty promise. It was such a disappointment. I realize you were new and we will give it another shot, but probably not a third. We are rooting for you.

The letter's author was smart, well-traveled, and had a developed taste for food and wine. His letter buried me. Scott, too. We both knew that we were a little bit the emperors with no clothes—our reach had so far exceeded our grasp.

My cooks were still learning, and I was impatient. The reality was it was harder to be good in a small town. Sourcing quality product was harder, training talent was harder, expanding the horizons of the clientele was harder. I wanted to be universally good, not just Springfield good. Indigo wasn't there yet. Neither was I.

Because it shone a light on a bitter reality, the letter nagged at me. I was verbally aggressive with the staff the next week, and so was Scott. Pre-shift had real muscle behind it, and volume. Scott had been through more than I had. He had been working at a famous restaurant when a critic deducted stars from its rating; at another when it closed involuntarily. Because he'd experienced ebbs and flows, and knew that improving was an hour-by-hour, day-by-day discipline, he tempered his aggression with optimism and faith in his troops, so his message landed better than mine.

Scott stayed for a few weeks, until I found a chef named Sean Keeley to take over. As a gift to Scott, I ordered a bottle of Château Lafite to drink on his final evening with us. Five of us from the restaurant gathered to send him off, and we all drank a first growth for the first time. We signed the bottle with little notes that expressed how much love and excitement we all felt. Scott wrote, "Much of my heart I leave with my new friends and with Indigo Springfield."

As our execution improved, I found some strong allies outside Indigo's four walls. During one service, Illinois state senator Jimmy DeLeo kicked a chair out for me to sit on, and told me he had bad news. "Sorry, kid, this restaurant's never going to make it in Springfield. It's too damn good."

At that time, I was trying to turbocharge my cultural clout. A lot of it fell in the *I know I'm supposed to love it, but don't* category. I watched *The Bicycle Thief*, read Ulysses, made myself eat offal, and drank weird varietals like Ribolla Gialla. You can take the kid out of Springfield I guess, but you can't . . . Wait, I was still *in* Springfield. Maybe that was the problem. I decided patient evolution would help me and the restaurant grow up in the right way.

We started to change the menu more regularly, the wine list evolved, and we identified signature ways to shock and awe. After executing a Frank Sinatra night and a Charlie Trotter's Tribute Dinner culled from the recipes in his cookbooks, we planned an elaborate black-tie Titanic Dinner and served the same menu offered in the Titanic's luxe main dining room on its final evening above sea level: beef consommé, salmon mousseline, lamb with mint sauce, and Waldorf pudding. For the menu cover, we reprinted an image from *Last Dinner on the Titanic: Menus and Recipes from the*

Great Liner by Rick Archbold and Dana McCauley that featured a woman daintily holding a champagne flute. It was quite the night; even Dee and Larry were among the guests.

As the final course was being served, I realized that Cathy Palmeri, Woody's daughter and my secret sister (whom I recognized from prior visits), was dining with us. She asked me to sign a poster that came with the ticket. Without thinking, I wrote, "Love, Kevin Boehm."

She asked me: "Why does my father keep a picture of you in his wallet?" She couldn't help but recognize the resemblance between me and Woody. She had determined that there was more to my relationship with Woody than met the eye—now her eyes were telling her that there was even more to the relationship.

I wasn't ready to confront this, especially with Larry and Dee sitting at an adjacent table.

"I'm not sure why he does that," I lied. "I met him when I was younger, when my mom worked for him. We're just friends."

We had pulled off this ambitious event without a hitch, until just before its final moments, when Chef Sean tossed a broken cup into an overstuffed kitchen trash bin, causing it to shatter and a piece to hit Manny, the dishwasher. Manny, enraged, slashed Sean in the ear with the cup's jagged edge, gruesomely detaching a portion of the lobe. A full-on kitchen melee ensued. Before I knew what was happening, the dishwasher had overturned a table covered with rental plates. The resulting crescendo alarmed the guests. I walked up to the microphone, and improvised:

"Sorry about the noise," I said. "This is the part of the evening where the Titanic begins to sink."

The next day I received a very sweet card from Cathy that left the door open for another conversation, implicitly a more truthful one.

"If you are open to talking further, I am always here."

She wasn't buying my story, but for the moment, it was all I was interested in selling.

INDIGO WAS NAMED BEST NEW Restaurant in Springfield in the *Illinois Times* and Best Restaurant in the City in *Springfield Scene Magazine*, accolades that provided an infusion of confidence and gave our young crew some much-needed swagger.

Springfield wasn't a cliquey place, and neither was Indigo. Our staff hung as one. Even Jeffrey, a mid-fifties convicted felon, was included in our Saturday morning basketball games, and we ended the night at bars in a herd of twenty-five. If you accepted one of us, you accepted all of us. We were crafting a community that felt a lot like a family. I was still only twenty-seven, and we all worked, played, and leaned on one another. Mom was pretty much the whole place's mother. I'd often find her sitting with a server, dispensing advice and wisdom. When a sous chef and his girlfriend left to go work for Scott in Florida, she put together a care package of towels, swimsuits, and snacks for the road.

As was often the case, my mania worked in my favor: One night, apropos of nothing, I hopped up on the bar to address the crowd amassed around it. From this perch, I congratulated anybody celebrating a birthday, anniversary, or any other milestone, and coaxed the patrons to cheer for each one. The spectacle quickly became a nightly ritual—it made the guests of honor feel good, added energy to the proceedings, and fed my need for attention and approval. But there's a time and place for everything: I tried this at another restaurant years later, and it flopped.

Around 10:30 p.m. each night, I would run an X on my cash register. (Old-school cash registers have an X setting that runs a ticket showing the sales for the night.) I'd review the sales, then empty my pockets of wine-bottle foils, corks, and cocktail napkins. When I played "As" by Stevie Wonder, that was house code that we had officially shifted from serving to partying, and I would pour myself a Johnny Depp–like mega-pint of Cabernet.

With no office, I did close-outs at the end of the bar, rubber-banded all the cash, and stuffed it in my pocket. (On busy weekend nights, I felt like a drug lord when I left the building.) Chef Sean and I would caucus over cocktails, and I would let him bitch about the servers causing him the most grief. By midnight, we would all pack up, and hit On Broadway, Springfield's answer to the New York City nightclub the Palladium; Chantilly Lace, a run-down pick-up joint; or Rosalie's, a bar that was literally a trailer. Six more cocktails took me to a broken sleep, and then I would wake up and do it all again.

MOM'S AND MY WORK RELATIONSHIP was mostly smooth sailing. She handled admin and payroll, cleaned the place, and took reservations over the phone. I hired, trained, did the ordering and banking, and oversaw service.

A few weeks after we opened, I asked her what she thought about the business. "Well, it appears to me this business is all about effort. Whoever efforts the most, wins."

"That's pretty close, Mom. Whoever cares the most wins. Usually that goes hand in hand with effort."

Mom's prior restaurant experience consisted of serving at a restaurant in central Michigan in the mid-1960s. On New Year's Eve in 1965, she waited on a table for six hours, and they all got so wasted they didn't leave her a tip. So, she had supreme empathy for servers and was a protector of the hard-working members of the FOH staff. The lazy ones got a less generous side of her.

There was a rhythm and order to Mom's work in the afternoon. I could tell time by where she was in the process. Chairs up and sweep was between 9 and 10 a.m. If she was checking inventory, it was just past noon. Pledge, polish, and payroll was around 2 p.m.

One Saturday I noticed she was a bit behind, and making more noise than usual—bottles were hitting speed rails, and chairs were hitting table bases. "You all right, Ma?" I asked.

"No, I'm not. I'm not your maid. You need to close this place properly. If you choose to party, that shouldn't be my problem."

"Well," I said, "it's only slightly less thoughtless than you never telling me who my real father was."

I don't know why I chose to respond with the most hurtful, immature thing possible. Woody and I, without ever making a pact, had both kept our first breakfast a secret from her, so it was also shocking. My brutal rejoinder elicited the kind of sobbing that's tough for a son to witness, much less be responsible for. Thirty years of guilt, shame, and worry came to the surface, and the only thing I could do was hug her and tell her it was okay. She tried to speak for some fifteen minutes but kept choking on the tears.

Finally, she caught her breath enough to say, "I thought I was doing the right thing. I knew if I ever told you in confidence, that it would come out in a fit of rage in one of yours and Larry's fights. I was protecting you, and myself.

"Just know this," she said. "Woody is not the man he used to be, but he was great once, and I see a lot of him in you."

"I'm sorry, Mom. I don't blame you for anything."

We hugged again. As was her way, Mom tapped my back, signaling for me to let go. This time, I didn't oblige.

SCOTT AND I KEPT IN touch. After quitting his Panhandle job, he drove up to see me to talk about collaborating.

We traveled a hundred miles south to St. Louis to look at a possible second location for Indigo. On the way, we peeled off the highway to grab a quick burger at a Wendy's in southern Illinois. What happened there is a story I've told at every opening for the past twenty-five years.

As we walked in, we immediately noticed that they had positioned a greeter, a woman in her mid-sixties, at the entrance. "Gentlemen, welcome to Wendy's!" She was probably the first and last fast-food maître d' I've ever encountered.

When my turn at the cashier arrived, he proceeded to describe, in compelling detail, their new spicy chicken sandwich with the polish of a four-star-restaurant captain. I ordered the sandwich, fries, and a—for old times' sake—water. Scott got the SuperBar, a buffet of greens, veggies, vinaigrettes, and even warm pasta and sauce that was a defining Wendy's offering in the nineties. The greeter also kept the salad bar immaculate. At one point, she refilled our waters from a pitcher.

That's when I turned to Scott and said, "What in the hell is going on?"

"The general manager must have spent time in real restaurants," said Scott.

"I don't know," I said, scanning the entire place—the order-pickup line was in a steady rhythm, the greeter was making new arrivals feel welcome, and another employee was cleaning up after customers who hadn't cleaned after themselves and straightening the napkin holders on each table as he did. Wherever they had come from, the manager of this place amid the plains of Illinois clearly had the ability to inspire greatness. I wanted to speak with them, as badly as I'd wanted to meet Gordon Sinclair.

"We have to meet this guy," I said, standing up.

I approached the cashier: "Can we see the manager, please?"

"Is there a problem?" he asked.

"No, just the opposite."

Mike, the GM, came out, a perfect Windsor knot in his Wendy's tie. He was young and tall, with a spine as stiff as his uniform. Like any good Midwesterner, his handshake was firm and he looked us dead in the eyes when he spoke.

"Gentlemen, how can I help you?"

"We just wanted to tell you how amazingly well run your place is."

"Well, as you can see, we are pretty proud of it." He beamed, pointing to a plaque on the wall honoring them as one of the best-run Wendy's in the US.

This GM was given the same music and lyrics as every Wendy's franchisee, and he decided to play the best fast-food cover version anyone has ever heard—a corporate Jimi Hendrix breathing new life into Dylan's "All Along the Watchtower." I had never been as fired up to return to my own restaurant and get to work on getting better.

THROUGHOUT MY NINE YEARS OF nomadic restaurant-ing since college, I had become a miner of manic moments and dopamine. I would roll through town with my pickaxe, set up camp, and grab every diamond I could. I was never going to stick around for the stuff that was hard to find.

I had carved out a new identity in Springfield—I was the restaurant guy, the guy from Indigo, the happy one, the dude who hopped on bars to wish people happy birthday. My avatar was joyful and carefree. It was an illusion, but it didn't matter. Billy Crystal's *Saturday Night Live* character Fernando was right. It was better to look good than to feel good.

My mom celebrated her fiftieth birthday while I lived in Springfield. I asked her how five decades felt on her.

"I have the same insecurities and prewiring that I did when I was eighteen," she said. "I only know I'm fifty when I look in the mirror."

I only sort of knew what she meant, but I've come to understand it a little better every day since.

In the summer of 1999, I was offered another ticket to ride. If there was any feeling that rivaled the opening-party boost for me, it was the going-away one.

Corky Joyner, one of our best customers, made me an offer to buy the restaurant just eighteen months after opening, and it was one I couldn't refuse. I hadn't realized it, but I was still flipping restaurants, and this flip came at a perfect time. I was starting to lose my discipline, and I felt like Indigo had already peaked under my care. I would run the floor like a technician from 4 p.m. until 10 p.m., when I'd become part of the party as a humorously inebriated master of ceremonies, like a Dean Martin character. (If all of this seems like the cycle of a budding alcoholic, it was. But it was also common restaurant industry behavior at the time, so went largely unnoticed and unremarked upon.)

Concern for Mom losing the purpose and community she'd found at Indigo caused me to hesitate momentarily. But the place had given her all she could take from it. I needed to move on more than she needed to stay put.

Like a budding news anchor, I was jumping markets, hoping to make it to a national network. I set my sights on Nashville. I had visited Kim Carnes and her husband, Dave, there and observed firsthand its upward trajectory. Springfield was the two-hundred-seventy-first most populated city in America. Nashville was the twenty-second. It wasn't Chicago, but this still would be a jump to lightspeed. Hopefully, my ship would survive the leap.

6

I'VE GOT DREAMS TO REMEMBER

I HAD HEARD A BOXING glove connect with a face before, just not my own. Now, what sounded like a wet towel hitting a stone wall—*SCHWAP*—reverberated in my right ear. My head felt like an enormous stubbed toe.

"Snap your arm back, just like you extended it. Reset yourself," Woody admonished me.

It was late June, and late afternoon. I had decided to visit Woody before leaving Springfield.

His jab wasn't the sledgehammer it must have been in 1946, but it could still do damage, at least to me.

"Take it easy, Woody. That fucking hurt."

Woody deployed a high-pitched giggle—"*hee-hee*"—as a playful taunt in competitive situations. "Seventy-eight versus . . . how old are you again?" Then a pause, for his chiding comment to sink in, literally adding insult to injury. *"Hee-hee!"*

"You still hit a bag?" I had asked on the phone earlier that morning.

"I can still hit a bag. I just don't. Want to come by and see what the old man has left?"

At this time, I had yet to discover how much time I had already logged at Woody's modest dwelling, just ten minutes from my childhood home on South Park. A small, dilapidated lean-to out back, precariously listing to one side, housed a desk, a typewriter, a scrapbook of biblical proportions, and framed photos of Woody alongside various boxers, most notably former heavyweight champ Jack Dempsey. It was also where Woody kept his faded and cracked leather boxing gear.

Sparring with my itinerant dad wasn't the Ray Kinsella *Field of Dreams* moment I'd hoped for. It was as much my fault as his: My counter-jabs were backed with pent-up anger, and so when my right cross connected, it rattled his cage. A twinge of puncher's remorse rippled through me as the aged southpaw before me shook his head. But then he took a dramatic pause and beamed.

"That right hand has some Valentine in it!" he roared.

Woody wasn't much of a boxing teacher. He imparted wisdom in his lecture-tour anecdotes, but had trouble understanding why others couldn't do things that came naturally to him.

And so I'd try a hook-jab combo, and he'd snap: "Come on, that's terrible. You're telegraphing! Disguise the hook so it looks like it's going to be another jab."

After, we had a cup of coffee in the shed. As usual, he went on and on about Mom, declaring for the thousandth time that she was the love of his life.

I let him repeat a few of his stories, then made up a dinner party I had to run to.

"I love you, son."

"Thanks, Woody. I will see you sometime."

I WAS GOOD AT PACKING up and starting over. I traveled light, acquired disposable yard-sale furniture at each destination, found framed stock photography to decorate my walls, and bought thin mattresses that I threw right on the floor. No matter where I lived, or for how long, my home felt like a crash pad, a place to sleep and refuel on strawberry jam, 2 percent milk, Gatorade (for hangovers), and week-old pizza refrigerated in the box. Occasionally, when a date veered toward "Your place or mine?" I lobbied for theirs. Mine was about as conducive to romance as a morgue.

By this time, I had developed a repertoire of coping mechanisms to navigate what I called the ones and twos, meaning the lowest of the low days: a midday movie, meandering through a bookstore, moody albums on vinyl, a revolving door of "relationships," and endless infusions of reposado and red wine.

This would be my fifth relocation in eight years. The blank slate offered by new cities thrilled and invigorated me. I arrived in each place with more business wisdom than I'd had on arrival at the prior destination. Clearly, I had inherited Woody's weakness for boredom—my nomadic tendencies, too, had some Valentine in them.

If my first three restaurants were independent movies, Six Degrees, the place I'd open in Nashville, was a bona fide studio picture with an A-list cast and a proper budget. For safety, I would stick to what I'd learned: contemporary American food and sushi, plus live music, but all of it taken to another level.

I had no compunction about pouring every penny I'd made into this extravagant venture. If necessary, I'd even assume some debt. I wasn't interested in a life outside my restaurants, so I figured there was no point in saving money for one. This was a town I could sink my teeth into and grow as a restaurateur and a human being. I convinced myself that my depression and mental anguish—all of it—was situational, brought on by location and the people around me. I had been contributing to a metaphorical pension in these small towns, paying my dues, and now I was going to recoup my investment.

Kim and Dave had introduced me to some developers who were turning a redevelopment district called "the Gulch" into mixed use in what seemed to be a soulful way. The developers had not completely bought into me, so I spent weeks in full pitch mode. After three months of courting with no letter of intent, I threatened to walk if they didn't commit. The developers decided to roll the dice on a twenty-nine-year-old college dropout for their anchor restaurant.

My first thought was to ask Scott Alderson to move to Nashville and be my chef partner, but he turned me down three times in the ensuing months.

Socially, I was humbled during that time. Restaurants were not only my mood stabilizer, but also a source of new relationships—fraternal, platonic, and romantic. I spent a lot of time by myself as a small fish in this large country pond, and it took me a while to find my Nashville people.

One night at Buffalo Billiards, I met Robb Osaba, a singer-songwriter and my Cuban doppelgänger. Every woman we met would say, "You must be brothers." Eventually we leaned into it, telling an elaborate story of how our parents had split at a young age, each taking one of us with them, and how we had been estranged until recently. Within this lie, I was creating a ruse that was closer to reality than the fiction I told most people about my family. It was harmless until someone at the restaurant's opening told my mother that she loved both her sons. Mom just gave me a look that said *What the hell's the matter with you?*

Between selling Indigo and opening Six Degrees stretched fourteen agonizing months of life without a restaurant. A hospitality lifer removed from that structure and rhythm is a pitiable spectacle, like a newly released convict unfamiliar with evolved societal norms and technology. For somebody of my mental makeup, it's like quitting narcotics cold turkey, and then all that energy has nowhere to go. And so I ran, wrote, dated, drank, worked, and traveled. The latter gave me some adrenaline. Part of

Six Degrees' budget was earmarked for research and development, including travel, so in summer 2000 I took a solo trip to New York City.

No doubt I was a conspicuous one-top at Sparks Steak House and Gotham Bar and Grill in my poorly tailored suit. Both restaurants were incredible, indelible theater. Gotham's high-ceilinged dining room, still packed with almost two hundred guests after nearly two decades in business, with veteran servers presenting state-of-the-art American cuisine, defied belief—how did they deliver like that at such a huge volume? At Sparks I dined on sliced steak, Bordelaise, mushrooms, and a bottle of Bordeaux recommended by the sommelier as I read my copy of *Wine Spectator* while the staff hovered around my oversized table.

Then I met Scott Alderson in Chicago for the National Restaurant Association (yep, "NRA" for short) Show. It was May and it was snowing, as it can in the Windy City, and we met at Bistro 110 to warm our bodies and souls with potted liver, duck confit, and baked garlic. Chicago still felt out of reach, and so it scared and electrified me. The restaurant of the moment was Donnie Madia and Paul Kahan's Blackbird. We couldn't get in, but we cabbed there and gawked at its glowing dining room, staring through the frosty glass from the sidewalk—literal outsiders.

I had an ulterior motive for the trip: to convince Scott to be my chef at Six Degrees.

"In Nashville, you can cook all the food they don't let you cook in the Panhandle," I promised. "How many orders of quail and grits can you make?"

I knew this was a pressure point—that was the one dish he wasn't allowed to delete from the menu at his current place of employment. "I hate cooking quail and grits," he muttered. "You promise I can find cooks there?"

"I promise."

As our faces glowed in Blackbird's soft light, Scott finally acquiesced. We shook hands on a fifty/fifty deal.

We got back to Nashville just in time to cosign the lease. That night, Scott buried two cigars we had half smoked in the rafters above our space to recover and finish savoring at a later date.

Scott and I had much in common, from our mental makeup to our wandering spirits to our foibles. Scott had left chef positions in bigger cities, post-divorce and mid-heartbreak, to recalibrate his life and redefine its meaning. He was prone to depression but manically excitable just like me. His animal self belonged in bucolic environs, but his culinary standards and esoteric cooking demanded the sophisticated palates of a metropolis. Music City seemed like a good compromise, because it was a small big town.

Limitation may breed creativity, but I was weary of thrift-store chairs and Target plates. With real capital, I was finally going to outfit this restaurant with proper wine coolers, All-Clad pans, and Bernardaud china. Whenever I could touch something authentic, buy something real, work with someone who had the goods, I felt better about myself. I had bullshitted my way through the nineties, but the 2000s were going to be the real deal, when I came of age as a restaurateur, and as a man.

To whip up pre-opening demand, we worked food festivals, did interviews with the media, and were part of a *Tennessean* cover story. I cozied up to songwriters, artists, and studio heads. I megaphoned everywhere I went, "Six Degrees, Six Degrees, Six Degrees."

At a party, I met Bernie Cahill—tall, handsome, and brash—a fellow Illinois downstater and young entertainment lawyer whose star was on the rise in Nashville for representing clients like Jamie O'Neal and Kenny Chesney. When people referred to "Bernie the attorney," everybody knew whom they meant.

"This place you're opening has a lot of buzz," he said. "How about I do your legal work for free, and you make sure I always have a table?"

We shook on it, and that was that.

Bernie would go on to date Sharon Stone, marry another movie star, and manage everyone from the Grateful Dead to Richard Lewis, Jeff Goldblum, and Chris Hemsworth, but leaning against that wall, he was just Peoria Bernie, a Midwestern hustler and horse trader reinventing himself in Nashville.

By summer, I had assembled another group of talented misfits. In Nashville it was mostly songwriters, artists, filmmakers, and—yes—a few bona fide career cooks. It felt like a band, and we treated it as such: We called ourselves "the Scorchers," and did all the things that would've earned us a *Behind the Music* episode: fights, love affairs, breakups and reconciliations, and—naturally—partying.

I was dating around, within and beyond the Scorchers, but I'd zeroed in on an ambitious singer-songwriter. She lived in Madison, Tennessee, far from the action, on a small plot of land with eight Siberian huskies. When the ones and twos descended, it was the perfect sanctuary. Sundays were reserved for chilling at her house, eating at a little Italian restaurant around the corner, and eavesdropping on her songwriting process. She even penned a couple of songs about me that thematically inferred, *This guy is crazy, but I love him.*

For the first time ever, I had printed out a critical path to opening a restaurant. Before that, it was all instinct and muscle memory, without so much as a to-do list. (Lists were too Larry for me.) Version 1, year 2000, delineated the 155 tasks required to open a restaurant. Everything from forming an LLC to buying pashminas for guests who might get cold. As we approached the fall, we got to #88, Scott's test kitchen.

Fried chicken with raw Sonoma milk cheddar and a homemade biscuit with foie gras dipping gravy; lavender-cured tuna as an appetizer; a study of avocado with avocado ice, avocado French toast, avocado ceviche, and an avocado fritter—they all made the menu. Scott also devised an Asian Caesar with fish sauce instead of anchovies and crab rangoon instead of croutons, and "three gifts from the sea lightly seared." It was crazy, broad strokes of cultures, complex for Nashville, and complicated to cook.

His staff reminded me of a heist picture: Big Mike, Bear, J-Rock (who was on prison furlough), Ray-Ray from Indigo Springfield, Etienne, and Jason Luna. They were rough around the edges, but Scotty loved playing drill sergeant.

We had ten thousand square feet to design, more than double the area of my first three restaurants combined. There was a large bar and lounge area, a slick and shiny surfboard-like sushi bar that set the dining room off from the drinking area, a dramatic mezzanine space with more seating, and a stage for big-name acts. For art, we had six album covers blown up to eight square feet, on four separate panels, each made of glass. In this rock 'n' roll church, Buckingham and Nicks, John Coltrane, Richie Havens, Johnny Cash, Miles Davis, and Jefferson Airplane looked over us like Jesus. This project would have been ambitious even for a seasoned operator; for me, it was an Everest. (To be honest, even with our generous budget, funds got tight. As we ran out of money, Mom swooped in as she always did to lend a hand: She re-upholstered some old banquettes we had purchased with new fabric and vinyl.)

The day of the grand opening party was the most frenetic, adrenalizing, chaotic day of my life to that point. The ten-year-old who told my parents he wanted to be a restaurateur had been picturing this night: people clamoring for a reservation, celebs on red carpets, the staccato click of camera shutters.

By 10 a.m., I told the staff that I was no longer taking phone calls. We had swelled to 350 expected guests, and it would take a crowbar, a shoehorn, and a canister of WD-40 to squeeze another table in. Studio and publishing heads kept having their assistants call to find room for them.

Around noon, Amanda Pearce, a young reservationist, told me I needed to take a phone call about an addition to the party.

"I don't care who it is, there's no room," I told her.

"Even for George Strait"—she lowered her voice to a whisper—"himself?"

Before you could say "Amarillo by Morning," I grabbed the phone.

Make that 354 people.

I finished setting up the room, and gave my best pre-shift—impassioned and perfectly calibrated, with pauses and upticks in all the right spaces, and ending with my personal-best rendition of the Wendy's story:

"He had an A-frame and the same Wendy's menu and mined greatness out of it. We have Scott Alderson's talent, a brilliant design by Manuel Zeitlin, and we have all of you. Let's show this city who we are."

I raced home, took a late-for-school shower, threw on my suit and tie, slicked back my hair, and walked in the door fifteen minutes before showtime.

Lined up at the sushi bar were two local news crews. Channel 5 was broadcasting a live feed to open the news: "It seems like the developers have a lot of eggs in one basket right now with this restaurant."

"Well, they have researched this thoroughly, and the thirty-year-old restaurateur they chose has opened and sold three restaurants already, and they are really banking on him to help make this restaurant and the Gulch a success."

Six Degrees was more Tao than it was a country bar, but you couldn't have told that by looking at everyone. The smoky room's stage lights reflected off rhinestones and pearls. Some of the attendees wore black leather cowboy hats and snakeskin boots. Photographers froze moments that would otherwise have been lost to the ages: Emmylou Harris dragging on a cigarette at the bar, George Strait striving for anonymity in a baseball cap, and Toby Keith leaning against the sushi bar, downing a frosty bottle of beer.

Soon-to-be superstars like Keith Urban, Dierks Bentley (who was dating one of our servers), and Kimberly from Little Big Town were simply bystanders taking in the show. From the stage, Trisha Yearwood belted out "Wrong Side of Memphis" and "Walkaway Joe" while sipping tequila. NRBQ's Big Al Anderson bent the strings on his acoustic guitar mercilessly as he delivered the line "It took a while to get here, but I'm right on time." Kim Carnes sang "Don't Fall in Love with a Dreamer," with Greg Barnhill sitting in for Kenny Rogers. *Billboard*'s Songwriter of the Year Jeffrey Steele then took the temp up a notch with his hit song "Unbelievable": "She's so kissable, huggable, lovable, she's got-to-have-able." Bekka Bramlett, Bonnie and Delaney's kid and onetime Fleetwood Mac–er, made everything she sang feel like gospel with her Texas-sized voice.

Scott and I had a moment on stage where he retrieved those two half-smoked cigars from the rafters, surprising and amusing me. We relit them, thanked the team, and even thanked Dee for her help.

Scott and I told each other we loved each other, drank champagne, and then spent the next several hours both hosting the party and participating in it. We were more than just partners and depression twins; we were mirror reflections in our respective houses, he in the back, me in the front.

On the manic meter, this moment touched the sky. I didn't want the night to end; after Scott left, I lay down right there on a lounge couch, clinging to the euphoria until, against my will, I fell asleep.

I WOKE UP TO VACUUM cleaners and stacked chairs. Regret at my overindulgence flooded right in. Nauseated and with a throbbing head, I was in no shape to work. The sixteen-hour day ahead of me stretched out like the Bataan Death March.

Six Degrees' hangover would last longer than mine: the drain behind the bar wasn't working, resulting in a lake. Servers and bartenders frequently left their posts to pitch songs to producers and do shots with the beautiful people. It felt like a nightclub—which is great for a short-term money grab but damaging to the long-term viability of the restaurant.

Our neighborhood, although cool and edgy, was still a bit of a war zone. Thieves tested car alarms by shooting BB guns at them in our valet lot. If nothing got tripped, they'd seize car stereos. It's tough to turn around a guest's experience when their only souvenir is a smashed-out passenger-side window.

Hundreds of well-heeled partiers invaded the lounge around ten every night, burying our three-station bar, and making it all but impossible to get drinks to tables or guests in a timely fashion. Worst of all, the developers presented us with a bill of $180,000 for extra work on the mezzanine. I didn't have the time, energy, or money to fight it. I simply wrote it on the problem list, then ignored it, hoping it would disappear.

The second weekend still felt like an invasion around 9:30 p.m. After that, runners couldn't get food to tables. I finally reassigned the barista to be the door guy and hold down the fort.

I needed to get my arms around Six Degrees. I locked myself in the office and began writing down every problem we had on a

A packed house for opening night at Six Degrees

The stage would soon be graced by Trisha Yearwood, Kim Carnes, and Jeffrey Steele.

yellow legal pad. I didn't stop until I'd recorded every one I could think of. When I finished and looked it over, I realized it was more exhaustive than Larry's most exhaustive list. I genuinely didn't know whether to laugh or cry.

A few highlights:

#83: Need separate cocktail staff; servers can't finish marathon sessions
#125: Bathrooms get trashed, need attendant
#141: Squirrel POS system on the fritz constantly

I found Scott in the kitchen, showed him the list, and said, "Let's start crossing these problems off. I can't take it."

Scott bent down to a low shelf under a prep table and emerged with his own yellow legal pad. "Babe, I got my own list," he snapped back, sticking the pad in my face.

Scott's menu required the knife skills, knowledge, and speed of one of the restaurants he'd trained in. But Stars had boasted a future all-star team; we had cooks on prison furlough. Even basics that didn't involve heat or knife work, like composing a shellfish tower, demanded his intervention.

The ability to adjust is crucial to success and I lacked the requisite experience or playbook. Essentially, I was playing chicken with the Peter principle, pushing my capabilities beyond the limit.

Scott and I were on our own. Our general manager, an old friend of Scott's, was losing a battle with alcoholism. Selfishly, I felt like that created a problem for me. I needed administrative backup. I was a killer on the floor, but, at this point, I didn't have the bandwidth for systems, spreadsheets, and QuickBooks, and my back-office team lacked the foundational knowledge to keep things organized for me as Mom had.

Even the best crews need boundaries and structure. Our FOH staff was not dissimilar to those in Springfield or Seaside. They were beautiful, talented, wild spirits. But where Six Degrees was concerned, they were problem-generating machines who often went off script—requiring my course correction, same as those shellfish towers in the kitchen.

A typical exchange: An elderly couple asked a young server named Wes—tall, good-looking, and affable—his opinion of a wine. Of all the possible answers in the universe, he selected, "I wouldn't wash my dog with that shit."

Nashville had become a big enough city to keep gossip columnists swimming in the muck. The most-read column was Brad Schmitt's "Brad About You." Between it and the entertainment rag *Nashville Scene*, we dominated the headlines for a while.

A picture of Six Degrees made the cover of the *Scene* in an article called "The New New Nashville." Bob Bernstein, a Nashville legend who owned Fido, talked about the changes:

> "Sometimes you feel like this town is too small and that you know everyone," he says. "But when you walk into a new place and no one knows you, it's kind of strange. It's strange to walk into Six Degrees."
>
> Bernstein recalls that earlier this year, after a Predators game, he dropped by the trendy restaurant for a drink. He says that not only did he not know anyone in the restaurant, but also it looked like the crowd was from another city.
>
> One question came to mind: "Who are these people?"
>
> Others have quipped that the owners of Six Degrees must have imported all those attractive, fashionable twenty-somethings from Atlanta's Buckhead neighborhood or the set of HBO's *Sex and the City*.

Clearly a tug-of-war was afoot for Nashville's soul. Many loved us, but others resented the change we represented.

I eavesdropped from the host stand as two old-schoolers walked in one night.

"It's so pretty, and clean, and modern," said one. "I hate it."

Honestly, I didn't care. We got so much press that my head swelled. I believed that there was no end to my ascension. I had completed my metamorphosis from the eager, humble kid into arrogant and insufferable know-it-all. As a result, I stopped learning. I scoffed at critical analysis, even when offered constructively. I refused to ask for help. I drank way too much. I enjoyed too much of my own party and I believed the massive crowds would just keep coming.

There is an adage in this game: The restaurant will never kill the bar, but the bar can kill the restaurant. Bar patrons often spill (or stagger) into the diners' space, their chatter can drown out conversation, and the hoots and hollers from the cocktail set can be downright annoying for a romantic table of two.

One night, Scott caught a man stubbing his cigarette out on our vibrant red rug in the lounge. He called over two of our security guards and told them to throw him out. They picked him up by the legs and arms and tossed him out the door.

"I meant escort him out, not literally throw!" Scott screamed.

The line between comedy and tragedy had never been finer.

We were serving the most ambitious food in Nashville, playing OutKast at outrageous volumes, all while people danced on the stage. A line of people waited on the sidewalk outside in hopes of gaining entry, but the line didn't project order and success; it looked frantic and felt one shoving match away from bedlam. We were fucked and I didn't have the first clue how to begin the unfucking.

One evening before the rough nightly transition from restaurant to club, one of my hosts informed me that an older gentleman had asked for me and that he was acting a little strange. I had not seen Woody in over a year, and in that time, he had lost more than a couple of steps.

"Hey, Kev-O, get in here," Woody shouted, pulling me in for a hug.

This time, I clung to him like a life raft. I would have done the same to Larry at that moment. I was so confused, so scared, and so exhausted from keeping a poker face in place all night long. Here, suddenly, was somebody in whom I could confide and maybe glean some wisdom.

But it quickly became clear that dementia—possibly Alzheimer's—obscured Woody's thoughts. He was grayer, too, and stared and fidgeted for long stretches. He tried to charm the crowd, as he had at Lazy Daze, but the magic was gone. He was a punch-drunk boxer operating on the fumes of muscle memory.

"You know this guy, young lady?" Woody asked a random patron, gesturing at me, as she walked by. "He owns this joint, what do you think of that?"

"Great, good for him," she said, shutting him down without slowing her step.

It was tough to watch. I joined him for a beer and an appetizer, but I kept getting up from the table to give myself a break. As per our family tradition, he didn't comment on the restaurant or ask how I was doing. He was monologuing, almost like I'd hired him for a speaking gig and he didn't know where the job ended and real conversation began. He told me about a skirmish he'd had with Joe Frazier's assistant once, and nights out with Harry Caray in St. Louis, and that time he and Sugar Ray Robinson went for dinner after he fought on his undercard.

Afterward, I drove him to his hotel. He told me he was off to see an old war buddy in Florida, but would call me for coffee before he left.

"I've got a good story for you in the morning!"

I needed a real person that night, not a talk-show guest. Someone to give me a halftime talk. Someone to tell me they believed in my ability to turn it around. A father. Perhaps Woody's diminishing faculties included the ability to issue sage parental advice. Even so, how poor must my luck have been that two men had failed me so completely on that front?

The phone didn't ring the next morning. I never heard the promised story. And I never saw or spoke to Woody again.

BY MIDSUMMER, DINNER BUSINESS WAS slowing, making it impossible to chip away at our construction debt. The contractor put a lien on the building. The developers had lost confidence. In retrospect, they were right to.

Six Degrees was a cliché. It was a barstaurant with all the core incompetencies: Booze was poured too liberally; cocaine was dealt and snorted in the bathrooms, by both patrons and employees; and there weren't enough eyes on the doors or the safe. I wasn't smart enough, strong enough, or sober enough to turn the tide. Big sales allow you to survive inefficiencies, but when the opening surge recedes, you are left with a P&L that's more L than P. I needed door guys, bathroom attendants, an office manager, an IT person, a sober GM, a drain behind the bar that worked, a training guide, and three of me.

Most mornings, the first thing I did was vomit. Was it the hangover, or anxiety, or both? Beats me. All I knew was that there would be no sudden buyer waiting in the wings this time. The current of failure was too strong. I was drowning.

I had stopped calling Mom. She had invested her part of the Indigo sale in Six Degrees, and the embarrassment of owing someone money, something that had never happened to me before, made me want to run and hide. I didn't want to hear

Larry's voice in the background while all his predictions about me were coming true. I had never gone two months without calling Mom.

Finally, she called the restaurant one morning.

"What's going on? If there is something wrong, tell me."

"I think I may have fucked all this up."

Once again, my mom donned her cape and did the job two dads had failed at: "The worst will happen if you run from it. You must face it head-on."

I formulated a crude plan to emerge from this disaster with a few bucks in my pocket and a sliver of dignity. I explored various outcomes with the developers, including them allowing us to sell the lease and our many improvements for key money. They verbally agreed to that option, but behind the scenes they were working to find us in default.

Meanwhile, after reviewing our cash position one Monday in September 2001, Scott and I decided to give it one last push to get back on track. The next day, terrorists attacked the Twin Towers and the Pentagon. Amid all the terrible darkness in the world, we decided to go dark as well.

The team at Six Degrees, much like Indigo, had become my entire world, and I knew that telling them about our imminent closing would spin them into a period of mourning. This best friend/employer relationship was a sticky dynamic that can't and doesn't exist anymore in my world, but in 2001, I didn't know any other way. We saw each other laughing, crying, drunk, sober, stupid, in the weeds, past midnight, and passed out on the floor.

It's hard to discipline your compadres when they are also your drinking buddies, so I resolved that I'd no longer mix management and friendship. Of course it's better that way, but it's also less fun. You develop a chemistry with people you love on the floor, and there was something more real about it. Like many things in

Nashville, my restaurant adolescence came to an abrupt ending. It was time to grow up.

Before deciding to shutter, we had committed to a private charity event scheduled, as it turned out, three weeks after closing. The headliner entertainment was rock legend Steve Cropper. Steve had cowritten "Green Onions," "(Sittin' On) The Dock of the Bay," and "In the Midnight Hour," among other hits; played the lead guitarist in *The Blues Brothers* movie; and was an anchor member of Booker T. & the M.G.'s. We tried to get out of this event, but the organizers pressured us, so we decided to make good on it as a final act for Six Degrees. It was Steve's sixtieth birthday and the fortieth anniversary for Booker T. & the M.G.'s, so we got our band back together for one final blowout.

I was broke, contemplating filing for bankruptcy, humiliated, and sad, and we barely had enough staff to do the event. But we did. It was the hardest service I had ever worked.

Around midnight Cropper walked up to me, hugged me, and put his massive, weathered hand on my cheek. "Son, I know this night has been tough for you. This street, me and you, it goes both ways, bubba. When you need a favor, ask me."

"Can I ask it now?" I said, not skipping a beat.

There was a guitar hanging next to the stage that I had bought at auction during the peak of what I believed to be success, just weeks after selling Indigo. It represented the me that I liked. More than one hundred people had signed it, including fifteen rock 'n' roll Hall of Famers. The bank was taking the rest of this place; the guitar was coming with me.

"Can you play the last song ever at Six Degrees on my Epiphone for this tiny crowd that's left?"

I'll give myself this much: I still knew how to seize a moment.

Cropper's wife, Angel; Wynona Judd; Scott; and Cropper were all that remained, besides me.

While intermittently singing the song, he proceeded to tell the story of writing "(Sittin' On) The Dock of the Bay" with his best friend Otis Redding. He claimed he wasn't a singer, but his weathered voice suited the moment. In full storyteller mode, Cropper gave us a song and insight into his long-lost friend.

"Otis had written 'Watching the ships roll in / And then I watch 'em roll away again.' I finished the rest of the lyrics," said Steve in a nostalgic whisper. (I didn't have the heart to tell him that it was Otis's part that made me want to hear that song, at that moment.)

I hugged Steve, grabbed my guitar, and hit the lights for the last time.

I had my box of pictures, clothes, my Snoopy doll, guitar, five hundred bucks, and a half tank of gas. I was going to have to start at square one again. For the first time in a while, my destination was unknown.

7

I CAN SEE CLEARLY NOW

ANY "EVERYTHING HAPPENS FOR A reason" Pollyannas who came into my orbit around this time were told to fuck off.

My firm belief was that the world was punishing me for no reason, that bad things were happening to this good person, the way they did to, say, Job in the Bible or Maximus in *Gladiator.*

As I gradually accepted that I had no short-term alternative to returning to my parents' house, I slowly morphed back into that 1980s kid.

My last order of business in Music City was to declare bankruptcy. In seven years, I had parlayed five hundred dollars into one million. But that was nothing. Because—ta-da!—I made it all disappear in a year and a half! Like many restaurant people, I regularly let my plane nosedive for the heart-pounding thrill of seeing if I can pull her back up before she shatters on the ground. I liked my cliffhanger existence and emerging the hero more often than not.

By the time I set off for Springfield, I scarcely had enough money to buy the gas to get me home. I crammed my furniture and bulky miscellany into a storage unit, and drove off with a trunkful of pictures, keepsakes, and my meager wardrobe.

"Welcome home, kid," Mom said, opening the door to their new house. Then she visually calculated the fifteen pounds I'd accumulated, at least one of them around my bloated face, and added, almost involuntarily, "You look terrible."

"Is Larry home yet?" I asked.

"Nope, you've got about an hour. Enjoy it."

I promised myself I'd be a model prisoner this time—no dust-ups with the warden.

When he got home, Larry blew past me without even making eye contact and vanished into the bedroom.

Several people I considered friends in Nashville stopped answering when I called. Mom gave me a well-timed admonishment to develop the ability to distinguish between people who love you and those who just want a good table.

I stopped by the Criglar house one night for coffee with Beverly, someone that I knew loved me, success or failure. She didn't recognize this slump-shouldered pudgy Kevin. "Let's stop this feeling sorry for yourself," she said. "It's a waste of time. Thirty is damn young. I promise: You'll be fine."

I didn't believe her, but it was the kick-in-the-ass/vote-of-confidence combo I needed.

I once met a Navy SEAL who told me that the key to enduring the unique stresses and stakes of their work is focusing on short-term goals—even just brushing your teeth in the morning. If you ponder the larger picture and its consequences, it's like looking down from a tightrope pulled taut across a canyon: you'll likely fall to your doom. The need for income and self-reliance was my immediate, short-term goal. That should have been motivation enough, but what really drove me was the need for someone—or something, namely a restaurant—to love me.

I shook out of my stupor and decided, fuck it—I'd take my first shot at finally conquering Chicago.

I arranged two meetings there with possible business partners. One was Michael Kornick, a talented chef and restaurateur I had met through the wife of a friend. Kornick had opened MK, a contemporary American restaurant and local institution, and Nine, a steakhouse whose profitability had spawned an outpost in Vegas. I met him at MK and was directed to his office, where I had a ringside seat to his managing the prep team. When he was able to break away and talk, he asked me about what had happened in Nashville and then told me he had an upcoming project in Vegas that I might be able to help him out with. He wanted to continue the conversation the following week, but we never did.

The other meeting was with Rob Katz, a prominent Chicago nightclub owner. In 1987, Rob had moved to Chicago from Vancouver to be a trader at the Chicago Board Options Exchange. For maybe the only time in his life, his timing was off. His first day on the job was Black Monday, the worst stock market crash since 1929. Rob was a born hustler with the hair and anger-management capabilities of 1980s-era John McEnroe. Street-smart with Michael Jordan–like confidence, when he wasn't in the pits, he was taking money off wealthy traders in underground backgammon games.

Rob won at most things. Currently, he was winning at owning midsize bars and nightclubs in Lincoln Park. They were edgy-cool, manageable, and engineered to make money. I liked a bar's labor model (three bartenders and a barback) a lot better than a restaurant's (hosts, chefs, cooks, and food runners). He was raking in outlandish cover charges from twentysomethings and serving up rivers' worth of flavored vodka cocktails.

Five years my senior, Rob was at least a decade ahead of me in wisdom and life. He was married, something I doubted I'd ever be mature enough for. He and his vivacious wife, Kathleen, were expecting their first child, and they owned a formidable house in Lake View. He was a real adult; I just played one on TV. (When I finally met Kathleen, she and I realized we had known each other in college. Without a trace of irony, Rob pleaded: "Please tell me you didn't sleep together." We hadn't, but delayed our answer just long enough to torture him.)

It had all the potential for a dream business relationship; Rob and I had similar values and sensibilities, which spared us the need to negotiate every decision, and we possessed complementary skill sets and personal tastes that streamlined daily operations.

In December 2001, Rob and I met at Nookies, a standard-issue diner in Lincoln Park that pumped out surprisingly solid breakfast fare to a clientele of Old Town old-schoolers. Talk about déjà vu: I was back in a diner just like D&J Cafe with Woody, omelets and coffee spread out between us. I guessed this was where all my monumental life decisions and revelations were destined to occur.

Instead of a résumé, I brought along something I thought would be more substantial and validating: a scrapbook of clips and reviews from my decade in the business.

For four hours we talked about restaurants we liked, sports, fantasy football, and love for all things Chicago. We talked about Rob's impending fatherhood, and why Six Degrees hadn't worked, despite the buzz.

He'd heard enough to propose an idea:

"Let's do a restaurant together," Rob said. "What's the worst that could happen?"

I said "Deal" before he even finished his sentence.

Of course, it would take a while, and I would need to serve or bartend to cover living expenses in the meantime. Rob offered me a gig at Katacomb, his subterranean nightclub, where I was installed Wednesdays through Saturdays on the graveyard shift that ran until 5 a.m.

At Katacomb, 2002

I rented myself an apartment on the sketchy side of Western Avenue and spent my days touring potential restaurant spaces with Rob.

Nights were another story. I started at Katacomb in January 2002, and it was a humbling comedown from hosting and hanging with country music stars in my own place in Nashville. Here, I was an anonymous hired hand scrambling to keep pace with the whims of young Lincoln Parkers who barked orders at me like "Raspberry Stoli and soda and three Lemon Drops."

With a partnership, you hope to align with someone who has your back. Rob proved that he had mine early on. One night a fight erupted out of view of Katacomb's college-age security team. As a drunken Lincoln Parker cocked his fist to throw another punch directly in front of me, I hopped over the bar and put him in an armlock. I managed to escort him toward the front door, but then lost control as he wriggled out. As I braced myself for the impact of the drunk guy's impending cross, Rob's right hand connected to his jaw faster than you could say *Woody Valentine*. The combo of Boehm and Katz were a lot of things, but delicate wasn't one of them.

I could fake it when I met Rob and real-estate brokers to see those spaces, but I no longer belonged to the mainstream. I was a nocturnal animal, subsumed by nightclub subculture into a black hole of sleep deprivation, hedonism, and enough secondhand smoke to cause miner's lung. The throbbing den that was Katacomb robbed one of all sense of time, space, sobriety, and direction. Many mornings post shift we would play liar's poker until 8 a.m., then stagger like vampires into the excruciating sunlight.

Rob and I became very close, very quickly. We excelled at midday brainstorming and late-night fun. The only area where we weren't in sync was sense of urgency. He was living large on the profits of his businesses, while I was clinging to a life raft. Potential deals for spaces fell apart in quick succession, until we finally secured one on North Milwaukee where we agreed to pay key money to lease the existing space of a restaurant called Prakash, which was owned and operated by a husband-and-wife team, Prakash and Amani.

The concept itself seemed to be built around Prakash himself. Upon entering the restaurant, you were greeted by an eight-foot-tall photograph of him on the wall, his silky shirt unbuttoned to display his hairy chest, thick as an angora sweater.

"The good news is, you don't need to design anything. Prakash designed perfectly," Prakash boasted, using the third person to suggest objectivity. "This place will kill for you."

His wife was less sure of the sale.

As we pulled out a letter of intent for them to sign, she broke down in tears, screaming, "What am I going to do, if not this?"

They retired to a back room and when they reemerged, the deal was dead.

Several other offers were declined. We got outbid on others. Most painful were the ones that made it to contract, only to drown in the fine print. As each went up in smoke, what meager coping mechanisms I possessed were failing me. I was a drunk with no prospects and no intimate relationships.

On Halloween night 2002—desperate for an outlet, any outlet—I scribbled on a guest check, "It can't get any worse than this."

I got home at 5:30 a.m. and couldn't sleep. I spent an entire evening searching for reasons not to kill myself. I googled "how to kill yourself by carbon monoxide poisoning," and even cased the empty garage adjacent to my apartment. Hours ticked by as I envisioned an alternate life in which I hadn't made certain decisions. I thought about what the best version of me looked like and what it would take to realize him. It seemed like a million-mile trudge through the desert, and I didn't think I could make it. I needed to adopt the Navy SEAL mindset, but you needed a strong mind to do that. Mine was in disarray and disrepair, and populated by voices so loud and persistent I couldn't think clearly.

Maybe I wasn't ready for Chicago. Did I need more seasoning in the minor leagues? More of my own money? I needed to feel back in control of my own destiny.

I made it to sunup, always a psychological salve, and booked a breakfast meeting with Rob.

"I appreciate everything, but I can't keep doing this," I told him across a diner table an hour later. "I think we are snakebit."

"I think you're making a mistake," he said, "but I'm not going to try to talk you out of it."

Then I was back in Nashville chasing express-lane redemption. Scott had become chef partner at Saffire restaurant in Franklin, Tennessee, twenty-five miles away, and he hooked me up with a job there as a server. In my off hours, I began taking meetings about opening another place, just as in the old days.

One night at Saffire, Scott introduced me to Cortney Moon, a college student who worked there as a server a few days a week. She was quiet, serious, gorgeous, and a hard nut to crack. She had an innate confidence, or so it seemed, and did not suffer fools gladly. Twenty-two at the time, she had been dancing for both Nashville Ballet and Utah Ballet since age fifteen, and had developed a merciless discipline in things she cared about. Her parents had recently divorced, brutally, which rocked her. For the first time in her life, she was allowing herself a little recklessness, and I fit the bill. I asked Scott for the rundown on her.

"Forget it," he said. "She wants nothing to do with restaurant guys."

I worked service that night while attempting to work her for the next seven hours. Around midnight, we sat at a table at Saffire having post-shift cocktails. I took a chance and reached under the table to take her hand. She didn't pull away.

At approximately 2 a.m., while her friends were screaming at her to leave, we kissed in the corner of the service station. It was sweet and innocent. And just like that, I felt young, alive, and optimistic again.

Cortney seemed possessed of a sculptor's eye that empowered (or cursed) her to see the man that might be chiseled from the unformed lump of clay before her. This reassured me. Despite being younger, she fell into a sort of caretaker role. After our first night together, she bought me new pillows.

Proving that some higher power has a sense of humor, that's when Rob called to summon me back to Chicago. It turned out that the operators of a restaurant at 1729 North Halsted who had rejected our offer were just a management team and were not authorized to make such a consequential decision. The rightful owner, Gordon Lang, was game for a bargaining session. I rushed back to Chicago, the three of us met at a Seattle's

Best Coffee, and we hammered out a handshake deal in forty minutes.

Order descended over my life like a weighted blanket: just as Cort and I naturally assumed our respective roles in our long-distance relationship, Rob and I gravitated to our areas of relative strength. He negotiated the lease, assembled a construction team, and reeled in investors. Four finance guys put up a combined $450,000 for a 40 percent ownership of the restaurant. They would receive 80 percent of the profits until they were paid back their initial investment, at which point Rob and I would receive 60 percent of the profit and the investors would receive 40 percent. That became our formula moving forward.

I roughed out the wine list, helped design the website, authored our employee handbook, and made a training schedule. Together, we constructed a budget, began a chef search, and tightened the screws on the tone and concept. We hired a firm out of New York City, Bogdanow Partners, who had designed Danny Meyer's influential Union Square Cafe, to reimagine the space. (One element I contributed was an indoor phone booth for cell phone users, a secluded archway to isolate their raised voices.)

A name eluded us until a visit from Rob's father, who asked me my last name, then said, "It should be a combination of the first two letters of your names, so it's either Kabo or Boka, probably Boka."

In New York City's Greenwich Village, Warren Ashworth of Bogdanow Partners met with us to begin the design process. Then Rob and I voraciously devoured the Big Apple, and paid the price on the flight back.

"I'm in serious pain," Rob whispered as the plane sped down the runway.

"Me too, brother. Just get some sleep," I mumbled back as I nodded off.

From the absolute darkness that followed, I heard an announcement: "Is there a doctor on board?"

I opened my eyes. Rob was lying on the aisle floor, gasping for breath, a look of horror in his eyes.

"I think I'm having a heart attack," he said.

Fortunately, there was a doctor on board, who swiftly deduced it was not immediately life-threatening, and arranged for an ambulance to meet us when we landed at O'Hare. At the hospital, the ER team transferred Rob to a gurney and pushed him to an exam room.

At the door, one of the nurses asked if I was family.

"I'm his partner," I said.

She and the other nurses let out a collective "Awww."

Rob, with what sounded like his last breath, removed his oxygen mask to clarify: "Business partner."

I put the mask back in place. "Save your strength, baby," I said.

Rob was diagnosed with pericarditis, an infection of the sac around the heart. It's excruciatingly painful but not life-threatening if treated immediately. Rob was back in action a week later, and we started to attack our first critical path together.

From the $450,000 Rob raised from investors, we used $65,000 to pay off a lien from the prior tenant. That left a little less than $400,000—a fortune in Florida or Tennessee, but a pittance in Chicago. We installed a custom-fabricated hardwood grill but otherwise left the kitchen as it was, and spent an imprudent sum on a fabric sculpture by acclaimed artist Gisela Stromeyer, whose work adorned museums all over the world and had provided the backdrops of Elton John's concert sets. It was a statement piece. If Instagram had existed in 2003, you would have seen it there.

My relationship with Cortney continued long distance, through phone calls and periodic visits.

Opening night of Boka, 2003, with my anxiety on full tilt

One morning in the summer of 2003, I woke up to a call from her.

"Hi, babe." I yawned.

"I think I might be pregnant."

I was no longer half asleep. "You think you're pregnant or you know you're pregnant?"

"I've taken four tests. I'm pregnant."

The news wobbled my knees. What was somebody who'd vowed never to marry to do in this situation?

Cort flew to Chicago so we could talk in person. We spent our first night there in denial: We went to dinner, saw a movie, and hung out at my tiny apartment.

I was half present with Cort and half lost in a mental tug-of-war between the kid who lacked an example of a healthy familial role model and the man who wanted to show up and do better than any of his parents had.

The next night, we dined at MK, my first life-changing conversation that didn't take place over omelets and coffee.

"Marriage has always scared the shit out of me, but I've always wanted to be a father," I told her. "If you are game for letting us grow at the same rate we would anyway, let's grab your belongings in Nashville and give this a whirl."

She reached across the table with both hands, taking mine in hers.

"I'm so glad you said that, because I'm having this baby no matter what."

It wasn't a pragmatic decision. This was all emotion. We went home, made love, and talked about what parts of us we hoped would mingle in our yet-to-be-named child. I kept my wish that depression would not be one of them to myself.

As Cortney nodded off on my chest, the tenuousness of our situation displaced the high of being in love. It was dire. Cortney didn't have health insurance. I was broke and living in a one-bedroom apartment. Boka wouldn't open for five months.

The next morning, I woke up as that hungry, obsessed kid driven by fear of failure. I cut a cash deal with an ob-gyn and we looked for a bigger apartment. I'd never had more motivation to succeed.

Two quasi-strangers being thrust into parenthood could have been a recipe for disaster. For us, in those early days, it was one of the pillars that supported our relationship. We would not always be this sweet to each other over our two decades together, but in 2003, we were each other's biggest boosters. We cobbled together a plan, scrutinized every penny we spent, ate cheap meals at home (Cortney was pescatarian and a great cook, so her salads and pastas were plenty satisfying), and listened to so many Cub games on WGN radio that we referred to the team's dedicated radio announcers, Pat Hughes and Ron Santo, as Uncle Pat and Uncle Ron.

Meanwhile, Rob and I had narrowed our chef search down to two talented industry vets. One was Giuseppe Scurato, who had spent time at MK and two Wolfgang Puck restaurants, Spago and Postrio. The other was Don Yamauchi, formerly of Gordon, a *Food & Wine* Best New Chef and current chef of Le Français, a historically significant restaurant in suburban Wheeling, Illinois. Don's food was precise and elegant. Its visual beauty was a bonus. All his dishes, precious as they may be, were conceptualized through flavor, not aesthetics. (That may sound elemental, but you'd be surprised how many professional chefs, even in a food mecca like Chicago, are all show, no go.) Scurato leaned rustic. He didn't care if we were serving his food on pristine white Homer Laughlin; he just wanted to cook delicious food. It wasn't rocket science, it was halibut with buttery lemon spinach and braised baby beets, and a dynamite roasted chicken with crème fraiche mashed potatoes.

We offered Don the job because he seemed a better fit, personality-wise, and his upsides were off the charts. He turned us down to become opening chef of Fuse at Hotel 71, a stylish boutique hotel in the Loop. We made the same offer to Scurato, who jumped at the opportunity.

Giuseppe's opening menu was contemporary American with accents from his native Italy. His stunners included grouper with oxtail raviolini, scallops with cauliflower purée, grilled octopus with frisée, and venison loin with juniper-braised cabbage. The only pre-opening press we received was one line in *Chicago* magazine's "Dish" column that had nothing to do with the food: They mentioned our cell phone booth as the first of its kind in the world. I wrote a wine list that celebrated female winemakers by having every grape varietal from each country have a representation from both sexes. It was gimmicky but lent interest to a small list.

On Thursdays at our construction site, we watched the Mark Burnett–produced reality show *The Restaurant*, starring New York

City restaurateur Jeffrey Chodorow locked in a furious collaboration with wunderkind chef Rocco DiSpirito. The show mirrored our dreams—Chodorow was, and remains, a prodigiously successful owner-operator—and our nightmares, as the restaurant at the center of the show, Rocco's, became the site of a chef-versus-owner cold war.

Chicago was having a culinary moment at this time, as molecular gastronomy had drifted to the Midwest from Spain and landed in the kitchens of Grant Achatz, Graham Elliot, and Homaro Cantu. The city was shedding its image of deep-dish pizza, old-school Italian, and beef sandwiches, and had sharpened its knives and fired up its liquid-nitrogen engines.

We had set our sights on something less ambitious. Opening a restaurant was always a leap for me, but what they were doing seemed more like jumping out of an airplane. I didn't have the stomach for that, yet. In a field of hall of famers, we'd happily settle for a life as utility players. As we gathered as a staff for the first time, it was apparent that our group, much like Rocco's, was straight out of central casting. Like Indigo and Six Degrees, we were once again the Island of Misfit Toys. It had been almost eighteen months since the closure of Six Degrees and I had forgotten how unique restaurant people were, and how much I loved them.

We'd held an open call that drew a procession of wide-eyed prospects with no experience and newly arrived servers from second-tier food cities—my favorite!

The concept, in elevator-pitch form, was straightforward: contemporary American food, à la carte menu, crafted cocktails, and a 150-bottle global wine list. The execution of a restaurant like this—in the same genre as Blackbird, NAHA, One Sixtyblue, and the recently closed Gordon—was anything but simple. We needed serious professionals in both front of house and back to meet the lofty standards demanded by the field we'd placed ourselves on.

Despite these challenges, Boka came together relatively smoothly: There was a generously sized reception room, two dining rooms—parlors, we called them—on either side of the bar (one sat thirty; the other sixty), and a large patio that was uncovered at the time and subject to the elements. We had a crew, a design, a name, a curated playlist, a talented chef, and two budding restaurateurs with much to prove.

Larry and Mom attended the opening and met Cortney and her mom, Pam, for the first time. My parents were awkward, even in the most basic situations, and Mom was always slow to warm to my love interests. (I think she liked being the only woman in my life.)

The opening party was a success. On arrival, Beverly Criglar put both hands on my cheeks and said, "Now look who had a comeback in him." There are people who flit in and out of your life. Some are only there to ride shotgun in the good times, some are there just to move the plot along, and some, like Beverly, are there to help pick you up when you run out of hope. A few weeks later, she died suddenly from a heart attack, and it was my turn to serve her, albeit as a pallbearer.

Post-opening, Rob and I jockeyed for control of various elements. I would do pre-shift and set the lights and the music. He would walk in, then turn the lights down and the music up. Moments later, I would reverse it. The staff were amused, but it probably made us look like clowns. After a few months we settled into a happy medium.

For the most part it was a love affair among our staff, each and every one of them strong of opinion and possessing well-defined personalities.

There was Nathan Crone, a writer, whose love of Hemingway informed the way he spoke, wrote, and drank, and Ian Goldberg, who—to borrow from Billy Joel—was quick with a joke or to light up your smoke from behind our twelve-seat bar. We didn't have a waitress practicing politics, but Donna Lee would wait on the Obamas at Table 45 a few weeks after opening—Barack was still just an Illinois state senator at the time. There was Mac, the aggressively drinking line cook, who would tell you about last night's adventure at the bars while he cooked your food. I was always moving in and out of the kitchen, so I only caught snippets of each story that, when pieced together, didn't make much sense. It was a fun game for me to try to fill in the blanks:

". . . and then I ordered three shots."

". . . and I was like, dude, you're John Cusack. *Serendipity* fucking sucked."

". . . and that's how you get arrested at the Hollywood Grill."

Mac was very twenty years ago, a guy whose volume and vocabulary wouldn't fly in today's restaurants, but to his credit, whether bloodied, bruised, sick, and/or hungover, he showed up and held down his station every night without fail.

Pedro, an immigrant from Mexico, was a sight to behold. If you shot a video of him from open to close, he'd be a blur, as if we'd hired the Flash. He would clear an eight-top unassisted, run more plates than any other server, and did it all with grace and professionalism.

Paul was the book-smartest of the bunch. He had read all the requisite service, wine, and food books and managed his station, and his server assistants, with an iron fist. His talent was A-plus, but his unforgiving nature left many of the others wanting to knock him out.

Many of our forty-person crew were the best that restaurants and humanity had to offer: Renaissance folks who knew their food, wine, music, and film. They were the dropouts who read more than the graduates; they were interesting but splintered; bargain finds in the irregular bin; and compelling in a dangerous way. We were a punk band playing a church gig.

The first customer to attain regular status at Boka was named David Bryant. An attorney who lived alone a few blocks away, David essentially owned barstool number 2, a perch from which he could gab with the bartender, fellow customers, and the dining room staff picking up drinks at the service bar. If restaurants offer something real and abiding, we offered that to David. Unlike some of those strictly transactional relationships in Florida, this was a true two-way friendship. We always had a seat for him. In turn, he supported us with objectivity about new dishes, encouragement for new team members, and an energetic Boka ambassador to anyone he met outside our four walls.

But David wasn't the norm and was counterbalanced by the occasional guest who resided at the other end of the spectrum, like one of the wealthiest Chicagoans, who clenched my shoulders, stared me dead in the eyes, and screamed, "Make the food come out faster!"

Normally, making that kind of physical contact with me would trigger a physical reaction, but ever wary of negative word of mouth, I just got her her food as quickly as possible.

When nights presented more dicks than Davids, we drank aggressively. To be fair, we also drank aggressively after shifts we felt like we'd won. We used to end Saturday shifts playing a game we made up called the Drive. The Drive was a classic-rock radio station in Chicago on 97.1. Every hour their marketing blip boasted, "No one knows [fill in a classic rock band] like the Drive." We each drafted ten bands, wrote their names on a sheet of paper, alternated picks, turned on the station, and whoever's band got played first won. It was a silly and fun way to end a grueling night of service. As we hooted and hollered around the bar with a spirit on the rocks, waiting for the next song, it never seemed like there was a hierarchy: Servers and bartenders, cooks and managers, owners and busboys, we all played along.

With our small dining room at Boka, I was once again in close quarters, but now I knew that when people had food in their mouths and drinks in their hands, they were less likely to combust.

Our fortunes changed one evening when a woman from *Chicago* magazine walked in with an advance copy of a glowing three-page review, capped by the headline "Boka is the Hottest Ticket in Town," anointing me, Rob, and Giuseppe as a very small part of the Chicago dining landscape.

I took the magazine into a bathroom stall and cried.

Every night of service I positioned myself at the door. No one place sets the economics or the tone of a restaurant more. I was equally concerned with making guests feel welcome as I was with squeezing as many covers (restaurant-speak for diners) as possible out of our ninety-seat dining room.

Giuseppe cooked with soul, but he didn't trust us. Discussions about food cost, which purveyors to buy from, or even how to improve individual dishes or make them more profitable often descended into arguments. After healthy relationships with Scott, Glenn, and Sean Keeley, I struggled to establish a productive working cadence with 'Seppe. I felt he had reached a point in his career where he'd be happiest owning his own restaurant.

Chef-owner tension often manifests in food-cost disagreements—how much a dish costs relative to what we charge for it, expressed as a percentage. When looking at a menu in the aggregate, some dishes will have a higher food cost than others, often based on what the market will bear. For example, during that time at Boka, the halibut main course and prime steak both ran at a relatively high cost because the proteins themselves were costly.

We wanted a chicken dish that cost $19 but still had a food cost of around 20 percent. Giuseppe insisted on an expensive breed of chicken from a small farm, resulting in a dish whose cost ran around 35 percent. We needed that dish to make up for the others. Eventually, I told him that if he didn't bring down the ingredient cost, I was going to assert my authority by taking the dish off the menu. In fairness, there is an art to achieving your wants through spirited, but respectful, debate. Rob and I weren't skilled in that art yet. Nor had we developed enough to mold our communication styles to different chef personalities.

My reluctance to turn anybody away at the door would occasionally cause issues with Chef. During the National Restaurant Association Show that May, the weather was nice enough that we were also able to sit diners in our sixty-five-seat patio. As I drifted back to the kitchen, Scurato screamed at me: "Why don't we just serve the whole city of Chicago at once, Kevin!"

He was right. I hadn't factored in the immutable timing needs of the kitchen, and I had set him and his crew up for failure. Today, we are scientific about how many covers one of our restaurant kitchens can handle without sacrificing quality, down to fifteen-minute increments, but at that point I was still in financial survival mode, and sometimes my eagerness to earn rocked the boat.

On April 14, 2004, my life became more rich and more complicated. Cort and I drove to the hospital in anticipation of our baby being born. I had seen many dramatic birth episodes in television shows and movies; still, my expectation was something slightly more serene. However, like most of my life up to this point, truth proved more interesting than fiction. Cortney was two weeks late, yet when we arrived for inducement, the baby had flipped, and they scheduled a C-section for the next day and sent us home for the night. Hours later, Cortney's water broke, the baby had flipped again, and they told us to come back immediately. That began twenty-three hours of labor—Cortney screaming, the doctor delegating, and me doing whatever I could to support her.

By the time our baby emerged, Cort was in agony, I was a teary mess, and I was the first to hold this extraordinary creature. Cort, all five foot two of her, had delivered a stunning eight-pound, thirteen-ounce baby girl, no easy feat. We named her Sofia. Cortney thought it sounded elegant, and I agreed. She had made us wait two weeks past her due date to meet her, and then twenty-three hours more just for good measure. Twenty-one years later she is just as beautiful, and just as stubborn.

After years of dwelling on the family I'd been (half) born into, I had now helped create my own, one that was more about others than myself. It wouldn't occur to me for years, but I now recognize that as one of the signs you are becoming an adult. It was also a tremendous unburdening. Tending to the needs of two normal people felt like nothing compared to chasing the tail of my own happiness. Maybe I had the makings of a man after all. Time would tell.

8
FATHER AND SON

SHORTLY AFTER WE GOT HER home, Sofia became a part of my nightly ritual. I began bringing her to the sofa with me, the same place I relocated every morning at 2 a.m., to snuggle. I'd set my iPhone alarm for fifteen minutes later, and let the world melt away. I knew that at any moment my phone would ring, and it would be Chef, or Rob, or a purveyor, but for a short while, I would be on that little boat hidden by an island in the middle of nowhere with my baby girl.

Then the timer would go off, and it all came rushing back.

Always top of mind was that I owed everyone. This was 2004 and I was still paying for the sins of Music City. I had borrowed money from Rob in dribs and drabs, taken on debt with the hospital, and was in arrears with the ob-gyn. On the Boka front, Rob and I wanted our investors to be happy, so we structured a deal that paid us far less than the norm. We took a combined eighty thousand dollars a year in salary, with no management fee. Industry standards dictated something like seventy-five thousand each plus a 4 percent management fee, but we wanted a home run with our capital investors, knowing that would be most advantageous to the company long-term.

I co-owned one of the hottest restaurants in Chicago. That meant I could get a table and red-carpet treatment at any of the other hot restaurants in Chicago. The utility companies, on the other hand, were unmoved by my aura. Few things will burst your bubble like the indifference of accounting programs that can trigger a shut-off of your gas. For two days, Cort would heat water in the microwave, then transfer it to the bath, so we didn't have to take cold showers.

My old college buddies would invite me to dinners, weddings, and other outings, but the answer was always, "I can't, all my money is going to diapers and heat."

After Letecia, our pastry chef, I was usually the first to arrive at the restaurant every morning. I would fill out a "Who's here" sheet, a roster of the scheduled cooks, hosts, and servers; write my nightly pre-shift; spend an hour working on the wine list (doing inventory, tasting new selections, and updating vintages); reprint the menus; spar with Chef Scurato; and huddle with Rob.

Like all restaurants, Boka was and remains a universe unto itself, with custom challenges to match. We were on the same block as Chicago's legendary Steppenwolf Theatre, so we experienced a profitable but punishing preshow rush and were also a destination for prime-time dining. And so we would flat-seat a stampede of one hundred people when the doors opened at 5, then reset the whole room and seat one hundred thirty more between 8 and 9:30 p.m.

"Mr. Boehm, would you go grab our Steppenwolf tickets, so we can walk right in?" asked neighborhood regulars, the Grosses, one evening.

"Of course."

Seventy-five minutes later, their captain alerted me that they were paying their check.

"Shit," I exclaimed. In the swirl of pre-theater, I had forgotten my promise within seconds of making it.

I tore ass across the street, only just evading an oncoming fire truck, sirens blaring, on a no-doubt more urgent mission than mine.

One of the firemen leaned out the side to yell: "You stupid motherfucker, what are you doing? I could have killed you!"

Hospitality! I thought but didn't say.

Restaurateur Will Guidara had not yet coined the term *unreasonable hospitality*, but almost getting flattened by a Chicago fire truck for guests' theater tickets fit the bill.

Late night, after their performances, Steppenwolf's casts would blow off steam at our bar. Over drinks, I got to know future Tony winners Anna Shapiro and Tracy Letts, who went on to collaborate on *August: Osage County.* I also met mainstay actors Terry Kinney, Amy Morton, Kate Arrington, and John Malkovich—and occasional players like Johnny Galecki and Laurie Metcalf. The scene was like two troupes seamlessly mingling: We'd all smoke and drink and entertain each other, them sharing stories of what went on behind the curtain and us regaling them with our own behind-the-scenes drama.

Theater people and restaurant people are soul mates, and not just because waiting tables is one of the primary sources of income for aspiring thespians. There's a kinship that bonds creative souls who simply aren't wired for more conventional working hours, office cubicles, computer monitors, and sitting still all day. Restaurant and theater people fit the bill. So do stand-up comics, working musicians, and, for that matter, career criminals. We all need to exist off the grid of conformity and in environments where we can be ourselves.

Before Boka came on the scene, Lincoln Park's intellectual set wet their whistles at two O'Rourke's Irish pubs. One was on

North Avenue, where Studs Terkel, Tom Wolfe, and Roger Ebert held down a rounded corner of the bar, and another was just doors down from where we'd open Boka.

Bruce Norris, part of the Steppenwolf ensemble and future Pulitzer Prize winner, was a frequent contributor and late-night reveler. He was also a world-class shit-starter. Three drinks in, he would abandon the reflective conversations he'd been sparking and provoke a random drinking buddy. Sometimes it was me.

"I don't buy this hard-luck backstory you're peddling. I have a feeling you were pampered," he chided me one evening.

"Fuck you, Bruce. I think the prickish intellectual you're selling is real. You are, actually, a prick."

"I think you might be right." He beamed.

Just as with Nashville and my songwriter crew, I felt an affinity with the Steppenwolf artists, especially Anna Shapiro and Kate Arrington. That winter, Josh Charles and Kate were the leads in playwright Richard Greenberg's *The Well-Appointed Room* for a three-month stint. They had both just ended long-term relationships and had been throwing their vulnerability and heartbreak into their performances and into the post-play Burgundies I poured them.

After their show on Valentine's Day, they occupied a small two-top in the front of our restaurant. At the table next to them, a man dropped to his knees and proposed.

Josh looked at me and deadpanned, "Are you fucking kidding me?"

We sent out a dessert to the newly engaged lovebirds, with "She said yes!" inscribed in chocolate on the rim of the plate.

I then sent a dessert to Kate and Josh with writing on the plate: "They said no."

Sometimes hospitality is biting humor, written in chocolate.

My workweeks were grueling. Our first GM was more of a nightclub guy, and only lasted a short while. The cumulative weight of being an owner, GM, sommelier, bookkeeper, and new father occasionally buckled my knees.

A new GM soon emerged, one who showed promise and lessened my load, allowing me to take Sundays off. I've always believed the best way to judge the effectiveness of a leader is to assess their place when they are not there. For this reason, I made a trip in to dine one Sunday a couple weeks after her start.

"Where's Lori?" I asked.

"She went home to watch *The Sopranos* and is coming back to close," said Nicole, one of our servers.

Lori wanted to be considered great, but didn't have the grit to give it everything. She wanted to ease into her day after a morning at the gym, get service started, and still have some time to bear witness to Tony Soprano's somehow-charming sociopathy.

Those are all logical, healthy things to want. But not if you want to manage a restaurant. That's not a politically correct thing to say, but most restaurateurs privately agree. (Eventually, she became successful as a partner in a small group of restaurants. She figured it out. Good for her.)

At times, I was not who Boka needed, either.

I was scattered, overtaxed, and easily flustered. Add to that my fear of failure, and it was more than my body could contain. Occasionally, my neck turned beet red, giving me away. If things really boiled over, like if a skirmish broke out with a guest or an employee, my entire body would turn bright as autumn leaves.

My daily respite was dinner with my family. The restaurant team ate together around four o'clock each day. That's when I ducked out the back door to meet Cortney, who had cooked and packed up dinner and then drove her little Chevy Cavalier to the alley behind Boka. I would get in, cozy up next to Sofia, and we would all eat together with the air-conditioning or heat blowing as the season dictated, and music playing at a whisper on the radio—all the elements of a restaurant within the car's four doors.

Then I'd slip back into Boka for pre-shift. My natural aptitude for crafting and delivering rousing remarks was no doubt inherited from Woody. In those days, I mostly designed my presentation to inspire rather than convey technical information. Sure, we tasted new dishes and talked wine, but we also talked about neuroscience and how certain words can trigger a guest. We discussed de-escalation techniques as a science, with very specific steps of service:

1. Gather as much information as possible before approaching a guest with an issue.
2. Allow the guest to tell us the whole story in their words because it will bring their blood pressure down.
3. Actively listen with nods and emotive facial expressions the entire time.
4. Provide them with an immediate action, an apology, and a gift.
5. Give them your contact information to ensure their next visit meets expectations.

I'm pretty sure at this point I could apply to be a FBI hostage negotiator. I've certainly put in my ten thousand hours of turning crazy people (holding my servers hostage) into happy guests.

We brainstormed elegant methods of nudging check averages upward, such as suggesting a slightly more expensive wine that is symmetrical to the one they usually order, or helping them create a multi-course experience when you feel the guests are looking for a tasting menu. We also caucused over what music we worked best to, and why the bar across the street, Black Duck, was the worst place for us to settle our grievances.

Years later, one of my pre-shifts talked about the Black Duck and an old *This American Life* episode called "No Fair!" It concerned an experiment done in a first-grade classroom where there was a "tattle phone" installed on which kids could call and tattle on any of their classmates. The first week they lit that line up:

"Billy pulls my hair all the time."

"Janie made me sit in gum."

Just weeks later no one was using it anymore.

One of the children explained why: "It doesn't do any good, nothing ever happens."

This was my message in 2004: If you want something to happen, talk about it here, not at the Duck.

The staff took this message to heart, almost to excess. For a stretch, as Boka continued to grow in popularity and the staff felt the resulting pressure, pre-shifts became more interactive than intended, lapsing into gripe sessions. Sometimes the crew directed their ire at each other, sometimes the kitchen, sometimes at me. It wasn't always pretty, but allowing everybody to voice their frustrations always brought the temperature down.

One common complaint was how tightly I booked the dining room. Nobody has ever sat a dining room more aggressively than I did in 2004. I would take reservations for all twenty-four tables and as many bar seats as possible, and then overbook by three parties at each turn to account for no-shows and cancelations. As at Indigo, the staff hated it when I pulled out Table 47, a four-top that I'd set precariously in front of a doorway. It was a better option than not seating someone for two hours, but it looked tacky and obstructed service flow. On the nights everyone actually showed up to Boka, I tap-danced like a Rockette.

I had dreamed of being reviewed by a major-city newspaper since I read reviews from up north on my back porch at Lazy Daze. Nashville had robbed me of some of my little-boy optimism. Now, my dreams were slowly reconstituting. One of them was to be featured on the cover of a dining section.

In 2004, there were four major restaurant reviewers in Chicago. If none of them loved you, it was tough to make a go of it. We had received some glowing ink in *Chicago* magazine, as well as making its 2004 class of Best New Restaurants, but if you took your dining-out cues from the *Chicago Tribune*, the *Chicago Sun-Times*, or the *Chicago Reader*, you might not have known we existed.

When it came to critics, we had done our due diligence, receiving some intel from our opening PR rep, and our crackerjack team knew just enough to be dangerous. We knew that *Chicago* magazine writer Dennis Ray Wheaton looked like Kris Kringle and often dined with a woman named Susan Weiss. We had a candid picture of the *Tribune*'s Phil Vettel taken at the James Beard Foundation Awards, and knew his pseudonym was Max Roach. We also possessed two snapshots of the *Chicago Sun-Times* food critic, Pat Bruno, and knew that he sometimes booked under the name *Pasquale*.

With three decades of perspective, I now take most critical analysis in stride. Having survived more than one hundred professional reviews, thirty years, and forty restaurants, I am mostly grateful. The lion's share of reviews have been accurate, or at least fair-minded, both the good and the bad. Our teams have received pans that we deserved, rock-star reviews that we earned, and write-ups that made us sound better than we were. We've had three-star reviews that read like four-star love letters, national reviews that jumped off the page, and one two-and-a-half-star review that left me so bewildered and upset I spent an entire day in bed.

About that last one . . .

In 2004, the *Chicago Sun-Times* food critic stepped into Boka as a two-top walk-in, meaning without a reservation. I was standing right at the front door, like the universe had gift-wrapped it for me.

That's Pat Bruno, I thought.

Instinct took over and I slipped right into critic-protocol mode.

We were just wrapping a ferocious theater rush, and I let them know that their table would be ready shortly, if they would allow me to escort them to the bar.

I sat them there for just a few minutes, and then showed them to the front dining room, our quietest space.

I assigned the table to Nicole, our best server, with Pedro, our finest SA (server's assistant) as backup. I periodically watched from the wings as that dynamic duo gracefully moved them through their meal over some ninety minutes.

When I wished them good night, I was sure that we had nailed it.

Imagine my surprise, then, when we received the text of the review online weeks later, preceded by the headline, "Attitude Isn't Everything."

Bruno effusively praised the two appetizers, salad, two entrees, dessert, and the cheese plate, but it took him three paragraphs to get there.

The first paragraph contained an inaccuracy—it said that we had been open "for a couple of years" when we had only been open for one—and possibly stretched the truth: It referred to two visits to the restaurant, but everything the couple tried that evening ended up in the review, nothing more, nothing less, suggesting one visit.

In what I took as a sign of a preexisting antipathy toward Boka, Bruno proceeded to carve us up: "Also, there is a steer-'em-to-the-bar approach. If you show up without a reservation (and that's not a good thing to do, especially on a weekend night), expect to be shoveled off to the bar while the staff 'checks to see what is available.' Really? At least a half-dozen tables were ready and available, but that's not how the game is played at Boka."

It seemed that two decades of restaurant dining hadn't made clear to Bruno that experienced restaurateurs stagger reservations. We had just sat and fed all twenty-four tables, and they were completely booked again and would be re-sat over the next hour. The only reason he was given a table at all was because of his potentially poisonous pen.

The next several paragraphs praised the food, culminating in our two and a half (out of a possible four) stars. Not a terrible rating, but it felt like an assault. Everything I loved about Ruth Reichl's reviews—her research, her wit, her wealth of detail, and her foundational love of restaurants—was utterly absent. It felt lazy, spiteful, and inaccurate, and temporarily caused me to abandon my love of big-time food journalism and entertain the most cynical thoughts of how the game is played.

By 2005, I had converted that disappointment and ire into fuel for our fire. We started to chisel away at our rough spots, and we hired Louie Hickner, a wine-savvy, service-oriented pro, as general manager, instantly granting us greater legitimacy.

Our special brand of hospitality was personal and kind, almost like small-town familiarity. It started to earn us regulars who ran the gamut from kind and easy to high maintenance.

If we are the sum of everyone we have ever encountered, no one customer's visits added more to the equation than Jack, a sports agent and loyal customer who felt compelled to send me critic-like dissertations in emails after every meal he had with us.

Dear Kevin,

Nice to see you last night. A Recap:

What happened to Shanna? I liked her a lot more than the girl running the door. Small thing, but Marjorie's menu had a smudge on it in the corner.

Are you guys doing something about the sound, it just seems to be getting louder, perhaps you are just busier.

The new menu items that have come on since the opening seem to not have the same vetting process as some of our favorites out of the gate.

The loss of the venison dish (my favorite) was not adequately replaced by the heavy, cloying pork chop dish.

Also, Marjorie's trout was dry, and the clams just didn't work.

Salads, octopus, desserts, and bread service were spot on.

Wine list is getting better,

Until next time,
Jack

The emails became an annoyance, mainly because, despite my innate and acquired gifts, I could never satisfy him.

In late summer 2005, I caught Jack's name on the reservation books and decided that the only email I would receive the following day would be one of effusive praise.

Pre-shift was dedicated to "solving Jack." My presentation crossed Benoit Blanc solving a crime with Nick Saban laying out his gameplan ahead of the Iron Bowl. My easel and whiteboard featured a picture of Jack and the proper placements for everyone during his two-hour meal.

I inspected uniforms, we swapped out faded aprons, and we ironed all the tablecloths. We selected specific runners, server assistants, and one captain, Nicole, to be the only hands to touch the table. Our lead bartender would make all the cocktails, and I would provide the wine service. We gave them a free-standing four-top, even though they were only two people, and I stood waiting at the valet stand to welcome him on arrival.

The madness of restaurants resides in how many hands touch one reservation, and how one misstep can undo several perfectly executed ones. To begin Jack's evening, I minimized conflict at the most difficult-to-control aspect, the valet, by being the first line of defense. His reservation had been properly placed by the day manager the previous afternoon, and we had his table ready to go exactly at his requested time. He was sat by our host, who was spiffily dressed, right down to his freshly polished shoes, and the night's menu had been fastidiously spell- and grammar-checked and priced accurately by the day manager who had printed them before service, with no smudges. His stemware, plateware, and flatware had been washed and polished by the dish team and polishers, and the captain's opening spiel was compelling, charming, and knowledgeable. Every item from the kitchen was hot-food hot and cold-food cold, and each component of each dish was prepped and executed perfectly by our kitchen team. When Jack visited the restroom, it was fully stocked, cleaned, and organized by our porters. His desserts were prepared deliciously by our pastry chef and his check was processed without a hitch.

When he left the restaurant, no fewer than six team members said "Good evening" as he walked toward the host stand.

He then very dramatically placed his hands on my shoulders and said:

"Now that's a goddamn dining experience."

As he walked toward the valet, I high-fived our floor manager, Jeremy, and then went back to celebrate with Chef Scurato.

"We have a great team, and with the right intention, we can do anything. Let's do that every time, with every guest. We solved that motherfucker!"

I returned to the dining room a conquering hero, only to see Jack storming back into the dining room.

"Kevin! What's going on? I am still waiting for my car!"

Noooooooo!

Stupid me: I had celebrated at the ten-yard line and got the ball knocked away at the one. It was a major lesson learned about completing the process. As my friend Andrew Friedman likes to say, restaurants are like tennis, not football. You have to win the last point; you can't just run out the clock.

The truth was, as much as Jack drove me crazy, he taught me more than any other guest. We changed things about service style, bathroom cleaning, and valet monitoring, based on his feedback. As soon as I received an email from him, complaining about unwiped sinks in the bathroom, there was instantly a new standard operating procedure regarding sink checks. I am so detailed these days because of moments like this. In reading his emails back recently, I was able to tell what a paternal-like interest Jack had in Boka. He wanted us to succeed, and I am now embarrassed that I didn't accept his help in the spirit in which it was intended. To this day, he still dines in our restaurants, but I no longer receive emails from him. Perhaps we graduated from his mentorship and another young restaurateur now receives his dissertations. I hope, for somebody's sake, that's the case.

"WHAT IS IT ABOUT THESE three Boka martinis that makes everyone around me an asshole?" asked Steve, another Boka regular, one night.

Steve drank too much, and his volume had one setting—LOUD!—but he was blessed with self-awareness. He knew he was the crazy one. I was starting to figure that out, too.

I had once again allowed myself to get on an all-too-familiar hamster wheel, a daily cycle of morning panic, afternoon onslaught of caffeine, a cortisol-producing service, and a bottle of wine or two to put out the fire. I truly believed that all I needed was one more restaurant, and a little more money, and happiness would finally arrive. Those delusions sat on the horizon and kept me running hard and fast.

By the end of 2004, after being open twenty-four months, the good reviews, our collective hard work, and my aggressive seating had paid back $240,000 of our $450,000 investment. We set our sights on a building down the street for restaurant number two.

Meanwhile, Cortney was lonely. The only real time we had together was early in the morning and on Sundays, when I was mainly concerned with recovering from the week. Money remained tight. So tight that when Cortney received a credit card with a $10,000 limit in December 2004, we thought nothing of adding to our substantial debt by planning, for the first time in my life, a real vacation.

We dropped Sofia off with Larry and Dee and spent a week in Negril sunning ourselves and getting better acquainted, all while drinking bottomless glasses of tequila and smoking the local ganja handed to us by a beach attendant. It was one of the few times during our two decades together that we were able to take a trip on our own.

When we returned, Dee and Larry seemed put out. They had not been active parents in a long time (or ever), and full-timing our young daughter had been more like a chore than a love lift.

I HAD NEVER HAD TWO restaurants at once before, so the idea of opening up Landmark, a clubby barstaurant, piqued my ambition and my ADD—an opportunity to spread my wings and work two distinctly different environments nightly.

We worked with Warren Ashworth again on design, spending three times what we had on Boka, calling on our existing investors and supplementing with a few new ones.

The menu took a broad stab at pleasing everyone: tuna tataki, pizza, potato latkes, steaks, ribs, BBQ, salads, and quesadillas. The food was tasty, but it came across as scattered and lacking identity, as if an amateur artist had tried to imitate Jackson Pollock.

The design was splash and clash, with bark-cloth booths, a soaring catwalk, an industrial hardwood floor of Douglas fir and hemlock, all housed in a two-level, ten-thousand-square-foot warehouse-like space ten doors down from Boka. The subterranean Moroccan bar in the basement was simply known as "VIP."

I was back in the club business, contending with long lines and DJs, late-night drinking and 2 a.m. close-outs. It all felt familiar.

There was a rhythm and pulse to it all. In at 9 a.m., grind, meal with family, pre-shift, run the door at Boka, work the late night at Landmark, close-outs, drinks, repeat.

On a snowy Wednesday afternoon in December 2005, just weeks after we opened Landmark, the record skipped. Missi called, sounding solemn.

"Kev, Woody died yesterday."

I was surrounded by servers, bartenders, and managers in a preservice rush, a cacophony of conversations, clanking glasses, and laughter. One manager caught my eye, as if to tell me he needed to ask me something.

Here I was processing again, amid a flurry of activity. The predominant feeling I had was not knowing how to feel. In true repressed Boehm-family tradition, I told no one about Woody's death, not even Cortney. I pushed through the rest of the day in a fog.

I had known only an eroded version of my biological father. For all my mother's assurances of his faded glory, it's tough to cobble together a memory of somebody you never really knew. My picture of him was like one of Mom's quilts, a patchwork comprising disparate fabrics and patterns.

He was a fighter in and out of the ring, a storyteller, an evangelist, a mystery, a part-time father, and a full-time character. I had never called him Dad or told him "I love you." He hadn't earned those things. And yet, years later, I still feel the need to confess to and defend those decisions.

Would it have killed me to utter those words and gift a regretful old man something he clearly longed to hear before he descended into dementia and expired alone in a hospital bed in an assisted-living facility?

Probably not. But I wouldn't be capable of such magnanimity until I understood that nobody, not even my biological parents, would or could ever truly fathom the depths of my emptiness. Until I accepted that, I only had so much to give.

9
WE ARE THE CHAMPIONS

I'M NOT SURE WHEN I stopped yearning for Larry's love and approval, but I do remember that at Christmas 1979, when I was nine years old, he was still Daddy to me, and I wanted nothing more than to be the object of his affection rather than his ire.

That fall, after watching Charles Ingalls swing an axe on the network series *Little House on the Prairie*, Larry had commented that he'd like an axe so he could chop down the dead willow tree in our backyard. I made a mental note of it, and asked Mom if that could be my Christmas gift to him.

I had a knack for getting it wrong with Larry, but I was sure this eight-dollar axe was going to be the key that unlocked our mutual love. Of course I couldn't have known it at the time, but I was flexing my nascent hospitality muscles, seizing the opportunity to shock and awe by letting somebody know that I was paying attention to them.

If the Boehms excelled at anything, it was Christmas. It brought out the best in everybody, even Larry, who kept his anger at bay through New Year's Day. As one of our only family rituals, we opened one gift on the Eve, then attended midnight mass. Standing alongside Mom, I sang "Joy to the World" at the top of my lungs, then headed home with the bells of Trinity Lutheran

Church echoing in the frosty Springfield night. At 7 a.m., Missi and I would attack our stockings, and Mom would make coffee and serve julekake (a Norwegian fruit-and-nut bread), her specialty.

"Dad, open your gift from me," I insisted.

He tore away the wrapping that covered a clearly axe-shaped object, revealing the tool within.

"Remember? You mentioned wanting it."

"I do!" He beamed.

Turning it over in his hands, he added: "This seems like a good one."

For a nanosecond, he regarded me with warmth and affection, and I felt like his true and rightful son.

"We got it at Sears!" I said, thinking that sold its dependability.

As the morning went on, seeking more of his praise, I continued to prompt him: "Do you really like the axe, Dad? Do you want to go outside and try the axe? Do you like how it feels in your hand?"

"I told you I did!" he snapped, smushing my sense of kinship. "Stop bringing it up. I don't want your sister to feel bad about her gift."

When it came to soliciting affection through hospitality, Larry was my greatest teacher. In every restaurant I ever worked in, I was the Special Forces guy who was dispatched to disarm the guest that others couldn't defuse. Riding his unpredictable waves enabled me to surf pretty much any situation.

Clearing an eight-top unassisted is a strange combination of difficult and meditative. You can strategize from ten feet away. The remnants of bone-in filets and uneaten ciabattas are not your friend. They will have to be placed on that bottom base plate with stacked cleanish plates overlapping it, resting just above your forearm. The precarious balancing of plates made me a nightly walking metaphor for my two dining rooms in 2006.

It was a transitional time: Chef Scurato and I still tolerated each other, but the writing was on the wall. Rob and I spent fourteen hours together daily, busting our asses, which solidified a partnership and foxhole friendship. Sofia was both walking and talking, and Cort and I held on to each other tightly when we could. I spent too much time with other people, she spent too much time alone, and we grinded check to check in our shoebox apartment.

By the end of that year, Rob and I realized that Scurato was too set in his ways to be the chef partner to take us where we wanted to go. Scurato was gracious and kind when we parted ways, perhaps recognizing that he, too, needed to be on his own.

We took a coffee meeting with another Giuseppe, this time Giuseppe Tentori. A native Italian, he had spent ten years at Charlie Trotter's, rising to the position of chef de cuisine. Ten years with the mercurial Trotter meant that he must be both thick-skinned and talented.

Sure enough, he turned out to be headstrong like Scurato, but also generous of spirit, with a sweetness signaled by the gleam in his eye. The Trotter culture was much tighter than ours. It was quasi-militaristic in every aspect of service and food preparation. In a legendary reflection of that compulsiveness, at Charlie's decree servers had fixed double-sided Scotch tape to the bottoms of their shoes to pick up stray crumbs and lint. Master sommeliers roamed the floor, guests ate off Villeroy & Boch, Bernardaud, and Haviland china, and line cooks of the past had become legends—among them Alinea's Grant Achatz, MK's pastry chef Mindy Segal, and Ever's Curtis Duffy. They literally wrote the book on hospitality in Trotter's slim and wise *Lessons in Service.*

We offered him the job with the promise that if he did well, we'd build him his own restaurant and make him a 20 percent partner in it.

The team of Tentori, Boehm, and Katz was not well known in the industry yet, so we still had to scratch and crawl to find talented staff. In a pinch, we made a rookie mistake, violating an unspoken no-poaching rule when we tried to hire a pastry chef away from one of Chicago's OG chefs, Carrie Nahabedian. Although Elizabeth had originally approached us, we didn't notify Carrie of our intentions, and once she found out, she let me, Rob, and Chef Tentori have it: "Charlie taught you better than that," she scolded Tentori. She was right, and we never forgot the lesson.

Tentori prepared a formal tasting for us at Landmark. A few courses in, it was clear that his food was on a different level: discernment, originality, and execution mingled in dishes like squash blossoms with tomato water and ash-baked eggplant with crispy polenta and cumin-accented pine nuts.

This was James Beard Award–worthy grub, *Food & Wine* Best New Chef bait, our ticket to the big leagues. Once upon a time, guys like me and Rob—the owner impresarios—could generate buzz and draw customers by dint of our service-floor mettle. By the time we were opening restaurants, the media and public were firmly fixated on chefs, and our success was dependent on picking and nurturing the right ones.

My crystal ball had been murky ever since Nashville, and now with Tentori in the picture, I could see the future clearly and confidently. I had learned to be a good squirrel in Seaside, constantly burying nuts, but Chicago for me was more like growing a giant Himalayan lily, planting flowers that would only bloom after years of cultivating. I was desperate for a sign that I was on the right path, and I'd had a few: The Boka investors had recouped their money, and I had finally paid off all the people I owed money to, thank God, including the State of Tennessee who had tracked me down for debt not excused by bankruptcy. I was sure I was the poorest restaurant owner in town. That might not have bothered me if I were still single, but with a life partner and kid, I felt like I was underproviding and longed to make my family whole.

By late 2007, Landmark was sprinting toward recouping its own investor debt, we were building a third restaurant called Perennial, and Cortney and I were tiptoeing around fraught concepts like marriage and another baby.

Because I engaged in a lot of small talk, heavy conversations felt overwhelming. On Sundays, for example, we would order delivery sushi from Kamehachi, watch a movie or two over spicy tako makis, and weave in some inconsequential dialogue. One Sunday evening, the small-talk dam broke:

"If you're not planning on marrying me, I need to know," Cortney said.

My longtime declaration that I'd never marry hadn't factored in that I might actually fall in love, or have children, or crave stability.

"You know how I feel about marriage," I said stoically.

"I do, but this is not just about you."

She was right. And as unsure as I was about marriage, I was equally sure that I loved her and our family. I also gravitated to situations that no one thought would work, and this marriage filled that bill to a T. Cortney was structured, serious, and quiet, while I was loud, brash, and shot from the hip. If opposites indeed attract, we were a match made in heaven.

We shot a wedding documentary with plenty of humor and a smattering of potshots at myself.

Scott Alderson would be the wedding officiant; Sofia Boehm, age three, would be the soloist, singing "You Are My Sunshine"; and a mere fourteen people would be present for our exchange of vows and rings in a hotel suite. On my side, Larry, Dee, Missi and her husband, her two kids, and my best friend James Belletire would attend.

The next evening, we threw a blowout party at Landmark for two hundred people. I opened it up by singing "She's No Lady" by Lyle Lovett. We drank till dawn.

There were no words from my parents at the wedding. No "I love you," "I am happy for you," no handed-down wisdom. Just a hug as they whispered to me mid-reception that they were heading back to Springfield.

I woke up next to my wife the next morning with a wicked hangover and a half-drunk bottle of 1982 Cos d'Estournel. We had opened it at 4 a.m. with our room service dinner, but only drank a glass.

We were both in for quite the ride over the next few years, and I was pretty sure neither of us was prepared for it. After four and a half years together, it felt like we were still getting to know each other. I had been married to the job through our time together, and we often orbited each other's universes, but we were rarely on the same planet.

BY THE TIME BOKA OPENED in 2003, I had mastered about ten of those cards in the deck I created back at Indigo. For Tentori, I needed all fifteen.

Boka with Tentori in the kitchen was indeed a better restaurant, but a more nerve-racking one. If anyone was good at applying constant gentle pressure in the dining room, it was GT, and his bosses were not excluded from his unrelenting standards.

A typical voicemail from GT might go something like this: "Mr. Boehm, it's eight a.m.," he'd say, channeling Trotter's combination of Midwestern formality and taskmaster intensity. "I'm at the restaurant, where are you?"

GT was also pushing the envelope in the kitchen.

His signature dish on Boka's new menu was stuffed squid. He boiled rice wine vinegar with sugar, clove, cinnamon, Thai chili, ginger, and lemongrass, then strained it over cubed pineapple. He'd let it steep for an hour or two while he puréed raw scallops with heavy cream and added blanched diced shrimp. Lastly, he would take dill, togarashi, and Meyer lemon zest and stuff that into the squid bodies, sear them, and roast them in the oven. The key, though, was juxtaposing the squid with tapioca pearls that had been cooked in squid ink, granting them the luster of giant caviar. Rounding out the composition were sauteed spinach and cooked pineapple—it was staggeringly beautiful.

Our neighborhood had become a more serious restaurant hub, and more competitive. Opening next door to us was Alinea, the brainchild of chef Grant Achatz—a Charlie Trotter's and French Laundry alum who had raised eyebrows with his molecular experiments at Trio—and his backer Nick Kokonas.

It turned out to be the most talked-about and covered opening in the world. Nobody was doing more progressive food than Grant, just steps away from our front door. For weeks, as I shuttled back and forth from Boka to Landmark, I would see mega-celebrities, from Oprah to Streisand, entering and leaving Alinea's optically amazing corridor that created the illusion of narrowing at the far end.

One night I spotted the unmistakably lanky, altitudinous figure and curly gray locks of Anthony Bourdain leaning against a tree, smoking a cigarette. Of course, he was there for Alinea. I had to take my shot.

"Good evening, Chef. If you have any room after twenty-four courses, we serve some fine cocktails next door."

"Good to know," he said, mid-drag. (No, he didn't show up.)

Being on our block felt like what I imagined life on a Hollywood studio lot to be: You never knew who you might see: Bono, Justin Timberlake, superstar British chef Marco Pierre White . . . They all made the pilgrimage to Alinea on Halsted.

One night, I encountered John Malkovich and the late Martha Lavey, Steppenwolf's artistic director. Martha and I hugged, and she reintroduced me to John.

"John, you know Kevin, from Boka, yes?"

"Of course."

John then proceeded to grab my face and kiss me right on the lips.

He had an unfiltered and boundless sense of humor, and I just think he was in the mood to shock me that night.

Not a bad kisser, actually.

THE FIVE HUNDRED FEET BETWEEN my two restaurants was often the only place I was alone in those days. I took it in like oxygen, coming up to the surface and breathing as deeply as I could before resubmerging into Landmark's raucous party or Boka's subdued luxury.

If the walk was my oxygen, pre-shift was my adrenaline. I had thirty minutes to inspire, educate, correct, or put the clamps down on any front-of-house consternation. Because Landmark opened at 4:30 p.m. to get the bar business rolling, I could do pre-shift at both places every night. If we were coming off a bad service, I might play the audio of Al Pacino's inch-by-inch speech from *Any Given Sunday* to fire everybody back up. To shore up wine-by-the-glass knowledge I would gamify it by having the captains compete against the server assistants in a blind tasting. To encourage empathy, I might read Bruce Feiler's "The Therapist at the Table" from an old *Gourmet* magazine, or "The Mouth That Matters" by chef Dan Barber, a tale of mistaken identity that made Blue Hill a better restaurant in its infancy. I did my best to never phone it in, knowing that emotional investment and being present are contagious.

I felt more comfortable on that stage than I did any other place in my life.

Looking out at the audience each night, I saw a diverse interest from our hard-working crew: the Kyles, Ians, and Abbys hung on every word, the Carries and Mollys were deeply passionate but also quick to poke holes in anything I shared, and then there were the there-for-a-good-time-not-a-long-time folks. I tried to speak to all of them, with varying degrees of success.

The key to pre-shift was knowing when to floor it and when to take your foot off the gas. Sometimes, after a particularly hard stretch like the overwhelming amount of covers during Restaurant Week—a promotion where restaurants offer an inexpensive multi-course menu—or a brunch after a busy Saturday, you just told some jokes and bought espressos for everyone.

ROB AND I HAD COME to believe that any lucky SOB can catch lightning in a bottle and open one successful restaurant; the second could be a byproduct of the first one's momentum; but three made you a bona fide group.

We opened Perennial, our magic number three, in 2008 in Hotel Lincoln, a place that had been abandoned and was being refurbished. Boka was now officially Boka Restaurant Group. We were asked onto the project by the investment team behind the hotel. They were a peculiar bunch, and their diverse business interests, most notably their South African diamond mines, seemed more like pickup lines than reality.

The negotiations were a chess match of mutual distrust. Our lawyers insisted on an SNDA (Subordination, Non-Disturbance, and Attornment Agreement) clause to the lease. This clause stated that if the hotel went out of business, they couldn't just kick us out. On their side, the operators of the hotel repeatedly expressed concern that they would open before we were ready. Rob, a seasoned poker player, called their bluff and suggested an agreement that we would begin paying rent only when the hotel opened, and not a day sooner. They agreed.

Sure enough, just before our opening, they were hauled off by the Securities and Exchange Commission (SEC) for a Ponzi scheme, and all of a sudden, our landlords became the federal government. Welcome to Perennial, please don't run in the halls in the abandoned hotel when you use the restroom.

As Rich Melman, founder of Lettuce Entertain You and the patriarch of Chicago restaurants, likes to say, "You can't do a good deal with a bad person."

We opened on time. The hotel, on the other hand, didn't open until the government sold it off—three years later. Rob's quick thinking saved us thirty-six months of rent.

THAT MARCH, TENTORI CAME RUNNING into Landmark saying that he needed to speak to Rob and me in private.

Rob, who often assumed the worst when presented with urgency, turned to me and said, "He's going to quit."

Once safely behind the office door, Tentori's solemn gaze morphed into a childlike smile of pure joy. "*Food & Wine* just called. I'm one of 2008's Best New Chefs and I'm going to be on the cover of the magazine."

It had been sixteen years since the back deck of Lazy Daze, and for the first time, national recognition would be bestowed on a restaurant I was involved with.

Around that same time, Stephanie Izard, a local chef whose restaurant Scylla had received national acclaim, dined at Boka. She had recently closed her little place and was now filming *Top Chef* season four. In one of the most fateful table touches in my career, Rob and I stopped by Table 35 to say hello, congratulate her on her success, and wish her luck on the show.

"How's it going in competition world?" I asked.

"I can't tell you," she said with a radiant smirk.

The season had just premiered, and not only was Izard kicking ass, but she was a natural TV presence with a high-wattage smile and a nimble sense of humor.

She met us at Landmark after her meal, and we all agreed to talk after the season ended.

June 2008 might have been the most intoxicatingly hectic month of my life. It brought four different life-changing adventures: The *Food & Wine* Classic at Aspen officially announced Tentori's selection as Best New Chef; Izard won *Top Chef* and texted us that night to meet for coffee; and Perennial opened on the same day that Cortney and I welcomed Lola Moon Boehm, as wide-eyed a baby as I had ever seen, a spitting image of Boo from *Monsters, Inc.*

We trained at Perennial from June 13 through June 20, we had coffee with Izard on June 19 and talked about opening a joint together, Rob and I went to Aspen on June 21–22, Cort was scheduled for an inducement on June 23 and brought Lola into the world, we drove our baby home on June 25, and then I worked about thirty services in a row.

Perennial was stacked with culinary talent. Originally it was a dual-chef situation with Ryan Poli—a French Laundry vet whose most recent restaurant, Butter, had earned inclusion on *Esquire*'s Best New Restaurants list—as co-executive chef along with Tentori. Alinea vet Jeff Pikus was sous chef, and future restaurateur Tony Galzin was making pastries.

Too many cooks in the kitchen? Absolutely. Ryan and Giuseppe attempted to negotiate dishes on the menu, but it was like bandmates fighting for songs on an album. It was getting a little too much like we had Oasis in the kitchen, and someone had to go.

Giuseppe graciously extracted himself from the situation and started concentrating on helping out at Landmark in addition to Boka.

Ask any legitimate hospitality professional about their worst service and they can give you a detailed blow-by-blow of every excruciating step. Ask them their best, and they will struggle to pinpoint one.

My worst was a late-summer night in 2008 at Perennial, as we were just getting our footing. The night started out straightforward enough, then I looked over and saw two familiar faces—Becky and Christina—who used to frequent Indigo Wine Bar.

"Oh my God, Kevin, is this place yours?"

"It is. A long way from 30-A, huh?" I said, stating the obvious.

"Are you happy here?" Becky asked.

I paused, mulling the question. Christina, a sarcastic mother of three in her mid-fifties, jumped into the silence: "He's happy, he probably just doesn't know it," she said, lifting a line from a John Hughes movie. She didn't realize how close to home she hit.

An hour later, a server grabbed me to convey the worst news you can receive in the midst of a modern service. "The POS just went down."

POS is short for *point of sale*, and refers to the computerized system that generates checks at the end of a table's meal, along with connecting servers to chefs and the dining room to the bar. It's the central nervous system of the restaurant and ours was kaput. Sometimes rebooting the system fixes it. But not that night.

I shifted into doomsday protocol. "Handwritten tickets, guys. If you need to close someone out . . . find me."

Once upon a time, of course, this is how every restaurant ran. But that doesn't mean that a generation of professionals born into a digital world knows how to do it. It felt like running on dry sand or riding a bike from California to New York. You eventually get there, but it takes an eternity.

To make things worse, I had to take myself off the service floor for an hour in order to troubleshoot on the phone with a rep from our POS software provider, Aloha.

We were running an hour behind on reservations, and at the near peak of full chaos, an investor walked in, telling me he'd called Rob, who'd promised him a table.

"Have a seat at the bar, and I will get you sat in a bit," I said, ignoring reality.

Perennial boasted ninety indoor seats and forty-five outdoors. Around nine o'clock at night, it started to sprinkle, and al fresco diners took it upon themselves to migrate into the dining room, plates in hand.

"Where can we go?" demanded one, waving his entrée plate at me.

"Rob said you could get me right down. I'm still waiting!" screamed the investor.

"We need our check," hollered one table.

I spent the next three hours comping meals and begging forgiveness. I caught a glimpse of myself in one of the mirrors behind the bar—yep, my neck was bright red.

When the onslaught was behind us, Rodman, our GM, chef Ryan Poli, and I walked down to Gamekeepers and took all our frustrations out on a boxing game where you punch a bag as hard as you can. Between that and the tequila, we gave ourselves a pretty good beating.

I woke up the next morning with black-and-blue hands, a hangover, and an endless stream of ranting emails from the night's guests. There needed to be a better way to open a restaurant, and I felt like it came down to time.

The prior night was par for the course—we were always rushing, running out of money, training quickly, and then opening the doors sprinting.

Perennial would be Boka Restaurant Group's last rush job.

I TRAVELED HOME TO SPRINGFIELD for my twentieth high school reunion, and added a second private reunion to the mix.

Camp Butler National Cemetery has a symmetrical beauty to it. Rows of small white graves, perfectly spaced, with the names of veterans who died as young as eighteen and one war hero who died at eighty-six, named Woodrow Valentine.

My pre-idealized vision of my visit included me sitting in front of his stone and having a conversation with him. Instead, I stood for about five minutes and replayed a few of our interactions in my mind, thought about him in the war, teared up for a second, then left. It would have been helpful to have somebody along with me to process whatever it was I was feeling, but there wasn't anybody who belonged there. My relationship with Woody continued to exist in isolation.

I got a hotel room instead of staying at my parents'. Ever since Nashville, the conversations with Larry had always been laced with skepticism about my success. I could tell that he was sure it was temporary, and I didn't need that negativity in my life.

"I'm just going to stay at the Crowne, Mom. I will be getting in so late, don't want to wake you guys," I said.

"Okay."

That was all I got from her, but I knew that she knew that I knew . . . well, you get it.

There is something about twenty years that evens out all the emotions, sands the edges a bit. At the ten-year reunion, everyone had had something to prove. There was a little less posturing at my twenty-year one. Eventually, I ended up in the corner with the usual suspects, talking about long hair, the 1980s, old girlfriends, and keg parties.

"What do you actually do?" someone asked. "Like really, how hard is it, opening a restaurant?"

"It's pretty fucking hard," I said, and then changed the subject. He didn't want the real answer—it's too long, with too many details, most of them far less glamorous than civilians imagine.

I have been asked this question many times over the years and have come up with humorous analogies to explain the pain of opening a restaurant. "It's like getting a root canal with no Novocain," I would joke. I would then long-pause and add, "But I kinda like it." Another of my favorites was: "For most people it's a horror story, but for me it's a romantic comedy."

The elements of the story are the 850 things we have listed in a critical path. It includes hundreds of minor tasks necessary for the smooth functioning of a restaurant—like #188, office supplies; or #232, linen contracts; or #38, finding a flower vendor. But it starts with the biggest building block of all, the concept.

At that moment, my next rom-com was all about Stephanie Izard, and the concept started with her: thirty dishes comprising ten fish, ten vegetable, and ten meat. The proposed name was the Drunken Goat, so we called our intellectual property lawyer and got them working on a trademark. Her last name was a type of mountain goat (the Pyrenean chamois), and she loved goat meat, so it totally worked. Eventually, an importer of food products blocked us because they had a brand of Spanish cheese called the Drunken Goat, so we changed the name to Girl & The Goat. (The owner of a restaurant in California called the girl & the fig tried to fight us on that one, but we didn't relent. She had no case. We had our name.)

Stephanie wanted a left-of-center location, so Gold Coast, Lincoln Park, and River North were out. We set our sights on West

Loop. The area was an industrial and meatpacking neighborhood in the eighteenth and nineteenth centuries and had a moment in the 1990s, but was pretty quiet in 2009, with unrealized potential. We convinced Stephanie that the occasional violent crime and empty storefronts meant it was still edgy enough for her, and she agreed. It had killer wide sidewalks, expansive streets, buildings dripping with character, and century-old ghosts. Rob found a place at 809 West Randolph with another adjacent building. We made the space one, and signed a ten-year lease with two five-year options.

Earlier, we had decided we were going to raise the money ourselves, but it was 2009, and the world's financial markets had not recovered from the fall 2008 crash. Our pitch details said that $1,450,000 would get you 40 percent ownership of the restaurant. It didn't go well at first, as the first ten people we approached said no. Lehman Brothers had just collapsed, and people were holding on to their cash tighter than the lug nuts on a rusted car. Our high-intensity lawyer Harlan put together the private placement memorandum, the LLC, and the partnership agreement with Stephanie. She owned part of the individual LLC, just like Giuseppe did with Boka. Rob and I were in full P. T. Barnum mode, selling the dream, selling her million-dollar smile, and we eventually sold all the investment units but not without some heartache or sleepless nights. One of Chicago's biggest sports stars agreed to five units, or 5 percent ownership, only to have his lawyer tell us a few weeks before opening that he was backing out. In the end, we would end up $200K over budget.

For interior design, we called AvroKO, a New York City–based firm on which we had a major crush. They have a knack for creating modern, vaguely British-feeling spaces with timeless flourishes that ooze smarts and sophistication and fit right into any modern restaurant city's landscape: London, Copenhagen,

New York. We gave them a ring and tried to hire them for the project.

"We don't really work that way," said Adam, one of the principals. "But you can come pitch us on your project."

We humbled ourselves and tried to convince a company to let us pay them. They wanted to do it, but when they gave us the price—$250,000, more than three times our $75,000 budget—Rob shrieked. Literally.

We ended up working with Karen Herold and 555 International. Karen is Dutch, fun, and wildly artistic and has a pronounced accent, with a lot of tricks up her sleeve.

"I love AvroKO, but I will do it just as good," she told us. She wasn't wrong.

When you choose the right designer, that process can be beyond fun. Karen has a slightly inappropriate sense of humor, which made mundane design meetings have a little more edge to them. Every time she mentioned black caulk she giggled like a schoolgirl.

We pulled permits, began the licensing paperwork, and got utilities in our name—the boring stuff. LG Group, a small outfit that we are friends with, built the actual restaurant. It was their first one, and it was more than they bargained for, and there were some screaming matches, but the price was right, and in the end, they nailed it.

We hired a general manager after interviewing more than twenty-five candidates. His name was Dan Russo, and he was quiet, controlled, and charming. And importantly, Izard felt comfortable with him. Steph chose a couple sous chefs that she had in mind, one named Jan Rickerl that she had worked with for years. They spoke each other's unspoken language.

We spent weeks with Karen and the room began to take shape. We asked about more color.

"The people are the color," said Karen.

I met with the kitchen rep for Jade—a high-end equipment company—and tried to get some sponsorship dollars, as Izard's Q rating was high enough to attract some free stuff. There was no money for a kitchen designer, so Izard and I sketched it out with pen, paper, and a tape measure. It wasn't perfect, but it worked.

We picked out flatware, plates, candles, and check presenters. I love that stuff—the fun stuff where you can express yourself without breaking the bank. The plates were colorful stoneware from a small maker that Steph liked. They looked beautiful on the shelf, but chipped easily and didn't last long. Steph had a budget of $25K for small wares, including a $5,000 vintage Hobart mixer. It was beautiful, if you like that sort of thing.

Steph used her apartment as a test kitchen. Neighbors complained that they saw her carrying dead animals in at all hours. They weren't seeing things. She got slapped on the wrist at a condo board meeting. It didn't matter. It's Stephanie Izard, who cares if the hallway smells like livestock?

We threw pop-up parties called the Wandering Goat where we picked secret locations and sold tickets online. They sold out in moments. It gave Steph a chance to work the menu at cool places, like our friend Michael's house in an old church, and celebrity chef Art Smith's condo.

We hired Karrie Leung to do the PR. She excelled at landing big gets, but honestly, Izard was a PR machine. At that moment, to the rest of the country, she *was* Chicago, and journalists loved writing about her.

We did an open call for hiring and more than one thousand people showed up. We interviewed for six hours on consecutive days, did second and third callbacks, and then did final interviews, *American Idol* style, with Steph, Rob, and I on the panel.

We hired seventy-one people.

We did a pro-forma budget, with projected sales of $4.5 million, having no clue we'd do closer to $10 million the first year—a rare wild miss for us on the prognostication front.

We hired a talented somm to build the wine list, as my days of writing lists were over. I'd reached my Peter principle on that one. The cocktails would be created by a six-foot-five towering figure named Ben, Boka's clever mixologist.

We created a floor plan, built the reservation book for OpenTable, ordered coat check tickets and tags, made custom pens, and commissioned a painting from an artist friend of Steph's for the west wall. We put together a critics book with pictures of writers and editors—some of them candids, like Penny Pollack from *Chicago* magazine hanging at a neighborhood party—and stashed it under the host stand. It would be the front door's job, as the first line of defense, to recognize these potential assassins before we sat them.

Fifteen years later, the book looks like an old high school yearbook—the critics appear young and vital in the photos, but in real life are grayer, rounder, or dead-er.

We wrote training manuals and job descriptions for each position, created an allergy matrix for the menu, selected papers for all printed material, designed a logo, and hired a company to make our website and set up the menu designs. Karen picked out flowers and greenery, and we put in security cameras, found candles and votives, identified locations for water stations, designed the dish area, set up the employee changing area, and leased ice equipment. We placed a linen order, designed chef coats, found polishing towels, designed and fabricated a floor mat with a goat logo, set up pest control, and contracted a nightly cleaning crew. We claimed social media handles, built an HR platform, set up a tip-out spreadsheet, and scheduled HR training for all employees. We created manager emails, built a schedule by position, discussed proper footwear, and wrote mock schedules. We chose a coffee company, coffee equipment, and a coffee menu, installed a draft system, and developed a beer line cleaning schedule. We chose martini glasses, wineglasses, coupes, highballs, dessert wine glasses, and flutes.

We designed T-shirts with fun quotes on the back for front-of-house employees to wear: WHAT HAPPENS AT THE GOAT, STAYS AT THE GOAT; GOAT BIG OR GOAT HOME; CAUTION, GOAT X-ING; and of course, in snarky reference to our friends the cheese importers, THE GOAT IS STILL DRUNK.

We trained for thirty days in the front of the house, longer than we ever had. Days mixed food training, beverage training, and reviewing steps of service. This was Rob's and my fourth opening together, and we were going to get this one right from day one, and leave nothing to chance.

We slammed the bar with cocktail orders and talked wine, spirits, and beer with the team there. Steph gave long dissertations about each dish—the hows, whats, and whys—to the servers so they could pass the information on to our guests.

Finally, we set up a mock service like a theater setting: one table in the center of the room with chairs all around. Sitting at the table were me, Steph, Rob, and Dan (the GM). For three days we had every person who might touch a guest wait on us with every dropped plate, description, dialogue, and movement that might happen during a service while everyone else watched and took notes.

We created our own language during this process. For example, we had decided that, after a trend of the time, dishes wouldn't be coursed, but rather would be delivered to the tables as the kitchen had them ready. It was a reasonable decision for Girl & The Goat, with its sharable food. But we didn't want it to sound like we were doing it for our convenience. A phrase that accomplished that eluded us until one of our servers, Marni, suggested, "The food will come out in waves."

"Genius," I said, knowing that we had found the perfect adjective to describe how our shared plates menu would hit the tables.

That might not sound like an important creative call, but these are the stylistic and logistical odds and ends that add up to a well-run restaurant that knows what it is and effortlessly conveys that to its guests.

We lost five people during this exercise. Some panicked and left mid-training. People still walk up to me in Chicago and say they remember the terror of that mock service performance.

We did three friends-and-family services. One was designed as a warm-up; one was to mimic the pace and rhythm of a real service; and one was intentionally engineered to go off the rails.

At Friends and Family I, we realized our ticket rail was much too short for the number of order-fire tickets that came in. As I stopped at the pass to ask Chef how it was going, she showed me a handful of almost thirty tickets.

"Well, this isn't going to fucking work," she screamed.

Note to self: Buy a longer ticket rail tomorrow at Restaurant Depot.

Friends and Family II felt like a real restaurant. We earned some confidence.

During Friends and Family III, one of our investors brought in a foodie friend, and Steph stopped by to ask him what he thought.

"You have a lot of work to do. It's a mess. I also don't like the chairs."

On the eve of our opening, this guy had decided to tell a chef on the brink of the biggest moment of her life that our creation was a disaster.

I emptied my annual supply of dirty looks at this man, shaking my head in disapproval.

As soon as he was gone, Stephanie began crying. "The chairs! I can't change the motherfucking chairs, you motherfucker!"

"Fuck him," I told her. "He hates everything that we love, the in-your-face flavors, the mixed proteins [Stephanie took the idea of surf-and-turf to new heights, mingling fish and meat in the same preparations], the rustic plating."

She couldn't hear me at this point; she was too upset.

We would never do friends and family in the same way ever again, at any of our restaurants. (Today, we only invite other employees from our restaurant group.)

When we opened up the books for reservations on OpenTable the next day, we booked the restaurant out for the next six months. It was a perfect storm of Steph's popularity, a wide-open restaurant landscape during a financial crisis, and being in the right place at the right time. I had never seen buzz like this.

We served five hundred dinners every night with just 120 seats—Monday and Saturday were indistinguishable from each other. The extended training cycle paid off: we were fast, precise, friendly, and the room felt like a giant party, every night.

We went through more than one hundred line cooks that first year. It was as grueling a position as I had seen in any restaurant, because of the relentlessness. The cooking was complicated and had to be fast and precise with an insane amount of volume. Cooks arrived to work at 1 p.m., and closed out at 12:30 a.m. The survivors, the ones who showed up every day and knocked it out, like future *Top Chef* winner Joe Flamm, climbed the ranks quickly.

As Anthony Bourdain was fond of pointing out, restaurants are the truest meritocracies. No one cares about your past, whether or not you went to culinary school, if you are certifiable, or if you just spent three months grappling with demons in rehab. If you can rock out fifty perfectly cooked halibuts during service, you are probably the right person for the job.

I drove to Springfield with three-star Michelin chef Curtis Duffy around the time of the Goat opening. Before the drive, we knew each other only through courteous small talk. As we shared our back stories during the two-hundred-mile drive, mine seemed like child's play in comparison. When Curtis was nineteen, his father had shot his mother and then himself.

His siblings did not fare as well in the aftermath, but Curtis found sanity and structure in restaurant discipline. He craved predictability, based on standards, to quiet the voices, where I liked my brain to be so occupied by constant demand that it couldn't think of anything else.

We were both emblematic of why trauma fed restaurant success. I have been watching the damaged excel at restaurants my entire adult life. The talented chef whose hero dad went to prison when he was a kid, the lightning-fast line cook whose family kicked him out of the house at age sixteen, the hard-driving sous chef whose drug-dealer parents were both killed before he turned twelve years old, and the manager who'd been sexually abused by her father until she could fight back—they all thrived by controlling the seemingly uncontrollable.

These are the people who could laugh off the long hours, the unpredictable guests, the call-offs, and the back-breaking work. They were trained by trauma long before restaurant training.

The Goat staff was filled with fighters, survivors, students, and teachers, galvanized by hard work and a purpose. We were all soon to be rewarded with some local and national acknowledgment.

WHEN THE *TRIBUNE* REVIEW CAME out, I grabbed the paper, read enough of it to find out that it was overwhelmingly positive, and sped toward the restaurant. I found Steph, we read it aloud, and we shared a happy cry together. Stephanie's not exactly the take-a-moment-and-have-a-good-cry type, but I think she had

Me, Izard, and Katz celebrating at Girl & The Goat

been so determined to prove she was more than just a *Top Chef* flash in the pan that this moment was a release of all the pressure she had put on herself. Five minutes later she was back to butchering chickens.

In Bob Seger's *Greatest Hits* liner notes, he tells the story of each song, including his first major hit, "Night Moves." He says that people always ask if you know when you have written a hit song. The answer for him had always been no, except with that one. We knew Girl & The Goat was going to be a hit. We didn't know it was going to be "Night Moves."

About six months after opening, while on a trip to New York City, our publicist Kerry called to tell us to pick up the latest issue of *Saveur* magazine. We figured we'd been featured in a Chicago roundup, or list of noteworthy openings around the country. When we finally happened by a newsstand and lifted a copy of the magazine out of the rack, revealing its cover, we went into shock. A banner running above the magazine's masthead read: "Girl & The Goat, The Best New Restaurant in America."

By the end of the day, my phone sounded like a pinball machine as text messages and email notifications poured in, many of them reservation requests. It was the sound of eighteen years of trial and error, fits and starts, successes and failures coming to fruition.

I was happy.

But I still didn't know it yet.

10

MAMMAS DON'T LET YOUR BABIES GROW UP TO BE COWBOYS

IF YOU WATCH THE YOUTUBE video of David Byrne from Talking Heads creating and rehearsing the now-iconic dance moves for the Stop Making Sense tour, you can't help but be impressed by his confidence. Without the context of the stage and the corresponding music the moves look odd, and nothing more. When I watch that clip, I wonder if the other members of the band were tasteful editors, or if Byrne just believed in his vision with uncommon surety.

During brainstorming sessions in our Boka war room, Rob and I tried to create a fertile ground for bad ideas. If you were comfortable suggesting anything, our reasoning went, eventually you were bound to hit pay dirt.

So, when one of us says, "Let's create an on-deck circle in the next restaurant. A table where you are sat before your official table. You only stay there briefly, until your reservation is ready. It's staffed by one chef making both an amuse and a pairing cocktail. It might set a unique tone for the evening."

The other one's job in this case is to support and/or poke holes.

"What happens if tables get backed up? Is there just one on-deck?"

"Is it only for two, fours, and sixes, or can eight-tops fit there?"

"What is the cost of this station and how does the person working it get tipped out?"

Some novel thoughts, like the cell phone booth and the wine list with a male and female winemaker for every varietal at Boka, the leather-bound cocktail book with a drink for every week of the year at Lazy Bird, and the birthday wine list with a selection for every birth year going back to 1960 at Swift & Sons, got developed to fruition. Others, like the on-deck circle, failed the vetting process.

More successful was the time when, in 2024, we built informational cards for our upcoming pizza place with hand-drawn sketches of the pizzas and all the nerdy information pizza geeks want to know: hydration point, fermentation details, type of flour. They're like a baseball card for each pizza variety, loaded with stats. It's a more sophisticated move than we would have done twenty years ago, but that's the evolution.

When inspired ideas help deliver hospitality, add to the bottom line, and engender loyalty, that's when you've hit the innovation trifecta. In 2010, we developed a Boka black card after seeing the movie *Up in the Air*, starring George Clooney. In the movie, his character earns a fancy silver card by reaching 10 million miles flown. The card entitles him to concierge service for all his flight needs. Our program was similar with a black titanium card awarded after one hundred restaurant group–wide visits, a dedicated phone number and email address for ease of service, and a team of reservation concierges who could get you in, even when our restaurants were technically booked.

Rob's and my tastes have changed over our twenty-plus years together, but fortunately they changed in compatible ways. Our concepts became less broad, our locations were hipper, and our wine lists were smaller and more focused.

We kept surviving by keeping our word on the one rule of our partnership: No one draws a line in the sand. If you want to win your case in a disagreement, make a compelling argument.

Our partnership has aged gracefully, and the two of us got used to the fact that we would occasionally be called the other one's name. We were Bo and Ka, inextricably connected, no matter what.

STUPIDLY OR NOT, SOME EIGHTEEN years after witnessing those vacation dreamers at the original Lazy Daze, I found myself doing my own late-night tequila dreaming at the Boka bar, where Rob and I would lob concepts at each other like softballs.

Some of those concepts made the long slog to realization, becoming actual restaurants, and we loved that process more than anything. We were full-on opening addicts.

Success begets ambition. It also creates more opening amnesia—when something succeeds, we forget the pain of bringing it into being. The failures, on the other hand, weigh you down like an anchor. We started deliberately, but mostly because of financial constraints. Once we were on a run, we couldn't get to the next project fast enough.

We were hesitant to add more corporate infrastructure as we both operated from a position of fear and middle-class work ethic. Therefore, I was still balancing our endless procession of openings with balancing trays in dining rooms, clearing tables, and chatting up regulars five nights a week.

One night in 2011, I checked in with Bill, a Boka Restaurant Group frequent flyer, at Perennial. Bill and I were familiar enough that I gave him a real answer when he asked me how things were going: "Chaos, served with a side of stress and heartburn."

Bill's son—who was about ten years old and dining with him—stopped drawing and was listening intently. "Why do you keep opening places if it's that hard?" his son asked.

"You see the picture you're drawing?" I said. "What if that was the only picture you could ever draw?"

He scrunched up his face. "That would be boring," he said. "I like drawing new pictures."

Bill chimed in, "Your pictures are riskier than his."

"That's part of the fun, too." I grinned. I still loved that feeling of pulling up on the plane's controls just in time to prevent calamity.

People often venture unsubstantiated numbers about the percentage of restaurants that fail. I'm not sure what the truth is, or what exactly should constitute failure (five years? ten years?), but if Chicago offers any indication, the number is pretty high. In 2004, *Chicago* magazine named Boka one of the city's Twenty Best New Restaurants. Twenty years later, only three of those restaurants are still open: Boka, avec, and Vermillion. The seventeen that shuttered along the way were among the best Chicago had to offer. My chosen profession can be as perilous as a Philippe Petit tightrope walk.

The oven that kaboomed in my face at Lazy Daze had proven to be a harbinger of disasters to come. I've had: an ANSUL fire suppression system go off during a friends-and-family seating, raining chemical foam over the cooks; a disgruntled contractor clog a kitchen drain with concrete on the eve of building-department inspections; the bathroom plumbing back up so bad on opening night that the hallway outside was ankle-deep in sewage; and an older woman's heel snap off on the stairs down to a dining room, sending her tumbling to a head injury.

Restaurants pump out crises at the same tempo as they crank out food. Many can be catastrophic. During openings especially, my persistent anxiety seemed perfectly reasonable. In *Kitchen Confidential*, Bourdain describes the absurdity of opening a restaurant, likening it to standing directly on the railway tracks hoping not to be run over.

For all evidence to the contrary, I resisted the truism that sustainability is a pipe dream. I was consumed with the idea of building restaurants that laughed in the face of mortality. How did Gibsons, or Union Square Café, or Zuni Café, or Frontera Grill do it all these years? It was possible!

By 2011, Indigo Springfield had been open an astonishing fourteen years, and my Chicago places were so far beating the odds, but each in their own way. The management style and personality types that defined each of them might have led one to conclude that they belonged to different restaurant groups.

Stephanie's kitchen was noisy, populated by brash cooks decorated with tattoos, bandanas, battle scars, and piercings who moved at light speed.

"Order in pig face, Walters chicken, halibut," Izard would bellow with a force that belied her five-foot-two frame. Pig face, by the way, is short for a menu item that's been available since day one: the visage (cheeks, snout, and tongue) of a pig from Slagel Farms in Illinois that's been lavishly seasoned with cilantro, lime, and coriander, then rolled up like a porchetta, roasted in the restaurant's wood-burning oven, and sliced crosswise into rounds.

Tables 4 and 5 at the Goat anchored either side of the hot line. Guests lucky enough to be seated there enjoyed a front-row seat to the action. You just had to be careful; lean in too close and you might get splattered with the fish sauce aioli.

Garde manger, or the cold station, was so far away from the pass that the team members couldn't hear over the thunderous rumble of the always-overstuffed dining room, three-deep bar, and hard-rocking soundtrack. So, they developed hand signals for dishes. Rather than call those orders, the expediting chef would sign them.

In contrast to Stephanie, who deliberately hired team members with rock band personalities, Giuseppe maintained a quiet, orderly kitchen. Other than the brigade's constant cries of "*Oui*, Chef," Giuseppe's voice was the only sound other than clanking and sizzling. His hard time with Trotter had conditioned him to monastery-like quietude. There was no chitchat in that kitchen, no music (even during prep time), and people worked clean, sweeping up debris and wiping down their stations frequently during service. Peer in at a random time and you couldn't discern if the team had just started their day or were thirty minutes into a Saturday night.

Giuseppe was terrible with names. I assumed that he expended all his bandwidth maintaining standards and order. To cover for this, he made up nicknames for employees, calling them, say, McCracken or Little One, until, finally, their given names penetrated his memory bank. The first time he called you by your true name was like the end of a long probationary period. His military-like standards were rewarded with a Michelin star in 2011, when Chicago became just the third American city to have an annual guide.

At Perennial, Ryan Poli blended Stephanie's and Giuseppe's styles. Ryan was serious and surrounded himself with serious cooks, but also blasted Phish in his kitchens and strived for an upbeat vibe. But mistake that kindness for weakness and Poli's inner South Side bully boy would make a cameo.

His sous chef Jeff Pikus was serious as a CT scan, the prototypical fine-dining aspirant: Clean-cut and close-shaven enough to pass for a G-man, he moved with grace and economy and rarely raised his voice, because he could level you with a scowl. His pedigree included being part of the opening crew at Alinea, one of those fabled kitchen teams populated by future all-stars, like the cast of *American Graffiti*. He was leather-jacket cool with long greased-back hair and a testosterone-tinged, deep-register voice. Perennial was a downshift from working at *Gourmet*'s Best Restaurant

Rob, Giuseppe, and I were inseparable around 2007.

in America, but he seemed to enjoy the change of pace. He was cooking at a hot stove again rather than performing the robotic tasks of sous vide. He kept a spiral notebook with detailed notes, and one day he left it open sitting on a prep unit. I glanced at it as I walked by and saw a message from his then-girlfriend written inside. "Kevin and Rob are not your future. Start thinking about what's next. Let's talk about it tonight."

Ouchie!

That note said a lot. Talented chefs were either moving up or moving on, always on the hunt for the next opportunity, the next step up on the ladder of kitchen hierarchy. This, too, was a reality I longed to buck, by finding chefs who did see a future with me and Rob, and whom we could keep happy enough to stay around indefinitely.

They all had varying degrees of respect for the front of the house. The tension between cooks and servers had been well established by the time I got into the game. Both jobs are hard, and the cooks seemed to think they could do our job if they had to, but we couldn't do theirs. Servers generally made more money and enjoyed a less taxing lifestyle. But the most talented and ambitious cooks had greater upsides, namely the promise of earning a partnership as Giuseppe and Steph had, or raising enough capital to open a place of their own. Servers had to contend with the public, while cooks stood in front of a hot line, risking all manner of injury and withstanding the hellfire of a wood-burning oven for hours on end.

Two different populations coexist in the same space and depend on each other for a smooth service. Sometimes they fight, sometimes they celebrate, sometimes they fuck each other, literally and figuratively.

In the spring of 2011, Rob, Steph, and I were collectively nominated for Girl & The Goat as Best New Restaurant in America by the James Beard Foundation Awards.

Since 2015, the James Beard Awards have been held in Chicago, but in 2011 they were still situated in their original and longtime home at New York City's Lincoln Center. Rob and I flew in for the ceremony that May, feeling like small towners, with rented tuxes and stomachs full of butterflies. We hadn't been invited to any of the parties that were thrown on the edges of the ceremony, and I'd made our reservation at Danny Meyer's Eleven Madison Park not by phoning a contact there but on the reservation app OpenTable, like any non-industry person would.

Cort and I double-dated with the Katzes, and, as we stepped just two feet in the door of the restaurant, the maître d' greeted us.

"Mr. Boehm, so nice of you to join us, and Mr. Katz, welcome. Mrs. Moon and Mrs. Katz, lovely to see you both. Congratulations from all of us on your James Beard nomination."

It was a stunning greeting considering I had made a simple online reservation and didn't know anybody at the restaurant.

This was my first introduction to the template-shattering vision of restaurateur Will Guidara, who was general manager of Eleven Madison Park at the time. I later learned that he had his team create a dossier on anticipated guests before they arrived. The technology to do this with a quick Google search had been right there for anybody to seize for two decades, but nobody had made it a daily practice until Will instituted it. (It's still rare.)

We were shown to a table for four. Awaiting us there was a beautiful handwritten welcome letter from Danny Meyer himself. We were then whisked to the kitchen, where each member of the kitchen approached us, shook our hands, and congratulated us on the nomination. One of the young executive sous chefs, Lee Wolen, had spent a summer cooking in Chicago and made a point of telling us how much he loved what we were doing there.

It was choreographed, but also sincere—a neat combination when you can pull it off.

The food, too, was different in that it was eclectic but in an exciting and appropriately technique-heavy way. I ate the most interesting chicken dish I've ever had, with brioche and foie gras piped in as a stuffing just below the skin, and lobster with carrots and curried granola. It was, without question, the finest hospitality experience of my life, and one of my all-time favorite meals.

When the maître d' checked on us post-meal, she also invited us to their post-Beard party. We had walked in gangly, pimply-faced aspirants and left glowing, feeling ten feet tall, and as if we'd been invited into the industry's inner circle.

Before she left us, I asked, "How did you know how to pronounce my last name? People always get it wrong."

"To tell you the truth, I got a little stuck on that, so I called Boka."

Damn, that's good, I thought, feeling both inspired and pissed off. Again, here was something anybody could do, but nobody did.

"We have to do better," I said to Rob.

We had no expectations of victory at the awards the next night. Our category mingled the most recent launches by long-running legends with earnest efforts from ingénues. There was Benu, the future three-star Michelin restaurant from Corey Lee, who had just left his post as chef de cuisine at Thomas Keller's landmark French Laundry; Jean-Georges Vongerichten's ABC Kitchen, where chef Dan Kluger turned out sensational food highlighting local farms; prolific Boston chef-restaurateur Barbara Lynch's paean to French cuisine, Menton; and downtown Manhattan red-sauce Italian/tasting-menu hybrid Torrisi rounded out the category.

"We are just happy to be nominated," I lied on the red carpet, to a succession of journalists I'd never met before.

We lost to ABC, post-partied like fools at Eleven Madison Park (who had just won Outstanding Restaurant in America), then woke up, flew home, and got right back to work on the many openings we had on the horizon, which by then had been my default state for almost a decade: running restaurants while constructing others, both mentally and physically.

ALL THE NEW PLACES CREATED lots of moments for big speeches, and I would sell the dream to others as I managed my own.

"We are not creating restaurant people, we are creating Renaissance people," I told each opening team. "Even if you don't stay in this business, I guarantee you will be twenty percent more appealing in life, just based on your knowledge of food, wine, hospitality, and humanity."

We built a new restaurant, GT Fish & Oyster, for Tentori, making him a partner, as promised.

Chef still had some emotional bruises from his tenure with Trotter, and openings brought out the Charlie in him.

"Chef, we need to do staff-on-staff Monday, followed by four practice nights next week. We can take a day to get settled and then open on Sunday," I told him.

"No, we're not ready."

"Well, we're out of money, so it's happening."

"No, it's not."

The classic screaming match between artist-chef and belt-tightening restaurateur ensued.

Ultimately, hard fiscal reality prevailed. We opened GT Fish to much fanfare, and it shot out of the gates almost as fast as Girl & The Goat. It was named Restaurant of the Year in the *Tribune*.

Girl & The Goat had paid back its investors in a staggeringly quick nine months; GT Fish would do it in fifteen. Memories of Nashville loomed close enough to keep me from thinking I'd solved the restaurant riddle, but it sure felt like we were on the right track.

UNFORTUNATELY, I MANAGED MY RESTAURANTS better than I did my life.

I loved having a few round tables in my dining rooms. Rounds are egalitarian, and conducive to collaboration and conversation. I was not a round table in 2012. If I were to somehow seat my intellect, physical well-being, inner child who loves to play, and spirituality, my intellect would own the seat at the head of the table, with all the others subordinate.

Rob and I felt very much on our own. There are a small number of multi-unit independent restaurant groups in America, and only about fifteen of our size. This limited the people who might have served as mentors. And we were too proud to hit up, say, Danny Meyer from Union Square Hospitality Group or Rich Melman from Lettuce Entertain You for guidance.

Each new project altered the size and makeup of the company, and we didn't always evolve quickly enough.

One time in 2012, a manager for one of our restaurants showed up to work intoxicated, and we fired him. Ian, who as director of operations was our only corporate officer at the time, had to go back and GM. At the same time, I received a phone call from an employee at another of our restaurants, asking to meet.

After sitting, she simply slid her phone over to show a screenshot of a text exchange with her manager:

Manager: Am I driving you home tonight?

Bartender: What?

Manager: You said I could drive you home tonight.

Bartender: Don't put words in my mouth

Manager: I would like to put something else in your mouth

He, too, was fired immediately. With no backups in the corporate office this time, we had to go to the pen, to a forty-one-year-old reliever who had lost a little bit of speed on his fastball. (That would be me.) I foolishly tried to be both co-CEO and a GM for six weeks, pushing myself almost to the brink of insanity. Rob had also lost me and Ian in the corporate office in the short term, making his life miserable.

This was in the middle of a stretch when we opened seven restaurants in three years between 2010 and 2013. After years of fighting the current, now I was being dragged by it. There is a photo from around that time of me sitting on the stairs at Balena, a new Italian restaurant we were building, crying. The guy installing our glass frames had screwed up the order, causing the frames to collapse, and then disappeared on the very day he was supposed to install. It was the last piece of the construction puzzle, and not having it in place delayed our opening until the specialist reappeared with a new team of workers and fresh materials to complete the job.

I was trying to train a new GM at Perennial, manage my side of the openings alongside Rob (who was also getting his ass kicked), and for the first time ever, even our relationship would feel the heat at times.

"Kevin, what's the spec on this cooler?"

"I can't remember."

"Well, I need it. Find it," said Rob, sternly.

"Well, I can't fucking find it right now."

Rob broke the stare-down that followed with a question. "What the fuck are we doing to ourselves?"

This frustration would continue to simmer, and then the boil-over happened.

Hotel Lincoln, the abandoned hotel where we built Perennial, was finally sold by the federal government in 2012. We lived through real estate tours and the acquisition and renovation of the place. As the hotel prepared to receive its inaugural guests, there was friction with the new owners because we, not they, were running the food and beverage. We agreed to put out a breakfast spread each morning at Elaine's, our tiny artisanal coffee shop also located inside Hotel Lincoln.

The morning before, the manager approached one of our employees at Elaine's.

"Do you have the continental breakfast ready for tomorrow?"

"I'm not sure what you're talking about," he answered.

"Kevin and Rob better get their shit together," he snapped back.

Nino, Elaine's manager, had made an honest mistake, mixing up our agreed-upon offerings and a continental breakfast. These things happen.

When Nino recounted this story to me at the first practice dinner at Balena, I snapped and called the hotel manager. "I'm driving over to the hotel and I'm going to beat the fuck out of you."

Trying to juggle all these openings, and our existing restaurants, had put me in alternating states of frustration and anxiety, and I was about to unleash it all on an equally frustrated hotel manager. After sailing through a few red lights, I regained my composure and detoured to our house.

I walked in and saw my family in the living room. Instead of engaging, I walked upstairs, to Lola's room, and sat on her top bunk. I don't know why I retreated to childhood in these moments, as when I found my way to my grade school after my breakfast with Woody, but it was clearly a pattern.

No one will find me here, I thought.

Moments later, four-year-old Lola walked in and saw me. "Daddy, what are you doing up there?"

"I had a fight with someone at work, and I am beyond frustrated, so I'm up here trying to get my composure back."

"Did you talk to your friends about it, Daddy? Did you talk to Robby about it?"

I laughed. "No, baby, I haven't yet."

The next day, around 3 p.m., my cell phone rang. It was Lola, who had just gotten out of school. She had been thinking about me all day. "Are you better today, Daddy? Did you talk to your friends?"

I couldn't always accept or absorb it, but I had a pretty strong team on my side. Lola, at age four, only knew how to lead with love, and fortunately for me, and the world, it was a virtue she wouldn't outgrow.

I let hospitality guide me. I brought a bottle of wine to that hotel manager with my apologies and regrets. Sure, he had been wrong, too, but I was only responsible for cleaning up my side of the street.

Boka Restaurant Group had become the only restaurant company in the country with three *Food & Wine* Best New Chefs working under one umbrella simultaneously. Tentori got his award in 2008; Izard in 2011. When Ryan Poli left Perennial to become a partner in a new restaurant group, we decided to collaborate with 2007 Best New Chef Paul Virant to rebrand the restaurant Perennial Virant. We were no longer just saying we were a chef-driven restaurant group; we *were* one.

Paul was socially conscious, led with his heart as much as his palate, and had honed a culinary style founded on pickling and preserving. He was laid-back and had a hippie-like cadence to his conversational style; for example, "Dude, I think we should be composting. That'd be cool, right?"

We also added Chef Chris Pandel to Balena. If you don't get along with Chris, I hate to break it to you, but you're the problem. Chris is the salt of the earth, possesses an encyclopedic knowledge of food, can cook anything, and has the calming powers of Obi-Wan Kenobi. These chefs were brothers and sisters of a sort, meaning that we had a family: Pandel the wise one; Paul the flower child; Giuseppe the stern older brother; and Izard the tough one, who didn't need her brothers to protect her.

For the first time, each of our restaurants had a well-defined personality and mission.

Perennial Virant walked the walk. We composted for the first time, had a $10,000 inventory of pickled vegetables, were low on waste, and had a small carbon footprint. Boka would receive a Michelin star and was our tasting-menu joint; Perennial Virant was true farm-to-table; Girl & The Goat was a small-plates-high-energy American restaurant; GT Fish was modern seafood; Elaine's was an artisanal coffee shop; and J. Parker, which we opened in 2012, was a rooftop bar with soaring views of Lake Michigan and Lincoln Park. We were also working on a diner, Little Goat with Stephanie, and had just rebranded Landmark as Balena, with Chef Chris Pandel.

Getting reviewed at this point had become a way of life. Every time we opened, we braced ourselves for the onslaught of critics. If you search "Vettel," as in *Chicago Tribune* food critic Phil Vettel, in my historical text messages, you will find threads of heart-racing urgency and high-stakes standard operating procedures that a paid assassin would respect.

Manager: Vettel just sat at Table 30

Me: Fuck. Table 30? I hate that table. Who's serving him?

Manager: Tom

Me: Double Fuck, i hate Tom.

Manager: Sorry, we didn't recognize until he was sat

Me: all good-I don't really hate Tom, he is just new. Order?

Manager: tripe, asparagus, mushroom pizza, suckling pig, tagliolini nero

Me: good order-On way, only Pedro and Tom touch table besides you, yes?

Manager: Heard

Me: Nothing special for him, make sure all tables in his orbit are treated the same
Manager: Im sweating
Me: so am I, take a deep breath, be there in 5.

A month later, we found out Phil loved it: "The pizzas are terrific, tantalizingly thin but with puffy, oil-glossed, satisfyingly chewy edges . . . The ribbonlike tajarin, topped with pork ragu, oozes rusticity, as do the olives, braised rabbit and fried rosemary that grace twisty strozzapreti . . . A crudo of lightly smoked mackerel is not for the faint of heart—mackerel is an oil-heavy fish—but matched to a soft-cooked egg, held in place by a nurturing garlic aioli." Balena got an enthusiastic three stars, exactly what we were shooting for, and it gave everyone some adrenaline to keep getting better.

IN 2013 WE OPENED LITTLE GOAT. It comprised two levels, two hundred seats, and eighty-five menu items and was open seventeen hours every day. There was nothing little about it. By then, our hype machine was so well oiled and fully functioning that one thousand people showed up for breakfast and lunch, combined, for our very first service. Because it was a diner, we never even contemplated reservations, making it impossible to forecast demand, and we got our asses handed to us.

Mid-service, Stephanie said, "Shut it down, we are running out of food."

I spent the next hour apologizing and handing out gift cards.

Editing is just as important as concepting. That beautiful picture you have in your mind? By the time you traverse the wide chasm between imagining and realizing, it will never look like you thought it would. Get your pencil out and bring an eraser. Eighty-five menu items are cut to sixty-five. Seventeen hours a day becomes fourteen. The editor is just as important as the writer when telling the final story.

Every menu decision triggers several other questions: which farm are we buying the protein from, how are we storing it, who is making the tortillas, do we have enough cooler space, and does the price point fit our menu? You can't just be a dreamer in the restaurant business—you have to be an executor as well.

The public will also let you know if they are buying what you are selling. It's very hard to make money, so you look for the edges that need sanding. If no one walks in between 2 p.m. and 5 p.m., you shorten the hours. If no one orders the tripe, you cut it. The first year, you keep your eyes open, you listen intently, and you read all the reviews. You take this information and make subtle changes while maintaining the integrity of your concept, even if you tweak it here and there.

It took a year, but we found our groove at Little Goat, and *Restaurants & Institutions*, a prominent industry trade magazine, featured us on their list of the one hundred highest-grossing restaurants in the country.

Every day in 2014 was scheduled to the minute, structured, and choreographed. We had just opened Little Goat, Momotaro, The Izakaya, and Cold Storage, and were building Swift & Sons, Duck Duck Goat, and GT Prime. I didn't think—just followed my iPhone calendar's directives. It was energizing, but I felt caged. When you have chef partners, it's not just about your ambition; it's also about theirs. Stephanie had been incredibly successful, so when she wanted to do another place, we tried to make it happen. That would trigger the other chefs to want new places, too. Everyone's ambitions needed feeding, and this kept us running hard.

If you really want to think of yourself as an asshole, and have others agree with you, have your professional reality exceed your dreams, and then, in a momentary lapse of judgment, complain about it. Tell the people around you that it's not enough. I never really leaned into the latter, but I definitely dipped my toe in that water, and it was scalding hot.

I told my friend, James, that the more successful I got, the more anxious I felt, and more disconnected from anything resembling happiness.

He responded: "Aw, poor Kevin. Are you crying in your hundred-dollar bills again?"

That sent me into an interior tailspin. *What's wrong with me?* I wondered. Had I lost all perspective? Wasn't it time I allowed myself to believe in the reality I'd made for myself since the Little Blue House days?

Four groups of tastemakers lorded over the Chicago restaurant kingdom in those days. The first group, which meant (and still means) the most to your business, is the general public. After your diners came the macro critics like those at the *Tribune*. Then there was the small and cliquey group of the hospitality industry. And last was a shadowy fourth group: the bloggers and uberfoodies. We had cracked the first three, but this final group could be elusive, and snarky. For them, you couldn't be too big or too powerful, you couldn't seem like you were trying in a performative sense, be too broad in a concept, or look like a trend follower. This was the cool kids' lunch table, and they could wreck your status on a whim.

My anxious brain often left me focusing on people who didn't like us instead of the ones who did. The fear of judgment of others was the most powerful behavioral pattern I had. It was like using heroin as a dietary supplement: wildly effective, but it will slowly kill you. It made me obsess, work tirelessly, run hard, and then run harder.

By this time, Boka wasn't aging gracefully and had begun shedding its relevance. It maintained its Michelin star, but sales had dwindled. We gave it a complete overhaul, gutting the space, installing a new back bar and lighting, and taking away the huge fabric sculpture that had been our design calling card. And we added a wisecracking little brother to the mix—Lee Wolen, that same kid we met in the Eleven Madison Park kitchen during the James Beard Awards weekend. As high as our expectations were after tasting Lee's food, the result was more than we ever dreamed of. It changed the trajectory of the restaurant, and our company.

Lee was a cook's cook, obsessed but not obsessive-compulsive. He had mastered every technique in the book, and everybody in the kitchen respected him. The big difference between Lee and many of his contemporaries is that he achieves this in a completely different way than, say, Charlie Trotter. He's a charming combination of goofy, folksy, innocent, funny, and grumpy, with more catchphrases than a 1970s prime-time sitcom slate.

He'd earned his chops and street cred working at two restaurants that had been voted number one in the world by The World's 50 Best Restaurants: El Bulli in Spain and Eleven Madison Park in New York. But it was as chef at the Lobby in the Peninsula Chicago hotel that he earned a Michelin star and proved he could do it on his own. It was there that Rob and I encountered Lee a second time and decided to meet for coffee the following week. Two brainstorming sessions later, we had a chef partner.

Our new version of Boka was a showcase for Lee's talent, manifested in dishes like roasted chicken for two with lemon and thyme brioche stuffed under the skin; shaved and roasted broccoli salad with Parmesan crackers; and ricotta gnudi with mushrooms, squash, and sage.

The new Boka was also an incubator for developing talent. Among the cooks who worked for Lee were two he brought from Eleven Madison Park: Eddie Lee, who would go on to be chef of the Charter Oak in St. Helena, California, and Genie Kwon, who won a James Beard Award for her restaurant Kasama.

The restaurant felt brand-new as it soared into its second decade. I didn't know if it would defy mortality, as I wanted it to, but this was a good start.

I HAD SHARED MY CRAZY family backstory with only a handful of people. My kids were not among them. To them, Larry was Grandpa, a man they didn't get to see much and—although friendly to them—who lacked grandfatherly warmth and affection. Whatever relationship he and I had was mediated by Mom, but I thought Sofia and Lola might be able to have more.

When Lola's preschool scheduled a Grandparents' Day, she asked me if Larry and Dee would travel the two hundred miles to attend. Since Mom was uncomfortable traveling alone, Larry held veto power over such requests.

I rang him up.

"Hey, Dad, Lola would like you to attend Grandparents' Day at her school."

I thought, perhaps naively, that Larry would seize this shot at redemption, for the low cost of an Amtrak ticket.

"I can't do it," he told me. He had "too much going on at work."

Larry was still an insurance underwriter, not a bank president. I knew that he had not taken vacation time in almost ten years. The smell of bullshit uncorked a lifetime of anger. "You know, I've come to terms with the fact you were a shitty dad, but your lack of interest in being an actual grandparent is unforgivable. It's a fucking layup. This is the good stuff, the easy stuff."

"I'm sorry you feel that way," he said, then hung up.

Mom called back. "I'm the one who takes the brunt of it when you do that," she said.

This time, I hung up.

I often used cinema as a teacher, a guide, and a therapist. Even in *The Prince of Tides*, Tom Wingo's sociopathic father could play the part of a benevolent grandpa. Disappointment is built by expectation, and I kept thinking things would be different with Larry, only to be fooled again.

A YEAR LATER, A CREATION came that needed no editing: Cortney gave birth to our beautiful son, Luca.

Having a son was more daunting for me than a dozen daughters would have been because I couldn't look at him without seeing myself. I always loved finding order in things that had previously been mishandled. Perhaps this was another way of correcting the past. I kissed him and held him more in his first week than either of my fathers had me in a lifetime. It was healing and it was restorative.

I took Luca down to Springfield with the family to show him off. It was Larry's seventieth birthday, and the entire family, including Missi, her kids, and her husband, Ray, all met at a restaurant for an old-school Italian-American feast. Larry held Luca for a hot second, made no comment, and appeared sound asleep ten minutes into the meal. We drove straight back to Chicago afterward.

Observing Luca's youthful exuberance and boundless energy inspired me to get my body right for the first time in years. I hired a highly credentialed personal trainer six days a week. All these years of cortisol-producing anxiety and ten thousand steps a day in dress shoes had beat up my back and hips. I was perennially seized up, like an old catcher's mitt that had dried in the sun. Three months of intense stretching and epidural shots to address degenerative disk disease in my lower spine unpretzeled me. Once I hit my stride, I shed twenty-five pounds and reclaimed my fitness. At forty-three years old, I had whipped myself into the best shape of my life.

I found a second wind through a bolstered corporate infrastructure and better health practices, and Rob and I found a creative surge that helped produce two more restaurants—Momotaro in 2014 and Swift & Sons in 2015—two of our most successful ventures.

Momotaro was as complete a concept as we had ever put forth. We had been pondering a Japanese restaurant for almost a decade. We did tastings with chefs, looked at buildings, and batted concepts around. It was always at the top of our list of places we wanted to do. Both Rob's and my favorite cuisine was Japanese, and we both had very specific ideas about what we'd do with it if given the chance, but we hadn't found the right chef to lead it.

In 2014, we did a chance tasting with a Philadelphia chef named Mark Hellyar, who had logged several years cooking in Japan. Hellyar was quiet, shy, and brilliant. The first bite we ever had was Momotaro tartare, which was a Momotaro tomato diced, dehydrated, and then rehydrated, producing a beef-like texture. This was served with Maui onion and shiso leaves. It was a revelation, and we knew we had found the right chef in Hellyar. His vision helped bring the concept into view. This was not just a restaurant with a Japanese fish program; it was a Japanese seasonal kitchen as well, and a restaurant that was going to take big swings.

We finally got to work with AvroKO, our design crush, led by Adam Farmerie, who loves to tell stories through design. There were three historical narratives that the Momotaro design would all lead back to:

1. The obsessed Japanese salaryman, present in the one million meticulous scribble marks in the bathroom hallway.
2. The economic miracle in Japan, illustrated by a back-bar replica of the Tokyo Stock Exchange.

3. The back streets of Tokyo, resembling a movie set, in our downstairs bar and lounge area, the Izakaya.

We did a tasting in Los Angeles with Jeff Ramsey, the sushi chef at the Mandarin Oriental hotel in Tokyo. We sat on the living room floor of his friend's apartment as he smoked aji in ash from a thousand-year-old cypress tree. He would end up being Mark's opening chef teammate in what appeared to be a perfect culinary marriage.

Momotaro received the best opening reviews of any of our restaurants. It was included in *Esquire*'s Best New Restaurants; the Momotaro tartare was dubbed *GQ*'s Dish of the Year; it was nominated for Best Design at the James Beard Foundation Awards; and it debuted at number two in the *Chicago Tribune*'s list of the 50 Best Restaurants in Chicago.

In true Japanese fashion, the restaurant benefited from patience. Some of the early scenesters were looking for something more Americanized. We didn't cave to their whims and rigidity, or the bros or bachelorette parties. We knew who we were, who we wanted to be, and we stuck to it.

Two early diners were Mick Jagger and Ron Wood. They decided to eat in our third-floor office instead of the crowded dining room. I rode up on the elevator and played DJ and cocktail server, while the managers scrambled for someone to take the table.

Mick asked for jazz. I obliged by putting on Miles Davis's *Bitches Brew*, and he gave me an appreciative head nod. I poured Mick a white wine and then engaged Ron.

"Is there any way I could get a Red Bull?" Ron asked, in a broken, gravelly voice that reflected forty years on the road.

We didn't serve Red Bull, but a restaurant two blocks away did, so I sprinted in my black suit, in ninety-five-degree swelter, to score Ron his six-pack.

Back at Momotaro, as I poured it for him, sweating profusely, he looked down at the can.

"Sorry, I meant a *sugar-free* Red Bull."

Seven minutes and another sprint later, I repoured.

Ron noticed the beads of sweat cascading down my face.

"Are you nervous, son?"

I just smiled.

It's not always possible not to let them see you sweat, but you don't have to explain why. Not even to a Rolling Stone.

IN OCTOBER 2015, WE WRAPPED UP a tornado of restaurant launches with Swift & Sons, a sixteen-thousand-square-foot behemoth of a steakhouse with Chris Pandel as chef; Duck Duck Goat in March 2016, a mostly traditional Chinese restaurant with Stephanie Izard; and GT Prime in September 2016, a boutique meat-centric restaurant with Giuseppe Tentori.

Rob and I had our nerve center on the second floor of Momotaro, where Ron and Mick had eaten omakase. Our desks on either side of the room faced each other, with a small lounge area in between. My desk was orderly and well-spaced, while Rob's was in need of a punchline, with stacks of paperwork and yellow Post-its sticking out on all sides. Our desks may have showed our organizational differences, but when it came to partnerships it was our similarities that had gotten us through. We had spent fifteen years together, fifteen hours a day, breaking bread and breaking down deals. We now agreed on the lights and the music levels. No one understood each other's lives more than the two of us.

In the spring of 2016, we sat at those desks and watched the James Beard Foundation announce its finalists on a live stream. Among them were two Chicagoans, up for Outstanding Restaurateur in America.

Working the dining room at Boka, with both "Bo" and "Ka"

We looked at each other and then simultaneously put our heads in our hands. We both had been running for years like someone was chasing us. Rob and I were rarely, as they say, in the moment; we were always sprinting to whatever was next.

This time, for just a few hours, we let ourselves stay still and soak it all in.

11

LIFE IN THE FAST LANE

IN THE FALL OF 2016, I drove to Springfield to attend a charity event for Hope, an autism-focused foundation. It was holding its annual black-tie gala. I was on the board and asked Stephanie Izard to do the food as a favor.

I'd been back to Springfield countless times since my parents sold my childhood home in 1993. This time I found myself craving a visit to the Little Blue House. After more than a decade, I figured, the worst memories would have receded, and the best would come to the fore. And so I beelined for the house on arrival in town.

Approaching the front door, I noted that the painted wood had been replaced with permanent siding and I could see through the large windows that the browns and 1970s linoleum greens had been supplanted by an off-white color scheme.

When I knocked on the door, the current owner, a woman I'd place around forty years old, looked at me skeptically, perhaps wondering if I was a Jehovah's Witness.

I explained that I'd grown up in the house, asked if she'd mind giving me a quick tour, and she obliged.

I was struck by how small it was, how claustrophobic, how one sneeze must have shaken it like a tremor.

"Someone lived here?" the owner asked disbelievingly, as she led me to what had been my matchbox of a bedroom, which she was using for storage.

"Something like that," I said, amusing myself.

My guide probably thought me rude, but I was too overcome to make even the most perfunctory small talk as we continued the tour. The cramped basement, which had once held Mom's twenty-year collection of *Good Housekeeping* magazines, was now another storage room, and a large trunk sat where that little couch I'd migrate to in the middle of the night used to be. The back door still stuck, requiring a frame-rocking tug to wrest it open. The basketball hoop was gone, as was the jungle gym made out of old tires. Two large rocks still marked where we had buried our two birds, Cub and Dodger.

Passing back through the house to the front door on my way out, painful memories pushed aside better ones until all I could think about was Mom's tears, Larry's volatility, and my yearning for basic love and affection.

For all my optimism, I left sadder than when I'd arrived, same as always.

THE PAST WASN'T THROUGH WITH me that night.

At the charity event, I played maître d', working the room, strutting my hospitality stuff for ghosts of my past life.

"Shit, man, I haven't seen you since high school! Give me a recap," asked a high school classmate with thinning hair.

Well, secret father, fraternity, dropout, homeless, bobcat attack, Envelope Guy, four restaurants, bankruptcy, comeback, more restaurants, marriage, kids, perceived success, hamster wheel, dark depression, exhaustion.

That was what I wanted to say, instead, I just said, "It's been busy."

At the end of the night, I stood by the door, thanking people for coming.

Amid the procession of departing attendees, a woman's face materialized. She looked familiar—no, make that familial. I knew we'd never met, but perceived an echo of myself in her wide brown eyes and olive skin.

"Hi, my name is Lisa Palmeri."

"Is your mom Cathy Palmeri?" I asked, naming Woody's daughter, my half-sister.

"Yes," she said. "I think you're my uncle."

"I am your uncle," I said. It felt good to connect so openly and uncomplicatedly around a blood relation. I hadn't seen her mom, my half-sister, since Indigo and the *Titanic* dinner.

"I would like to tell you a story, if we could grab some privacy," she said.

I commandeered a private room off the event space.

"I want to tell you this because I think it might be important to you," she said. "Woody was my babysitter when I was little. Every couple of weeks he would pull out a picture of you and say, 'Do you want to see a picture of a handsome boy?'"

Every version of me needed to hear this. The eight-year-old kid whose dad hated him, the homeless kid sleeping on the beach, the bankrupt Music City kid who felt like a failure, the troubled middle-aged man fighting his way out of a dark depression.

The only words I could manage through a stifled cry were "Thank you."

How many tattered pictures of me had populated that wallet over the years? Did my mom order him a school glossy each year, or did he show the same outdated photo over and over? How many strangers saw that picture at small-town speaking gigs where he pretended that his alternate life happened, that I was his only son, and that the love of his life, Dorothy Boehm, was his bride?

Part of me always wondered if Woody thought he had gotten off lucky, that he was relieved he didn't have to raise me. He was able to keep his love affair going and not blow up his other family and continue his travels unencumbered. This was the first evidence I had that this might not have been the case.

My best times were often the moment before something anticipated: that 1991 drive to Florida, going to bed before Christmas morning, the nights before all the big restaurant openings, the plane ride to a vacation. I was often warmed by the glow of what might happen more than what actually did. I had driven the two hundred miles from Chicago to Springfield many times. My sunny expectations never matched the stormy results. That afternoon at the Little Blue House was the norm. This exchange with Lisa was the exception.

I WAS LOOKING FOR ANY excuse for a timeout in the fall of 2016, and then one of the most joyous and extraordinary things happened. The Cubs started to win—and win a lot. On October 7, 2016, the reservation book at Swift & Sons included President Barack Obama at 6 p.m., and I had tickets to the Cubs playoff game at 7:05.

Agenda: Throw on my suit, make small talk with the most powerful man in the free world—"Kevin and Rob, the restaurant business is a tough business. You seem to have navigated it well—congratulations"; "Thank you, Mr. President"—change into a full Cubs outfit in an Uber, and make it just in time for the national anthem. In the third inning, I caught a foul ball, the Cubs won 1–0, and Cortney and I talked all the way home.

That is a proper day. The president, a foul ball, and a victory. *Let's keep having days like this*, I thought.

I would see fourteen playoff games that season, ending in a victory so epic and so stressful that it contained ten innings, a rain delay, one Jason Heyward Knute Rockne speech, and one massive panic attack.

As I crawled into bed at 10 a.m., still frazzled and adrenalized, my phone rang. It was, jointly, Theo Epstein and Jed Hoyer, the president and general manager of the Cubs.

"We are sitting in an empty Wrigley," said Theo. "And we want to eat goat."

According to legend, the Cubs had long been cursed by William Sianis, a tavern owner who put a hex on the team when his billy goat was refused entrance to game four of the 1945 World Series at Wrigley Field. The Cubs and the Sianis family had tried to end the curse over the years by bringing in a goat to Wrigley, and now that the Cubs had won it all, team leadership wanted to officially put the curse to bed with a ceremonial goat meal, washed down with domestic beers, the early-morning hour be damned.

This is one of the many moments in my life where the years of serving people served me back. I called up Ian Goldberg, our COO, and asked him to pick up a goat leg from Girl & The Goat. Customers could preorder whole goat legs, and we already had three roasting for that night's service.

"What's the largest one you have?" Ian asked one of our sous chefs.

"Nine and a half pounds!"

"Wrap it up, it's going to Wrigley."

Ian picked up Rob and me, with the goat leg in tow, and drove through a sea of people, then through a gate on Waveland Avenue right into the stadium.

We celebrated another few hours, and then finally my tired body gave out and I hit the sack.

The playoff season had been a three-week de facto vacation with my childhood friends Joe and James, with whom I traveled to Los Angeles and Cleveland to follow the baseball action, and it

Eating goat at Wrigley Field, the day after the greatest baseball game ever played, 2016, with Theo Epstein and Jed Hoyer

was a beautiful distraction from everything else. With my intellect on the bench for a while, I got to be a kid again, this time with much more satisfying results.

WE HAD BEEN DRIVING THE Boka racecar two hundred miles per hour since 2010, opening thirteen successful places in seven years. The Cubs weren't the only Chicagoans riding a winning streak: Rob and I were building a bigger and better company, with real infrastructure.

There were many things that growth helped with; most importantly, we were able to build new positions for our people to evolve to. One of the challenges was that every time the company got bigger, my job description changed. There was a transition in my life at this point from a cog in the wheel at service to more of a macro-manager. It was more difficult to flit in and out of the service team at a given restaurant whenever I felt like it, at whichever restaurant beckoned. It was simply too long between visits, and I was unfamiliar with the idiosyncrasies of each place.

My day no longer started at 9 a.m.; it started at 7, and meetings went until 5 p.m. I would cruise home for dinner with the family, and then back out to hit a few restaurants for a couple hours. We now employed two thousand employees, with an annual payroll of $40 million. Where I used to make decisions on the fly, now directives had to be filtered through departments and triple-checked. Sometimes instituting new procedures felt like trying to parallel-park an ocean liner.

I hated giving up certain things in the name of progress. I had been running a front door for almost two decades. It had always calmed me, as there was a rhythmic choreography to it in which I could lose myself. The goal was always to set the tone of kindness and energy from moment one, maximize covers, never leave a table empty for too long, create a seating drag just long enough that it both populated the bar and gave the room energy, and provide the kitchen and servers with enough information to provide maximum hospitality.

I knew the attrition rates at each restaurant, how many people on average would no-show or cancel last minute, and I would replace and take walk-ins accordingly. It was a high-wire game of being aggressive but not too aggressive. There was also a move we called *upsells*. If a table opened up for a limited amount of time, we could tell a walk-in that it was theirs, but it was only available for forty-five minutes. It was *Let's Make a Deal*, dining style.

The spread was equally important. How many people can each restaurant properly serve every fifteen minutes? Some of our restaurants maxed out at eighteen, others could handle as many as twenty-six. When we were running late, I was an honest caretaker, telling people we were behind and offering them a drink. These are the moments when you need to find a way to people-please without being dishonest. Creating unrealistic expectations only postpones tension and erodes trust. I am both on your side and an honest caretaker.

It wasn't always perfect.

"Sir, we are running about fifteen minutes behind schedule," I told a diner one night at GT Fish.

"Nope, my reservation is for seven p.m. I will be sat now."

The best and worst feature of the restaurant industry is its interactivity. You do everything you can to make your guests happy, but every night brings different guests.

The reservation system is just one moving part in a complex machine, and the truth is that a reservation is a best guess. Reservation times are based on averages. In an à la carte restaurant, a table that opts for one course will surely vacate the table well ahead of the allotted time, and also spend less than you would have hoped. Another table might linger over a cocktail, take thirty minutes to order, and put you behind. Generalizing is a dangerous business, but it's safe to say that restaurant guests fall into two broad categories: those who get it and understand, and those who either don't get it or don't care.

"Sir, all of the tables are occupied, but several are on check, and one should be up any moment."

"That's not our agreement, our agreement is seven p.m."

"Well, I guess we are at an impasse, then, sir. I will do the best I can, and I'm happy to buy you a drink while you are waiting."

"Honey, we are walking, let's go someplace that understands the value of a reservation."

Just then, a table got up, and we all watched as they moved toward the door.

"That table will be ready in two minutes if you would like it. Please give us an opportunity to make it up to you."

"We want it," said his wife, her eyes shooting daggers at her husband.

The time was 7:05.

"Fantastic, I am so glad you are staying." There wasn't a smidgen of *fuck you* in my voice. I truly wanted to win him over. My allergy to judgment made me a very effective maître d'.

Running an aggressive door could mean the difference between a successful restaurant and a failing one. I knew having myself at the door in those early years added up to an additional fifteen covers a night. Fifteen times a seventy-five-dollar check average times 208 services a year where we operated at full efficiency was another $234,000 in gross revenue. You can both maximize covers and maximize hospitality, if you master the door.

As we started 2017, we had three projects written at the top of our whiteboard: Dutch & Doc's, a joint venture with the Cubs organization right across from the historic marquee at Wrigley Field (how could that fail?); Bellemore, a fine-dining restaurant; and food and beverage at the new Viceroy Hotel.

For the first time, we played divide and conquer, testing our systems, our trust, our mentoring skills, and the ability of our culture to not get watered down as it was batched and served all over the city.

In the 1960s and '70s, the Cubs would suffer from what they called the June Swoon. The heat of constant day games started to wreak havoc on players' energy and the Cubs would often fall from first place to an also-ran. In 1977 they started 47-22 and finished 81-81.

Our version of the '77 Cubs was our 2017 squad. We started out filled with piss and vinegar, confidence oozing out of our pores. But Dutch & Doc's, which opened in May 2018, had difficulties that were hard to overcome. We were packed before the game, but empty during, and on non-game days, the neighborhood had trouble pulling real diners.

Our hotel deal was more complicated. The hotel flag, or brand—in this case, the Viceroy—is rarely the owner of the property in hotel deals; they're usually a contracted manager. Often, that flag will run the food and beverage, but in this case, we did. It leaves you with three entities trying to work together in a high-pressure, high-stress environment. It was a multipronged partnership with us, the developer, and the hotel flag often arguing about each of our individual needs, both financially and customer-facing. We were constantly rowing in different directions, resulting in meetings that sounded like a *Real Housewives* reunion show.

In the summer of 2017 our acclaimed Italian eatery, Balena, suffered catastrophic damage when an electrical fire destroyed most of its second floor and kitchen. No one was hurt, thank God, but the damage, length of time left on our lease, and fights with the insurance companies on the eventual settlement led to its closure. Between Landmark and Balena, I had many memories in that building, and watching the destruction was jarring and heart-wrenching.

Bellemore seemed like the bright light in it all. We opened the week after Thanksgiving 2017 and *Robb Report* named it the Best New Restaurant in America. Jimmy Papadopoulos was our new chef partner, and his signature dish, the oyster pie, was all over Instagram. Bellemore shot out of the gates like a freight train, and then unfortunately puttered out like my old gray Chevette did when it ran out of gas.

The unfamiliar territory found us going from oyster pie to humble pie, and the temporary light that the Cubs gave me turned into the darkest period of my life up to that point. I was like the guy with flat feet and one leg longer than the other that keeps getting adjusted at the chiropractor. I'd be momentarily soothed, then throw out my back, slipping a disc over and over.

Anxiety, paranoia, and despair blanketed my every waking, and sleeping, minute. I was tough on team members, I had a short fuse at home, and I completely disappeared from any type of communicative relationship with Cortney. I conserved dialogue for conversations with guests where I faked being a normal and happy guy.

I tried everything in pursuit of relief and respite, from the healthy (float therapy, meditation, strenuous workouts, acupuncture, hot baths) to the distracting (more projects and board positions) to the destructive (alcohol and late nights). If I thought of it or read about it, or if somebody suggested it, onto the pile it went. None of it would work.

I always felt that I was disappointing Cortney. Of course I was. How could all of this not be a disappointment? And so our marriage suffered. I couldn't open up to her, though somewhere inside I wanted to, and, being a more stable person, she couldn't begin to fathom my inner darkness. It made for a relationship that was constantly defined and redefined by how well I was maintaining sanity. She was always waiting for me: waiting for me to come home, waiting for me to open up, waiting for me to notice her, and waiting for the work me, which was high energy and fun, to also be the behind-the-scenes me.

By the time I got home at night, it was a struggle to get words out. I was a quiet shell of myself at family dinners, as I silently catastrophized every work fire and irrational emotion. The kids would get just about all the energy left in my battery. After I roughhoused with them and they went to bed, I shut down and clammed up. Cortney had to settle for close to zero.

In the realm of finite games, I was losing my battle with depression. The tried-and-true pacifiers were no longer working, so I began to lunge at happiness, often missing my target. Grand gestures, big openings, trips, and speaking gigs all failed to give me that rush I desperately needed. I was a dopamine addict who could no longer get high.

Our work slump only deepened my valley. I only found respite in three things: drinking, yoga, and a hot bath in a dark bathroom.

One morning I woke up drenched in sweat, sobbing. I needed help and I didn't know who to talk to. I was so afraid to admit that all the things I had done in my life had led to this place. I had run in the opposite direction of Larry so hard and still ended up in the same place.

I tried therapy again—this time with Jennifer, who was young, divorced, friendly, and intuitive. But I wasn't honest with her, sanitizing my stories and editing my feelings. I wanted her to like me, as if she were a guest in one of my restaurants. The notion that this person was there for me, and no other reason, and that I was supposed to take rather than give, was so foreign to me that it never really occurred to me.

By the summer of 2018, I was self-medicating to a fault. I spoke to Mom once a week, but that was her therapy, not mine. She shared the weekly Larry highlight reel, and I tried to laugh or console her, whichever was called for.

On one of those calls, our weekly routine took an unexpected turn:

"I don't feel right," she told me, describing pains in her abdomen. "Something is wrong. I went to the emergency room, and they just sent me away."

A high school friend had become a prominent Springfield doctor. I pulled that string to get her seen.

Forty-eight hours later came knee-buckling news, in a rare midweek call: "Kev, I have stage four pancreatic cancer. They are giving me three to six months."

I had never contemplated the possibility that Mom wouldn't live to be 110. She was stronger than oak, never sick at sea, always finished the race. Even though she was in her seventies, I thought we'd be able to spend some real time together, maybe traveling. She wanted to see Israel, Mount Rushmore, Paris. Little did I know, the hourglass had already been turned over.

I was a mess, but she was as calm as I had ever heard her.

"I feel good about it, Kev. It's time. I'm going home to God."

Chemo would extend those three months to eighteen.

The first six were the happiest six months of her life. For the first time ever, she felt loved. I watched her with some level of fascination, as in death she was finding life. It had taken her seventy-four years and a grim diagnosis to bring her peace.

"I know now that people really love me and weren't just tolerating me," she texted one morning.

Her peace was not contagious. When I wasn't with Mom in Springfield, I felt guilty. When I wasn't with the kids, I felt guilty. When I wasn't helping clean up the mess of the June Swoon restaurant trio, I felt guilty. The answer was simple: I was maxed out, and then some. As a result, I was dabbling in every role I played: son, husband, businessman, host, leader. There were not enough projects or tequila to wash it all down.

By this time, I had become quite adept at faking discipline.

It actually had a construct that seemed regulated. During the week, I could fool everyone else and myself.

But by the weekend, my inner narrator had worked me like a speedbag. I was the villain in his story, and nothing I did was enough for anyone. So, by Friday, it was time to quiet the voice with a dozen or so drinks. Between 10 p.m. and 3 a.m. I would find the temporary peace that only alcohol gave me. I was a weekday model citizen and a weekend drunk. In that regard, I was not special or unusual.

However, the mental post-trauma that drinking gave me would make me want to die until I took that next drink again. I would wallow in deep guilt all week.

I told this to my sober friend Andrew Zimmern.

"I'm not an alcoholic, it just affects me in a strange way."

Andrew smiled.

"Wait a second: You're telling me that every time you drink you feel terrible guilt and shame afterward and want to die. How long has that been going on?"

"About ten years."

"Kevin, you have a problem. Think about what you are saying. It is worth it to you to feel like you want to die for four days after heavy drinking just to feel good for a few hours. You have a bigger issue."

Just like the time Sharon called me bipolar, I was quick to disagree with his assessment.

"I'm not a fucking alcoholic."

IN 2019, AFTER FOUR OTHER nominations for the James Beard Foundation Award for Outstanding Restaurateur in America, I thought about how nice it would be for Mom to see me and Rob win before she died. With everything going wrong in life, perhaps this superficial love would be the perfect antidepressant.

Just in case, I called Mom on the day of the awards and walked her through how to stream the live feed.

We had lost four times previously. It's hard to resist recalculating the votes afterward. The James Beard voting academy, made up of writers, a committee, and my peers, ultimately decided the end result. You wanted it to be a meritocracy, but, like all awards, it's also a popularity contest. Still, as silly and arbitrary as awards can be, they were incredibly important to me, representing a coronation that mattered to every iteration of me—from the kid who got picked on in grade school to the guy reading the *New York Times* on the back deck of a Florida restaurant to the guy still struggling with sanity and security. Rob and I tuxedoed, red carpeted, threw pre-parties, and wrote a speech.

The last five categories to be presented are all national awards; the ones that precede them are either regional or special awards. By the time ours came up, we had been sitting for four hours. Daniel Boulud presented, and when our name was announced, the Boka section of the Lyric Opera went into hysterics, and I just stood there for a second, stunned.

We had just been named Outstanding Restaurateurs in America. The pinnacle of my profession.

When Rob and I hit the stage, we gave each other an enormous bear hug.

"Does this mean we know what we are doing?" I whispered.

Rob went first and killed it. He thanked my hair and got a big laugh.

"This hair has opened so many doors for us."

During my turn at the lectern, I was feeling so good, I even thanked Larry. I also said the following about my mother:

"My first hero was my mom. She was the gold standard when it comes to hard work. I asked her for five dollars to go to Dairy Queen in the summer of 1985, and she told me no. She explained to me that she told me to get a job at the beginning of the summer three weeks previous, that she didn't raise me to be lazy, and that just like God, she only helps those who help themselves."

The audience roared.

For the next two hours, I received more texts than I ever had. By the time we went through the press room, I had more than five hundred, but none of them were from Mom.

Did you see? I texted.

No response.

Mom had once advised me to learn the difference between surface love and real love, and to not allow myself to be too moved by praise from strangers and sycophants. I skipped through the messages, finding the ones from the people I really loved. I got a voicemail from Kim Carnes's husband, Dave Ellingson, that said, "I couldn't be more proud of you if you were my own son," and one from my brother-in-law where he was legit choked up as he congratulated me.

I called home and the kids were cheering. I told Sofia, who was fifteen, to go to her mom's closet and find a dress, and that she could stay home from school tomorrow, and that we wanted to party with her, too. "I'm sending a car," I said. Lola and Luca were still a little young for this rambunctious of a party.

There were so many emotions and adrenaline, I felt like I was on some serious drugs. This night was nothing but pure joy.

Sofia walked into our Girl & The Goat afterparty just as I was talking with Jesse Tyler Ferguson and Zooey Deschanel. She might have thought I was cool again for a night.

I met Brian Canlis and his team from Canlis restaurant in Seattle at the Wieners Circle at 4 a.m. The guy making our hot dogs wore my James Beard Award medal, and we laughed at the absurdity of it all.

Come sunup, I still hadn't heard from Mom.

She and Larry weren't great telephone or text people, so perhaps they were just waiting on me. I was ready! Larry would finally have to give me my due. I decided to be generous and say some kind words back.

Celebrating with my beautiful daughter Sofia the night I won
the James Beard for Outstanding Restaurateur

I dialed, hit speaker, and eased back in my leather chair, waiting for a Boehm family lovefest.

Larry answered: "Hello."

"Hi, Dad."

"Let me put your mother on," was all he said.

Wait, what?? That's it? That's all I get?

Mom jumped on. "We couldn't get the streaming to work, but I saw your text. Congrats."

I paused for a second before trying to explain the significance of the award, told her I would send the video, and then ended a short conversation.

"I gotta go, Mom."

I might not have gotten the love I wanted from home, but my peers gave me a much-needed lift. Letters, texts, and emails from heroes, friends, and even some rivals softened the sting.

One of the things that made me happiest at work were the conversations with other restaurateurs. Those moments of mutual respect often carried me. Over the years, there have been some amazing collaborative moments, and a few uncomfortable ones. On this day I celebrated them both. (This sentiment is summed up brilliantly by the playwright John Patrick Shanley, who once said while accepting an award, "I'd like to thank everybody who ever punched or kissed me in my life and everybody who I ever punched or kissed.")

It was all an evolution, and Rob and I had learned a lot in our time together, about both how to run a company and how to be good industry citizens. There are unwritten rules and etiquette in restaurants just like there are in baseball. Don't give another operator advice unless asked, be diplomatic about the shortcomings of peers' restaurants, be punctual for reservations, tip generously, and do not under any circumstances poach other people's talent. Don't pursue them unless they pursue you, and make sure you call the other party to notify them you are hiring that person if it does happen.

I got a sweet text from legendary chef Carrie Nahabedian that night. She had been part of that learning process.

There have been many shades to these peer relationships. There are mentor ones, like we enjoy with Danny Meyer and Rich Melman; there are many true friendships; there are a sprinkling of adversarial ones that I won't mention; and then there is the one that drives you.

Donnie Madia is one of the best restaurateurs on the planet and is the cofounder of One Off Hospitality, owners of legendary Chicago restaurants like Blackbird, avec, the Violet Hour, and others. He won Outstanding Restaurateur in America in 2015.

For years, our relationship resembled two prisoners in the yard, neither Donnie nor I wanting to acknowledge the other, back down, or show weakness. There was the occasional head nod between us, or a quick handshake, but otherwise we used each other as a competitive dangling carrot.

We fought for the same spaces, chefs, team members, and awards. We were similar in the fact that as hospitable as we could be on the floor, we could run a little hot off it. One morning, our competitive dance turned into a tussle.

Hey, can you talk, texted Donnie.

We had been discussing our two companies throwing a joint Beard party, and Donnie wanted to respectfully back out because they were overcommitted.

I am just walking into something. Can I call you later? I texted back.

I was at the doctor's office having a hurt knee tended to and didn't see his response for another half hour: *With all due respect, I am always just walking into something.* It landed wrong and I immediately called him.

"I don't fucking work for you, Donnie."

"Everybody's fucking busy, you are not the only one," he responded.

We both took some not-so-subtle jabs before hanging up.

Two years later, our rivalry started to gnaw at me, and I suggested we have coffee.

We spent a few hours discovering how alike we were. He had his own father story, was motivated partially by grievance, and struggled to find the balance in life. His new son and marriage had helped him manage his priorities.

After we dropped the avatars and the guards, we found a special friendship that has endured.

Congratulations, my friend! he texted that night. *Can't wait to give you a hug.*

It was emblematic of how far we had come.

AS 2019 CLOSED OUT, THE company was thriving. Although the June Swoon trio were not perfect, they were momentarily stable. We now had eighteen restaurants and were building a nineteenth in Los Angeles, taking our Girl & The Goat show on the road.

I was also building a private wellness club called BIÂN with my friends Joe Fisher, Robby Leone, and Mar Soraparu. I wanted to gather all the things I needed to stay sane into one holistic space. I desperately needed a rehab center, so why not be the guy who helps build it?

Mom was failing fast, and she asked if I could come speak to her Ladies Aid group in Springfield.

I took the train, wrote the speech on the way, and Ubered to the Trinity Lutheran School.

Mom was in a wheelchair. She stood to embrace me and then collapsed in my arms. "I'm so glad you came."

I was so choked up that I wasn't sure if I could get through a forty-five-minute talk.

As they introduced me, I noticed that nine seats in front of the stage were empty.

"Before we bring you up, Kevin, we have some special guests. Please welcome your high school principal, second-grade teacher, fourth-grade teacher, sixth-grade teacher, elementary school principal, middle school vice principal, two of your high school teachers, and the pastor that confirmed you."

Gulp.

"This is your life," teased the pastor.

"Should I turn my speech in to be graded first, or should I just start?" I nervously joked.

I told my best stories, ad-libbed some teacher humor, and then hung with Mom the rest of the day at home. It would be the last time we really spoke for hours. It was clear that the end was near.

That horizon that I always kept in my mind, like a beautiful oasis, had been replaced by darkness. Even so, I had no idea how dark things were about to get.

12
SHE'S NOT THERE

"THE ANGELS ARE COMING FOR me, Kev. You will never make it in time. I want you to know that I love you."

It was the first week of March 2020. It had been sixteen months since doctors had sentenced Mom to perish within three to six months. The estimate had always seemed overly pessimistic to me, considering her fortitude and physical strength.

Still, if she thought she was about to leave this mortal world, I had to heed that.

I drove 110 miles per hour from Chicago to Springfield.

Usually, I'd have killed the few hours in the car with a podcast, or a favorite album, or by making business- and restaurant-related calls. This time, I just thought. Or tried to.

Death wasn't just reaching out to claim my mother. It was coming for us all. The COVID-19 pandemic had already ravaged China, was attacking Europe, and was now on American soil. There had been an outbreak in Seattle, and cases were popping up here and there on the West Coast and increasingly in other places. It was only a matter of time, it seemed, until the United States would be shut down like more and more parts of the world.

The human toll was incalculably grim, and the financial cost, too, was unfathomable.

Certain industries exist at the intersection of humanity and commerce. Travel and live performances are two examples. Restaurants are another. Serving food in a restaurant requires humans to be together cooking during the day, and for employees and guests to interact at night. And the requisite mask-wearing that became mandatory in many large cities during COVID was antithetical to eating and drinking communally.

Rob and I, and the entire industry, perceived the coming crisis as a cataclysmic tidal wave growing ever taller as it bore down on us. The invisible nature of the threat, and its unknowable timeline, left those of us waiting in a surreal state—still permitted to do everything, but scared of actually doing anything. More and more people were becoming fearful of going to crowded places, or even leaving their homes.

I knew only a little of the impending doom. I had been burning up the highway between Springfield and Chicago for a few weeks, splitting time between work, family, and visits with Mom. I was now in a race to say goodbye. By God's grace, Mom was still alive when I arrived. At her side was her pastor, along with Missi and Larry, who had been her caretakers for the past few months.

"You made it. I can't believe it."

"Thank God, Mama. Thank God," I said through stifled tears.

"You always had my back, Kev. You were always my buddy.

She handed me a letter, kissed me, and said goodbye. The letter was a bit rambling, talking about religion, politics, and the importance of family. "You have a full life now. Use all your many powers for good."

She wasn't being melodramatic. Her spirit was ready to go. But her body had other ideas. It would be eight days before she closed her eyes and exhaled for the last time. The constants of those days made them run together: the Hallmark Channel playing on the television, Pentatonix's "Hallelujah" endlessly repeating on Spotify, and the aroma of Swanson's chicken broth—the only thing she could get down—warming in the microwave. Those sights and sounds still drop me through a trapdoor right to that time, and probably always will.

For Larry and me, it was like 1980 again. Bitter adversaries in small quarters. Every time I tried to help, he would block my interference. Even in his advancing age, and with a dying spouse in the home, he managed to get upset when a meal-delivery service we enlisted misspelled his name on the packaging.

"Tell them how to spell my fucking name!" he barked at me.

After going to the dispensary to procure Mom cannabis for her pain, he screamed, "There will not be drugs in my house!"

I bought Mom a massage chair and he said it was too noisy and wanted it removed, and he canceled the extra hospice care I provided because he didn't like the nurses. Fifty years on, it was still a competition, and all he saw in my place was a facsimile of Woody Valentine.

It all reached a fever pitch when Mom asked me for help one evening.

"Kev, I am really hurting. Can you get me the morphine?"

As I walked to the fridge, Larry blocked my path.

"You are not giving that to her without the doctors here."

"She asked me for it, Dad, and I am giving it to her."

"No, you are not."

I grabbed him by the arm and squeezed as hard as I could.

We weren't in the Little Blue House, and I wasn't a helpless little kid battling his father in basketball or chess with nothing on the line but ego. This felt like a fight for my mom's soul, for her love, for her allegiance.

"Get out of my way, or I will knock you the fuck out of the way."

He retreated to the bedroom and slammed the door.

A few days later, Mom asked me to accompany Larry to the mason who'd fashion her gravestone to make sure it was cut to her exact specifications. Larry still had trouble with those sorts of transactions, always believing people were trying to pull a fast one on him. In this case, he groused that all of the words we wanted on a particular stone wouldn't fit.

As I walked back into the house afterward, Mom looked up.

"How did that go?"

"About exactly how you think it went," I deadpanned.

We both laughed uncontrollably, the last occasion we'd have to do that.

Then she squeezed my hand and said, "I'm sorry."

We both knew how much the apology contained.

"It's okay, Mom."

WHILE I WAS TENDING TO Mom's needs, Rob had generously done his best to manage the havoc COVID-19 was inflicting on our business. By Saturday, March 14, there was no more shielding me—serious decisions had to be made. I spent that afternoon on the phone by Mom's bedside, discussing closing the entire company. As I spoke, I held Mom's hands and lost myself studying them. They were beautiful, but not dainty beautiful. They were beautiful in the story they told. They were hands that began milking cows on that farm in Roscommon, Michigan, in 1952, and were still making quilts for World Relief deep into the ravages of chemotherapy. And they were the way she conveyed love. Through her strong grip, through those warm hands, I could feel the love she had so much difficulty demonstrating.

When the calls were over, and we were alone, she said, "I'm pretty tired. I can't keep my eyes open."

She closed her eyes.

"Love you, kid," she said as she drifted off.

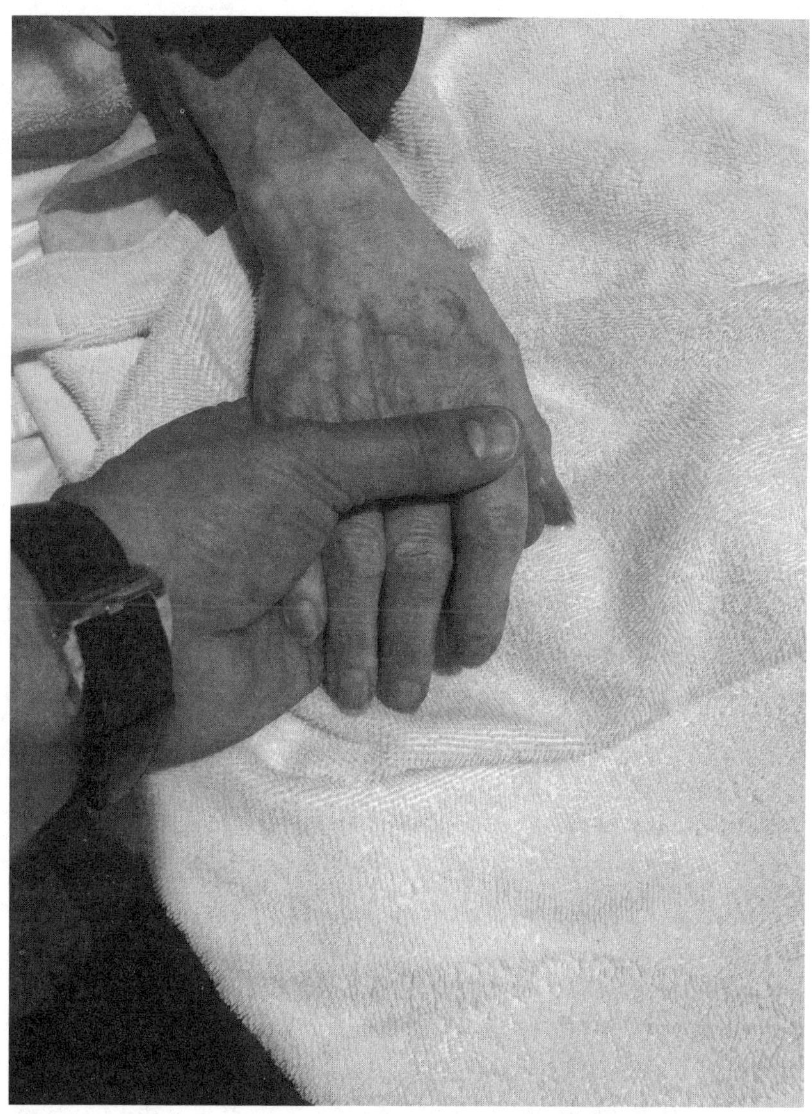

Holding Mom's hand for the last time

She opened her eyes one more time, but we never spoke again.

At 3:57 p.m. she took her final breath. I let go of her hands for the last time as I closed my eyes.

There was a limit to large gatherings due to COVID's rising tide, so we weren't permitted a funeral the following week. Fortunately, the night after she passed was also the last night restaurants were allowed to be open, so our family gathered at Indigo. The walls were still lined with her Blue Dog paintings. Larry cried the whole time.

At the end of the meal, Indigo's current owner Mike Novel approached our table.

"I am so sorry about your mom," he said. Then, glancing around the room, he asked, "Which one of her paintings was your favorite?"

"The blue dog in the poppy field," I said, remembering that conversation she and I had had about it.

"Well, it's going home with you tonight," Mike said. "To be with your family, where it belongs."

Mike's reflexive impulse to give comfort, and simply to give, is all you really need to know about true hospitality. It's what separates restaurateurs who serve customers from those who welcome guests.

BACK IN CHICAGO THE FOLLOWING Monday, the Boka Restaurant Group office felt equally funereal.

This was the first time I'd allowed the enormity of our business crisis to take precedence over seeing Mom out of this world. It was truly overwhelming: For a few hours, I had trouble articulating simple phrases, let alone making massive decisions.

Rob and I spent the next forty-eight hours temporarily dismantling our company. We had been in construction together for twenty years. Now we were in the de-struction business.

Leaving Indigo with one of Mom's paintings, the day after her passing, 2020

Just as there is no set playbook for coping with a death, there is no guide to running a company during a global pandemic. We were closing nineteen restaurants and furloughing 1,800 employees, an incomprehensible challenge compounded by the grief I was processing. I consciously funneled that energy into triaging the company's constantly shifting needs and keeping the organism alive and solvent.

Boka Restaurant Group ran with a payroll of approximately $3.5 million per month; rents were close to $800,000 per month, we had close to $2 million in accounts payable. The cost of keeping everyone insured was about $100,000 a month. And so stopping the spigot of cash flow put us instantly on life support.

For the next eighteen months, every move Rob and I made felt like the extraction of a block in some cruel, psychic game of Jenga. The trick was to safeguard the health of our team members and guests (once we were allowed to serve them again) while being fiscally responsible.

Rob and I each donated a six-figure amount to an employee relief fund, kept everyone's health insurance intact, sent Amazon care packages to furloughed employees in grave and immediate need, arranged food pickups for employees at both Swift & Sons and Girl & The Goat twice a week, and then tried to figure out how long we could stay above water. We kept our corporate officers and chef partners on board to help us navigate land mines along the way.

We asked our bank for a line of credit, and they gave us the maximum allowable according to their formulas. Cash-flow projections indicated a survival rate of four months. There was legitimate concern that we would not make it through, but I believed that, after Mom's example, we'd beat the forecast. We were too strong not to. Whether or not we'd survive in the longer run, I wasn't so sure.

There was so much noise in those first days that it was tough for Rob and me to know where to expend our limited time and attention. Within that noise there were myriad opinions about what the future of dining looked like, how restaurants should pivot, who deserves what type of relief or support, and—from a governmental viewpoint—to what degree restaurants were worth saving.

For me, and many others in my industry, it was hurtful. People spend some of the most important moments of their lives in restaurants. Plus we give so much: We give our all to making people happy. We participate in fundraisers and sponsor Little League teams. We assist our communities during natural disasters, serving food to the displaced and destitute. And we donate our surplus inventory to food banks and shelters. And now, in our moment of need, it was as if none of that mattered or even registered. I guess this is the danger of hospitality for those of us who practice it: If you're good at it, it feels personal. But most guests view it as strictly transactional, not as something akin to friendship. We're important to Mitch McConnell when he needs a primetime table for four on a Saturday night, but seemingly disposable when it comes to an existential crossroads.

Just days later, on March 18, a group of us decided that, rather than wait for the cavalry, we'd take matters into our own hands. Multiple chefs and restaurateurs set up a Zoom video call to start organizing an advocacy plan for independent restaurants.

Andrew Chasen, an agent at Creative Artists Agency (CAA); Sam Kass, former chef to President Obama; and Will Guidara initially got the ball rolling, as eighteen people, including myself, Tom Colicchio, Bobby Stuckey, Donnie Madia, Adam Saper, Andrew Zimmern, Naomi Pomeroy, Gregory Gourdet, Caroline Styne, and several others, started to hash out a plan.

The group, which would expand in the coming weeks and months, quickly morphed into a bona fide organization: the Independent Restaurant Coalition (IRC). For about a year and a half, we held almost daily Zooms, where operators around the country would not only work together to lobby, advocate, and plan, but also to build a support group for each member to lean on.

The Zoom background of each person was like a welcoming morning Hallmark card: Caroline sitting up in bed, Robert St. John at his mahogany desk, Will in his attic, and Bobby on the couch in front of a tropical painting. I, on the other hand, was more of a *Where's Waldo?* adventure, mixing it up almost every day.

It was a bit like an all-star game in the beginning, only with stakes and nerves as high as in the Super Bowl. It was an all-creatures-great-and-small venture, with everyone from the owner of a six-table diner to the chairperson of a behemoth restaurant group.

Our first and most complicated order of business was to seek and lobby for $180 billion for restaurant-relief grants. Everyone pretty much told us that we were crazy and to stand in line and mind our manners. I was about to see how the sausage got made in DC. It's a lot uglier than actual sausage.

As we saw it, the US government had bailed out companies and industries who had created their own emergencies. Chrysler, hobbled because the company failed to pivot to smaller fuel-efficient automobile production, received $1.5 billion in the late 1970s in what was a foreshadowing of the government bailout of the entire automobile industry. The airlines received federal assistance in both 2001 and 2020. And we famously threw life rafts to Fannie Mae and Freddie Mac during the subprime mortgage debacle.

Contrast that with the unique plight of restaurants during the pandemic. We bore no responsibility for the situation and were the second-largest private employer in the country, more than twelve times what the airline industry employs. (Because the industry comprises mostly small, independent businesses, this is easy to miss, but in the aggregate, we are a massive community.) So it was only fair, we thought, to imagine a similar carve-out for restaurants.

We raised some funding, hired a political PR team and some lobbyists, and presto chango, we all had new jobs.

Our first Zooms together were occasionally pretty awkward. Anytime you fill a room with super alphas used to running their own shows, there is a certain amount of frenetic energy generated by people talking over each other within the fight to be heard. There were a few screaming matches, which could be jarring, especially when you are watching chefs you've only known from television or Instagram tell someone to go fuck themselves. Tensions were high, bank accounts were dwindling, and there were many people on the IRC that were simultaneously helping to build a plan for all restaurants while holding on for dear life to their own. Some people sat back and listened, some would interject surgically, and others dominated the discussions with volume and frequency. After a few weeks, we all found some harmony and a rhythm.

In the beginning we thought of ourselves as a complementary arm to the National Restaurant Association. We internally thought that anything that gave independents a clear voice helped amplify them. We were certainly surprised when things got a bit combative with the NRA, and it felt like they were telling us to chill out and know our place, with a mob-like intensity. We would *both* be forced, in the end, to at least play nice in the sandbox as a divided industry could only hurt our cause.

If anything, the external conflicts and the treacherous road to getting a bill passed simply galvanized our team.

Master sommelier and restaurant legend Bobby Stuckey was our ace lobbyist. We would eventually coin the phrase "lobby like

Bobby." He applied his hospitality skillset—for example, researching guests—to charming lawmakers into submission.

Tom Colicchio and Andrew Zimmern put their prominent faces and voices to work as our mouthpieces in the media. Smart, fearless, and appropriately combative, either could take on Bill Maher or CNN or even Fox News and compellingly plead our case. Tom went a step further, playing Springsteen's "Youngstown" on an IRC call with a senator. After he finished crooning, the senator said, "Well, Kennedy got serenaded by Marilyn Monroe. Guess I got Tom Colicchio."

I did my own share of media, including interviews on CNN, MSNBC, and Fox News.

In June 2020, President Trump invited three members of the IRC to join a roundtable of restaurateurs at the White House in a room that would include the president, Treasury Secretary Steven Mnuchin, Jared Kushner and Ivanka Trump, and a few handpicked hospitality professionals.

We wanted and needed help, even though Trump's politics, especially with regard to immigration policy, were in direct opposition to many in the IRC leadership and the restaurant community as a whole. Trump, as we all knew, liked people to bend the knee and kiss the ring, and some of the people we planned to send were certainly not going to do that. After a deep dive into some of our members' politics on social media, the White House advance team nixed several of our suggested candidates that would have balanced both the gender, race, and ethnicity scales. In the end, a group of operators handpicked by the Trump Administration, three of them IRC members, made up a room that was 90 percent male and 90 percent white—certainly a poor reflection of the diverse restaurant community. The IRC would take some heat for that, but we decided it was worth it if the alternative was not receiving an audience with the president.

In the end, Will Guidara, Sean Feeney, and Thomas Keller represented the independent restaurants. Sean and Will called me from Pennsylvania Avenue from their car right before the meeting and asked for a quick pre-shift.

"You are representing everyone today, there are so many people out there that need your help. Remember them as you plead our case today. Last night on *The Last Dance*, Michael Jordan said, 'It only takes one match to start the fire.' Well, Sean, you are that match. And Will, you are the lighter fluid. Go light this shit up."

Will was the second speaker and in typical Will fashion, he killed.

"We represent the mom-and-pops, the local diner, the pizza place, the pasta place, the three-Michelin star restaurant, and everything else in between. The things that represent the cultural fabric of our cities and our towns, and the things, I think, as a country we need to fight to keep."

Although we didn't receive dedicated relief at this point, we were now in the conversation, and we started to see the articles, radio voices, and Instagram posts plead our case for isolated help. Like a dominant 1970s college football team, IRC had a great ground game. We were annoyingly persistent.

Personally, the IRC kept my world from rotating off its axis. Having something to concentrate on in the morning was a stimulant and a sedative.

Populated by people who'd been giving pre-shift for years, the IRC began ending each morning's Zoom session with a bookend post-shift. They were honest, raw, devastating, and inspirational. It was a place where we could all drop the veil of ego we lived with, constantly telling each other that our restaurants were so busy nobody could fit in the door, when the reality was that most of us were functioning with such tight margins that it was a wonder we slept at night.

Letting go of that illusion was the lifting of a crippling burden.

IT WAS A RARE DAY that I didn't speak to someone in tears. It was usually either an operator going out of business or someone on our management team who could no longer take the constant pivoting, fear, and dealing with the public. There was so much misinformation that it often weaponized those with very little context.

One morning in the fall of 2020 as I walked with my morning green tea outside our office, a random woman got in my face.

"You should not have your restaurants open," she scolded me.

"Excuse me?"

"You are choosing money over people, asshole."

I was so taken back that I just stood there dumbfounded.

If there was ever a ball with too much air in it, it was the restaurant business around that time. We had gotten to a point where people had turned their guns on the industry itself. One article suggested that all of the restaurants going out of business was a good thing. "Let's blow it all up," wrote the author.

I guess he got his wish. More than one hundred thousand independent American restaurants closed in 2020 and 2021. Three were from Boka Restaurant Group. We had a deal at a hotel with two restaurants where the fine print operating agreement was complicated. We would not get paid until the initial investment from the landlords was paid off, making it a sprint to profitability.

The pandemic began to dig a financial hole in our hotel deal that we were never going to get out of. Two million dollars in rent per year for the restaurants at the hotel started to accumulate debt like running water after a pipe burst. A clause in the lease allowed us an out, and we strategized on how to secure all the jobs of the staff with the hotel taking over as operators and accepting that staff with open arms.

However, the WARN Act was in play, an onerous law that required us to file that we were about to lay off "up to 500 employees" and give them notice, even though it was a formality. It didn't matter that technically we weren't laying off anyone. Legal filings often need context to find the real truth, and instead of fact-checking, the news just read "Boka Restaurant Group Could Lay Off 500 Employees."

The first comment I read on a Facebook share was "Fuck Kevin & Rob."

I wanted to mix it up with commenters and explain, but I knew it was futile.

Next, we closed Bellemore. Fine dining was getting hit harder than any either genre, and our pivot to jerk Caribbean chicken to go wasn't exactly setting Grubhub on fire.

We had a great celebration when the Restaurant Revitalization Fund passed in the House of Representatives. Many of us cried as we watched C-SPAN together that day. However, the legislation stalled in the Senate and never landed as a standalone bill. Ultimately, we had asked for $125 billion, and finally on March 6, 2021, almost one year after our first call, $28.6 billion in grant relief passed the Senate as part of the American Rescue Plan Act. This money would touch 177,000 restaurants across the country. The bill was signed into law by President Biden five days later.

My friend, the actor Michael Ealy, told me once about a play he was in years ago in New York City. The set of a basketball court on one side and a cramped apartment where an old man was watching the game on his TV on the other. As patrons entered the theater, the actors were doing warmup drills, putting on a show with choreographed dunks and layups. At the end of the play, it all comes down to a last-second shot with the super-fan old man losing his mind waiting for the outcome. At one performance,

Michael took the final twelve-foot jumper, made it, and everyone celebrated, including the old man watching from home.

Philip Seymour Hoffman was in the crowd that evening and waited for Michael outside the theater. When Michael exited, he saw Hoffman leaning against a light pole.

"What happens if you miss it?" Hoffman asked.

Michael replied, "It's a different ending."

"What's the other ending?"

Michael cracked a smile and said, "You have to come on a night when I miss."

Across one hundred performances, he didn't make the basket every time, but they were always prepared for both endings. Life, and certainly trying to operate restaurants during a pandemic, is not always that simple. In hospitality, there are innumerable variables. Some nights flirt with perfection; on others, a woman at Table 43 catches her hair on fire. Mishaps are inevitable and largely beyond our control; how we respond, though, is a choice. As Buddhist wisdom says, "Pain is certain; suffering is optional." I haven't evolved to that place yet, but we try always to be prepared for any ending. Hopefully, as we get older, we have more alternate endings at the ready.

Like many, we still struggled even as the industry overall was regaining its sea legs: BIÂN had opened in November 2020 and was hemorrhaging money, as it wasn't eligible for government relief because of its lack of sales history. Whatever wellness it was giving me, it was producing a greater amount of cortisol.

We were also building Girl & The Goat Los Angeles and paying rent during a time when we weren't allowed to open. All those plans we made pre-pandemic were now haunting us. The sense that the financial walls were closing in on me started to feel like suffocation.

I called my lawyer and publicist in the spring of 2021 and asked what my legal and PR issues would be if I walked away from it all.

"First of all, are you okay?" asked Harlan, my attorney of twenty years.

"No, I'm not."

Katy Darnaby, my crackerjack PR rep, tried to calm me.

"You don't owe anything to anyone. Do what you need to survive."

Two serene voices telling me that I could pack it in acted like a Xanax that night.

The truth was that I was contending with more than I could possibly explain to either of them. My feelings of failure were greater than they'd ever been. My business, my own success, and my responsibility to those who relied on me—everything I'd worked so hard to create for myself since venturing out from the Little Blue House—it was all crumbling, and I was all out of alternate endings.

13
SHELTER FROM THE STORM

THE MORNING I WOKE UP and decided to kill myself looked and felt like a lot of other mornings I'd experienced before. It was 80 degrees and sunny, I was in a hotel room in Los Angeles on the Sunset Strip, and the twelve drinks from the previous night were in full assault mode on my body. My liver was working overtime, trying to metabolize the toxins, desperately trying to excrete alcohol from my fatigued and weary frame, but it was my mind that was in real peril. If there is an American setting fade-in that screams loneliness and despair, this was it.

The sun streaming through the window, beating down hard on my pillow, prematurely woke me, and I checked my phone and saw fifteen unread texts. One of them was from someone sharing an anonymous blog hit piece on Boka. I had no idea who had written it, but it took some good shots at me, and I was in no shape to withstand the hits.

I couldn't concentrate at that point on what fucked-up part of my life needed the most attention. All the individual catastrophes had morphed into one giant impenetrable knot of problems. For the first time in my life, I hated my job, and the hatred of myself, a long-standing problem, had now reached a fevered pitch.

For thirty years, I had not been a day drinker, and I never drank hungover, but on that day, on that morning, I opened the complimentary bottle of Cabernet and put Jackson Browne's "For a Dancer" on repeat. It was the saddest song I could think of, and the lyrics, about being unable to find a lost love, represented me talking to a part of myself that I feared no longer existed. It had been a long time since I had seen the happy me. I was tired of this sad-sack-of-shit version.

I thought of the people I'd known who'd chosen suicide. In April 2015, Homaro Cantu, who I had just spoken to weeks prior, hanged himself in his restaurant. He had just organized a benefit dinner for Charlie Trotter's foundation, and we had talked about the many projects we both had in the works. He seemed adrenalized at the prospect of new adventures.

I never detected a trace of sadness. Evidently, he played that game just as convincingly as I did. Like many workaholic overachievers in the restaurant business, he could hide his inner turmoil under his work. This can be a gift. It can also be a curse. And the two aren't mutually exclusive.

Over the years, I served as the sounding board for many tortured souls both in my restaurants and outside of them. I was an effective amateur therapist because I knew whereof I spoke.

By 2022, I had lost an old Seaside chum and Indigo Wine Bar musician, one of my closest U of I fraternity brothers, and a frequent Chicago drinking buddy, all to suicide.

There was shock and great sadness each time, but never a lack of understanding. I was all too familiar with the concept of private despair, and each loss left me wondering if I'd come to a day where I myself would no longer be able to peer into the abyss without feeling the need to launch myself into it and disappear.

Jumping off a balcony seemed messy, and I didn't care for heights, but beggars could not be choosers. I didn't have the right pills to overdose on; nor did I have the patience or stomach for slitting my wrists with the dullish hotel wine knife. I sat on the floor of the balcony and started to write. A note for Cortney, and one for each of the kids. It took hours, and was excruciating, so I ordered a second bottle.

I didn't have great balance, so climbing up onto the railing in some ways meant no turning back. I got both feet secure and held on with both hands.

Just lift your hands and jump, Kevin, I thought. *It will be better.*

I unclenched my grip off the railing and was crying so hard that the shaking almost tumbled me off. I didn't want to look down, so I looked straight across.

Standing up partially straight, I took a deep breath as Jackson sang the chorus, and then . . . for the first time in hours the song stopped and my phone rang, startling me enough to reach back down to the railing.

As I looked in the distance, I saw my kids' faces. I cried even harder.

I stayed in a crouched position for a little while before awkwardly hopping off and lying on the concrete. I ignored the phone, reached inside the hotel room and grabbed a pillow off the couch, said a prayer, and passed out, ignoring the soft bed option, thinking the hard concrete was all I deserved.

When you wake up on concrete in a full flop sweat, you are not given that ten-second memory reprieve that you normally get when you wake up in your own bed. I instantly knew something awful had preceded my rough reentry.

"Fucking asshole," I screamed at myself. "How could you think about doing that? What is wrong with you?"

For all of you bipolar and depression nonbelievers, I didn't need to take vitamins or pick up a hobby. I wasn't desperate for the Lord, and I didn't require a kick in the ass or a self-help book. I couldn't outsmart it, outrun it, throw manic moments at it, or drink it under the table. There was something inherently and dangerously wrong with me. There was no way of looking at standing on a balcony railing as just a bad night.

Actual rock bottom is a supreme gift. All of those supposed rock bottoms before it were fucking pretenders.

My first step was to be honest. It took me fifty-two years to realize that throwing ambition at trauma was like Band-Aiding a bullet wound. Ambition can sometimes be an engine, and sometimes it's an anchor. I needed to move toward the light, but I was grounded by the hundreds of decisions that needed to be made daily. I was usually excellent at keeping secrets and I considered my time on the ledge as the embarrassment of embarrassments; if anyone was to find out, it would destroy the idea of me that I had spent years creating. However, I needed something to cease the onslaught of work communication, and I decided to go with the truth. Further, I was no longer interested in trying to justify my existence in the world. I just wanted to exist.

I sat with Rob and our C-Suite at Boka Restaurant Group and my partners at BIÂN and told them I was crumbling and that I needed space. I'm not sure if it fully landed, as I received multiple calls the next day.

I responded to each of them in a fairly serious tone: "Please leave me alone."

My next step was to book a hiking trip at the Ranch at Live Oak. It was a desperate attempt to Band-Aid things one last time.

I hiked twelve miles the first day at a furious pace, and on the second day, dehydrated and tired, I collapsed at mile ten and had to be carried off the mountain. As I lay in my small room getting medical attention, one of the hikers I'd bonded with on the hill came to see me.

I had been pretty real with him during our hike, and he gave me some tough medicine. "My sponsor told me something once and I think it might apply to you. The magic you are looking for is in the work you are avoiding."

No one sentence has ever hit me right between the eyes like that one did. There was work to be done, and I wasn't going to do it alone on a mountain or sitting on a beach in Mexico. It was time for real help.

I reached out to the therapist we had engaged to work with us at BIÂN. When we connected, I gave her ninety minutes of unvarnished truth, and it felt like removing a basketball-size tumor.

"I will set you up with a perfect therapist."

"No, no, no. I want you. I don't want to do this whole get-to-know-you thing again."

"That doesn't work, Kevin. We are working together."

I got really angry, feeling like someone just gave me an oxygen mask and then put a bag over my head.

"I promise you: I will find you the right person."

At that point, I didn't believe her. I was near hopeless, but willing to try everything to find the light. Fortunately, she was right.

I embarked on a kitchen-sink strategy to find my sanity, and it was intensive. There was an obligatory eye roll that often happened when I mentioned all the experimental things I was going to try. At a certain point, I thought it prudent to keep them to myself. It was one thing to be crazy, another to sound like I was.

Over the course of the next year, I stopped walking dining rooms for a spell; I did ayahuasca with sixteen strangers in the middle of nowhere with a shaman; I went on anxiety medication. I did two days a week with my powerful new therapist. I stopped drinking. I changed my sleep routine. I received energy clearings from my Chinese medicine doctor. And I went to the Hoffman

Institute, a deep-dive retreat that studied the psychological patterns of your life.

Hoffman was a one-week, no-bullshit, no-phones program that went from 7 a.m. to 10 p.m. every day. It was hard-ass work. It was not for the meek. Before I went, I read an article that reported Justin Bieber blew off Hoffman after just a few days.

As I got on the elevator to go downstairs before my trip, Lola looked at me and said, "Be better than the Biebs, Dad." I wasn't optimistic that I was better or stronger than anyone at that point, including a heavily tattooed pop star.

At the beginning of the week at Hoffman, an instructor recounted a teaching moment of their own. As he gave a lecture one morning, a student began to lean in with an intense look on their face. The instructor thought to himself, *I am killing this speech, look at him leaning in to grab all the power of my words.*

"Excuse me," said the student. "You have a big piece of spinach in your teeth."

Immediately they had gone from confidence to insecurity in the flash of a second.

This place gets me, I thought.

Often during the week at Hoffman, a therapist would draw a distinction between actual fathers and surrogate fathers. In my circumstance, a therapist swapped the usual model: Larry was my true father, she told me, and Woody was my surrogate.

Five days later, twenty-five of us were asked to close our eyes and lie on our backs. As I scooted myself to the center of the room, almost childlike, I was accompanied by a kind man in his mid-fifties, who ironically was also named Larry. "It's you and me, bro, let's get a perfect spot right in the center." Our Hoffman instructors darkened the room and asked us to open our eyes. The overhead skylight of the quaint guest house gave us a perfect starry night as John Lennon sang about world peace. Other Larry looked over and whispered, "I fucking love this place."

"Everyone is responsible, but no one is to blame," they told us.

"Holy crap, I love that," I told one of my instructors. "Is this the part where I stop blaming and start forgiving?"

"That's the idea," he told me.

It was the weirdest summer camp I'd ever attended. Hoffman is difficult, emotional, playful, cathartic, and the biggest surprise I had found in a long, long time. For most of the week I felt like I was twelve years old, my gaping wound of depression out for all to see, a subject matter to be poked, prodded, and discussed. As far as uncomfortable conversations go, it was a week of the most awkward I could think of.

The beauty is, no one knows who you are, like the thieves in *Reservoir Dogs*. They only knew me as Kevin, someone troubled enough to come to Hoffman. There was no backstory, no one asking restaurant questions. All our conversations were Hoffman related.

"I might not want to lose my patterns," another attendee said to me one day. "I think my negative patterns are the key to my success."

It was like I was talking to myself twenty years ago.

"That's certainly a theory and a choice," I told her. "But if the keys to success at this point are also the drivers of my depression, I no longer care about the so-called success. I think you should think about that for your own sake. You are here for a reason."

"Thanks, Dad," she said jokingly.

I had walked in overproduced, overchoreographed, and riding a fake smile that felt like a Herculean lift every time I flashed it. I was on an epic run of waking up sad and going to bed angry. I went from skeptic to ambassador in just a few days. Hoffman, at least temporarily, had stopped the madness. I would leave Connecticut with what they call "the Hoffman High."

Unlike my manic highs all these years, this one would stick.

They tell you all week that you are not your patterns, and if you believe them, you are left at the end of the week with all those coats of varnish stripped off. What if the actual you is the exact opposite of the role you have played all these years? Will you feel a bit stupid when it dawns on you? Maybe for some, but as I drove away that morning, I just felt grateful.

As I took this new Kevin for a spin, it would get a myriad of responses, not all of them good. Everything from people being worried about me to missing the old version. After not drinking for an extended period of time after I got home, I had some tequila at a friend's birthday. As I grabbed and downed a shot of reposado, she grabbed my face.

"You are drinking again! I love drunk Kevin."

I looked her deep in the eyes, and responded in a tone that was as serious as I could make it. "Most people love drunk Kevin, but you know who hates him? Drunk Kevin."

I had six main emotional rooms in my life that were all going through a gut rehab: my relationships with myself, my friends, my work life, my marriage, my kids, and the things I did outside of all that which replenished me. By late summer in 2022, at least four of the six had been knocked down to the studs. I had lived the last thirty years on construction sites, and now it was me in construction.

There were parts of me that were going to be demo-ed forever.

THE REST OF THE WORLD doesn't stop when you are having a crisis.

For the first time in thirty years, I took my eye off the ball for a little while.

It's almost impossible to be successful at restaurants without an obsessive eye to detail. As your company gets bigger, this is a collective effort. Within that change, if you move your intentional sail just two degrees, you might end up in a completely different place.

With new leadership often come new opinions and new styles. We added many positions to Boka in 2022, including a new vice president, directors, a chef partner, marketing and HR positions, as well as some financial strategy folks. One of the problems of playing divide and conquer is that a lot of communication can get lost. More than any other period in our history, the terrain was rough, and our success was spotty. Sometimes figuring out what doesn't work is just as powerful as success, and for us 2022 was a necessary learning tool. I wasn't the only one having a sobering experience.

In an eighteen-month stretch, we opened seven new restaurants. One of those seven restaurants would end up failing, and it was a hard pill to swallow. Whether you are a manic depressive or the healthiest guy on the planet, closing a new restaurant stings like a bitch.

I hold a thirty-seven wins and three losses record in my restaurant life, but it's the three losses that stick with you. It had been twenty-three years since my shellacking in Nashville, and this time I didn't need to play failure detective. I knew the buck stopped at the top. If the restaurant itself doesn't resonate, playing the game of who fucked up the most is just nonsense.

Anyway, I was in a rebuilding kind of mood. Fuck it, let's change everything in my life.

I had been taught at an early age in sports that playing with a chip on your shoulder was an effective way to create functional adrenaline. Playing life with a chip on your shoulder, however, can produce short-term gains and long-term deficiencies. In its most elevated sense, it's Steve Jobs, a man who loved products more than people because of the love he never received from his real parents, and in its most innocuous sense, it's a small-town chip on your shoulder, causing you to tell people your résumé before they even asked.

I had a bit of both of those. My burden now was: Could I operate just as successfully without that massive chip?

For twenty-five years I had been trying to feel that same high that I did at Indigo during the opening in Springfield. It was at this moment I was going to stop chasing it. If I could find some legitimate peace and balance through the work, then, wow, that would be pretty righteous. I was no longer swinging for the fences. I just wanted to hit a ground-rule double, one that allowed me to cruise into second base.

A part of me died on that balcony that evening, a part that I wanted to leave in that hotel room. As I began 2023, my entire being was different. I was quieter, stronger, and less distracted.

Some people come of age at eighteen, some when they get married, and some when they have a child. For others the moment occurs after a near-death experience, sometimes even one of their own making.

14
BOTH SIDES NOW

EVERYONE SHOULD WRITE THEIR OWN life story. If you can be patient, possess a detailed mental time machine, are willing to fact-check with ghosts, and are able to shit-kick yourself when necessary, it's a smorgasbord of self-awareness. You might also tell a story that shows a version of you that no one else knows, or even more importantly, discover the authentic you for the first time.

I've been the happy sad guy for most of my time on earth, and the hiding of that, the lack of care of it, almost cost me my life. If you like your morning coffee with a morning purge of truth, it can be quite meditative for you.

At times during this autopsy of the past, I hated the version of me I was writing about, but there were other moments that I looked at with wide-eyed amazement, empathy, astonishment, and forgiveness.

I see clearly that my need for love and reassurance, which I often cringe at now, fucked me up in a perfect way to be a restaurateur. I wanted so badly for my restaurants to be the antithesis of the sad Little Blue House, and for a couple decades I bled for that to be true. It put me at war with myself, and many times that ambition got in the way of me being a well-rounded human, which cost me a lot of sleep, my sanity, and ultimately my marriage.

Cortney and I both became very different people throughout our twenty-year journey together, and although I believe our time together was meant to be, our new iterations had stopped making each other happy. In the words of songwriter Dave Mason, "There ain't no good guy, there ain't no bad guy / There's only you and me, and we just disagree."

Cortney told me once, "You're never boring, but you're no picnic." She wasn't wrong.

Divorce, as I was quick to find out, is not linear and can leave you befuddled, angry, confused, and answerless. It is a journey that will take you twenty steps backward in order to eventually move forward. This much I do know: If I were to pick anybody to partner with in parenthood, it would still be her.

In retrospect, I wish I had been better at marriage. The institution, like life, is a practice, and if you are not constantly working at it, it will work you. I never saw a real marriage growing up, so it was an uphill climb for me, and I did a lot of falling along the way.

Cort and I separated in the spring of 2023. Telling the kids was as heart-wrenching as anything either of us had ever experienced. The loneliest walk of my life was the one leaving that night.

I'VE SPENT A GREAT DEAL of the last year, as my friend Dennis puts it, "cleaning up my side of the street." There was much to do, including establishing a closure with Larry, that I hoped would leave both of us all right.

I was reluctant to make the first move, but then a blast from the past gave me another reason to return home. Chris Blisset, my eight-year-old buddy who almost died in that car accident back in 1978, sent me a friend request on Facebook.

"You were only seven at the time," he wrote to me in a direct message. "But thank you for your efforts on the day of my accident. I remember asking you what happened because I have no memories of that day until the emergency room. And I recall that the two of you told me not to cross and I did anyway. You had a calm even in those days that I didn't. Thank you, brother. I will be in Springfield to perform, as I am a touring musician. I would love to see you."

Perhaps, I thought, it was time to tie up some loose ends.

I decided to visit Larry for what I thought would be one last time. I went into it steeling myself against any disappointment in the end result. I had no idea what to expect, having not spoken to him in the twenty-four months since Mom's funeral, but I called him up.

"Hey, Dad. I thought about driving to Springfield tonight. Want to grab some Saputo's?"

"I don't know," he grunted. "I am pretty tired."

Saputo's was a local institution that he was usually unable to resist.

"Come on, one quick dinner. You love lasagna, and you will be in bed before the nightly news."

"All right," he said quietly.

The trek from fear and anger to love and forgiveness is longer than the two hundred miles from Chicago to Springfield. I wanted to figure out how to leave things in a neat and orderly place. I wondered if I could tell him things without actually saying them. I wanted him to know that I was all grown up, that I forgave him, and that the past no longer moved me like it did before.

We dined at a restaurant almost as old as him, and as I followed him to our table, I no longer saw a nemesis. As he struggled to get into his seat, I watched a sad, elderly man who I hardly knew sit across from me.

The truth was that he barely knew me, either.

Two strangers, indelibly connected by a wife and a mother, bound by a secret we both endured but never spoke about. The universe had dealt us a bad deck of cards, and maybe we both could finally stop being punitive and cease blaming each other for one evening.

"That small cabin that was my dad's, in Michigan, do you think you could help me sell it?" Larry asked. It was the first time in fifty years that he'd implied that he trusted me with something. I think Larry was trying to show me that he respected my intellect in a symbolic gesture. "You are good at that stuff; it will just make me crazy," he said.

I was sure that Mom was there with us. She adored "Here's That Rainy Day," by Sinatra, and it played as I ordered tiramisu. Just the idea that Mom might be DJ'ing made me smile.

"You remember this one, Dad? It's the one Bette Midler sang with Carson on his last show."

"Oh yeah, your mother liked this one."

As we drove home from the restaurant, I felt like a thief trying to get away from a robbery unscathed. Three hours without a fight might have been our record. Our relationship had always been like deactivating a bomb—you had to keep a steady hand and no sudden moves.

As I dropped him off after a quiet ride, I got out and hugged him for the first time in years.

It was awkward, but it wasn't forced. Through the living-room window as I drove away, I saw the space where Mom took her last breath. She always prayed that we would be kinder to each other. That night, she got her wish.

THE NEXT MORNING, I WENT from a fractured relationship to one that had never really had a chance. Chris was still Chris: red hair, freckles, and boundless energy. It was hard to believe that under his T-shirt was a forty-five-year-old scar that ran from belly button to sternum. He was standing at the front door of Butler

Elementary School speaking to our former second-grade teacher, Mrs. Van Pelt. It was 1978 all over again. Chris was on a healing journey of his own.

We walked the same path we did the day of the accident, and talked openly about our childhoods in our respective little houses, and how it affected the trajectory of our lives. We both did everything we could in those days to be out of the house, chasing fun, chasing peace, trying to figure out how fast we could ride our bikes away from our combustive households.

The similarities in our circumstances, it turns out, didn't end at high school graduation. Chris's family saga rivaled my own. He had three paternal figures: one biological, one adoptive, and one surrogate. The biological dad met a tragic self-inflicted end. Chris's mother had left him for another man a few years after Chris's accident. One night, his dad jumped in his car in a jealous rage to find her and perished in a one-car accident.

I shared my own trials and tribulations with him as well.

"I am sorry you went through all that, brother," Chris said.

"You too, my man. I feel like we helped each other without even knowing it."

We hugged. It was forty-five years overdue.

AS 2023 ROLLED ON, I began to navigate both life and restaurants completely differently.

I'm not sure it's made me better at restaurants, but it sure as hell made me better at life. I was no longer finding energy from crowds, aspirations, or putting on a show.

I had been looking for love in restaurants for three decades, and it's been quite the education. When you figure out that most of the world is not in fact rooting for you, the disappointment is so profound that it can make you question everything that you thought was true.

I had believed in a linear ascent: work hard, gain respect, move the ball forward, achieve ultimate happiness. It doesn't quite work that way, but there is a lot of beauty in the way that it actually does work.

That love I was looking for didn't end up happening in a full dining room; it happened decades later in an empty one. Amid my recovery period, I had spent a month at our first New York restaurant, Laser Wolf, a collaboration with Michael Solomonov and Steven Cook.

I would have my green tea in the morning at Jack's Wife Freda in Brooklyn, practice yoga in a cramped neighborhood studio, get a straight razor from my guy Miguel at an old-school barbershop, and then I would travel to our Laser Wolf rooftop, with epic views of the Manhattan skyline. I would sit alone, melodic music in the background, and just defragment. My new medication had changed my chemistry a bit. The morning barrage of irrational anxiety I had played mental ping-pong with for decades was in remission, and so even at this frantic opening, it felt like rest. Dare I say I was laser focused.

My life was never simpler than in those few weeks, and I found something interesting in all the silence of those days. I wasn't thinking about what was next. I was just soaking up everything around me.

Three weeks after we opened, on a random Tuesday, our dining room was filled with food royalty: At one table, Ruth Reichl, whose reviews I dreamily read every week back at Lazy Daze, was dining with Kate Krader, food editor of *Bloomberg*; at another, Dana Cowin, former editor of *Food & Wine*, was sitting adjacent to Amanda Kludt, national editor of *Eater*; and at a corner table was Yotam Ottolenghi, the acclaimed Israeli chef whose cookbooks can be found on shelves around the world. All were communing over warm pita and salatim.

In my office back in Chicago, in a small frame above my desk, was a copy of Ruth's review of Union Pacific. I always loved it for its humor, its sharp writing, and the fact that I had actually dined there. As I touched Ruth's table, I told her about it.

"Why do you have that on your wall?"

"Because I love the writing."

"'The woman at the next table is moaning,'" she said, quoting her first line of the review.

"That's the one," I said, laughing.

At the end of the evening, as I brought them their soft-serve finisher, I also delivered the fries she loved so much to use as a dipper.

As I came back through the dining room, she grabbed me by the arm.

"This time, it's me that's moaning."

Serving Ruth was always the pinnacle for me, the dream of dreams, the ultimate guest that I wanted to impress. It had been almost thirty years since reading her first reviews in the *Times* in Seaside, a round-trip flight from humble beginnings. I came home revitalized, my cup at least temporarily filled.

And then, I disappeared from the front of house. I spent almost a year working quietly behind the scenes. I was parenting, getting used to a new home, further developing Boka and BIÂN, going to one-on-one meetings, and doing lots of spreadsheets. Dining rooms, however, were not part of my life.

When reality has been chaos all your life, living a normal life feels like a mind-fuck for a while.

I went from wanderlust to fixed in the blink of an eye. I had never been comfortable at home before, but I now clung to it like a life preserver. I took great pleasure in building my place from scratch, choosing items with intention that meant something to me to hang on the walls, place on my desk, and display on my coffee table. It was a new weird reality, this domesticity, a shade I have never worn before.

I threw a dinner party in 2024 and harnessed all my hospitality superpowers within my new condo. I booked the Chicago Children's Choir to serenade the group between courses three and four, gave each attendee a historic quote that I thought spoke to their character, and chose a fictional character that embodied their personality and made it part of their individual menu. I had never let my two personas—Restaurant Me and Home Me—bleed into each other before; like the two incarnations of Demi Moore's character in *The Substance*, only one had ever been allowed out at a time. It was a bit like a plastic surgeon throwing a wet T-shirt contest, but I quickly found out that harnessing my skills to delight the people I loved gave me even more pleasure than doing it for strangers. It was time to bury all the bad models the Little Blue House had shown me and start creating a new paradigm for the sake of me and my children. At last, I was comfortable in my own skin and in my own home.

I made some new friends. They never knew the twisted me, and I didn't have to convince them that this new version wasn't a passing fad. When I'm with them, it's like I've switched schools in the middle of the school year, and I got to completely reinvent myself.

I've never spent so much time alone in my life, an exercise that has fast-tracked me to getting to know who I really am. It's like driving a new car, but I am still getting used to all the new features on this model. It's slower and blends in with the traffic, but it never breaks down. I'm like a gray '94 Volvo, cruise control set to an easy-breezy fifty-five miles per hour.

FOR CHRISTMAS ONE YEAR, MY kids bought me glasses that help color-blind people like me see in color. What they didn't know is that they had already accomplished that. Life was more vivid seeing it through their eyes. They are both teachers and students, and, in a way, my GPS. They've kept me from getting lost a few times.

They have only known the truth about my childhood for a few years. When they were little, Sofia and Lola saw a young picture of Woody on my iPad as they were going through old pictures and asked, "Dad, who's that guy that looks just like you?"

I wasn't ready at that point to explain it, still trapped by a secret I thought I was supposed to keep. "That's one of your great-uncles," I said, gliding through a white lie with confidence.

They were pretty unfazed once I did tell them. Luca thought it was cool that his grandpa had been a boxer. Lola wanted to know about his service in World War II.

"That makes a lot of sense," Sofia said, having recognized the sharp physical differences between Larry and myself.

I've lived most of my life to a soundtrack, part of which is the curated playlists that echo throughout my restaurants, but it's also accompanied by a symphony of sounds that include joyous conversation, the clanging of pans, the shaking of cocktails, and the demonstrative voice of a chef at the pass. Occasionally, a server or guest drops a piece of silverware, mid-song, which is the symphonic equivalent of the first-chair cellist hitting a sour note. Thirty years after my first restaurant, and forty restaurants later, it remains my least-favorite sound.

I can imagine similar sounds from offices throughout history: the wood-pecking rhythm of typewriters at the *Washington Post* in the 1970s, or that *Trading Places*–like frantic roar of a 1980s trading pit in the NYSE. I have no doubt that others found and find that same comfort in their industry-specific sounds as I do. The rush of a dining room has always been my opiate, and for years it was the reason I woke up in the morning.

The most important people in my world: Lola, Luca, and Sofia

However, from 2017 through the pandemic, the alchemy of a busy restaurant stopped sounding like music and just came out as noise.

I love the quote from author James Clear that says "We do not rise to the level of our goals, we fall to the level of our systems." I believe there is so much truth in this, and to my company as a whole, it rings true. However, my execution was always moved the most by how much love and connection I felt. I rose to the level of my love.

IN THE SUMMER OF 2024, I got a text from Missi: *Dad went into cardiac arrest last night and had no pulse for seven minutes. They revived him, but he is not doing well.*

I drove down and met Missi at Larry's house before heading to the hospital.

In the middle of the kitchen island was a stack of yellow-lined paper, with a Post-it on it that read: "Missi, make sure Kevin reads this."

The little house on the west side of Springfield had seen better days. There was a small makeshift bed on the floor near the fireplace with a tattered comforter and a forty-year-old pillow with stuffing that no longer provided much support.

Larry had hundreds of Post-it notes sitting around his house, but at this moment I could only concentrate on one.

The letter was on the same kind of yellow-lined paper on which I had received all my lists and edits from Larry in my childhood years. The similarities stopped there. This was not an admonishment but a final plea for forgiveness.

The first couple of pages were rough drafts and edits. Perhaps he left them in there to show that he toiled to find the words.

"I'm not good at communicating," he wrote. "I know this. I'm especially bad at writing, but I haven't talked to you in a while, so here goes nothing. You don't talk to me anymore and I know it's all my fault. I'm sorry. I know I don't even know your kids and I wish I would have done things differently. Please don't shut me out. I'm so lonely. The morning of Mom's funeral, seeing you walk around the corner with your beautiful family was both the happiest and saddest moment of my life."

A man who had recently told all of us that all he really wanted to do was die had almost gotten his wish. However, the universe had decided he needed a little more time, or perhaps it decided we still needed a moment.

I read the letter a few times as Missi drove me to the Memorial Hospital ICU.

As we entered, Larry looked right at me.

"Kev, I am so glad you are here," he said as he started to cry.

I wiped his nose for him as Missi walked out to give us a moment.

"You and I are okay, Dad. I forgive you, and I'm sorry too."

I took a long pause, and then pushed three words out of my mouth with strained effort, like I was trying to throw a curveball with a broken arm.

"I love you."

The last time I'd said this to him, I was a little boy.

The three powerful words I couldn't give Woody. I wasn't sure if it was real or if it was a gift, but I knew it was what he needed to hear.

Death seemed imminent, but there would be no rushing Larry Boehm.

After Larry was discharged, he went into the hospice unit at Concordia Lutheran. It was the first time I had ever seen him clean-shaven. He looked nothing like the man I grew up with.

Most people have an intuitive sense of when someone does not like them. I learned these verbal and nonverbal cues from Larry. In my last few visits with him, it felt like his tune had somehow changed. Perhaps he liked my quiet version more, maybe the seven minutes without oxygen to his brain had altered his memory and he had forgotten our tense backstory; but more likely, he had just been given some clarity.

He was no longer thinking about bills, the yard, the dog, the irrational impending doom he saw around every blind corner. In that clarity, maybe, just maybe, he saw a son.

Larry was tough, petulant, obsessive, and stern. He was also responsible, dependable, and hard-working.

I was always sure that no one ever really got to know him, but through four years of thought, research, and time travel, perhaps I did.

As he took his final breath, a wave of sadness rushed over me. He was eighty years old. It seemed like a life unlived, a life unexplored, and so many opportunities unfulfilled.

THE DAY OF DAD'S FUNERAL blew up a few tightly wound narratives that I had held my entire life. In my mind, Larry had little use for laughs and didn't possess a romantic bone in his body. This day would be about saying goodbye, mourning a life, and gleaning fresh insights into the mind of Larry Boehm.

His secretary of twenty years greeted me at the church. "Kevin, I am so sorry for your loss. Your father was a serious man, I don't need to tell you that. Be he also had a great sense of humor sometimes."

"Do tell," I said.

"Well, one day we were at lunch together at McDonald's and I accidentally grabbed the wrong sandwich, your dad's Quarter Pounder. I started eating it. He called me out and we had a good laugh. The next day when I walked into work, he had put a Hamburglar magnet on my filing cabinet."

"You have to be kidding me!" I cracked up.

I found my sister immediately and told her the revelation.

"Dad was funny?" she asked.

Later that day, among Larry's possessions, Missi and I found a picture he had given our mom in 1965. On the back he had written:

You have given me a whole new outlook on life, and a will to live for higher principles. You are, to me, an inspiration. Your love has warmed my heart and quickened my pulse. You are to me THE girl. You are my very best friend in life.

FOR TWENTY YEARS I HAVE been writing a to-do list every Monday. One column lists the things I have to accomplish that week and a second lists long-terms goals. As my company got bigger and those lists got longer, the balance of things that I've got to do and the things that I get to do shifted so much that I barely recognize the job that I originally signed up for.

One gloomy Monday morning, instead of writing my weekly list, I wrote a list of things that I loved in this world as an inspirational pick-me-up. It was a random list of the serious and the frivolous, highbrow, lowbrow, and everything in between: Haribo gummy bears, Van Morrison's *Astral Weeks*, a perfectly made spicy tako hand roll, the sound of my kids' laughter, driving on the highway at night, and the smell of buttered popcorn. The list had no particular order, but eventually drifted into entries that had framed my work life for almost three decades: walking a dining room to Miles Davis's *Kind of Blue*, spitballing ideas with my teams, the adrenaline rush of a full dining room, table-side chats with guests, and pre-shift.

I still loved my job; I just didn't love how I was working it.

As I walked the dining room of Laser Wolf one recent Saturday, I heard a familiar song and started to sing the lyrics. I poured water at Table 201, high-fived the chef as I went by the kitchen, and then the chorus of the song hit. I looked out at the skyline on our rooftop and closed my eyes. I could hear all the individual glorious sounds. Bill Withers chanted "Lovely Day" as Chef asked for hands to run food and a server described individual salatim (vegetable preparations) that accompanied the pita at the table next to me.

It wasn't noise; it was the symphony.

Now that I've opened up about my own depression, it seems like a week doesn't go by where I don't talk someone off their own ledge. I think this is my purpose in my life. Hospitality has a broader definition to me now. If it's only reserved for within the four walls of restaurants, was it even real in the first place? In my opinion, it's never been harder to be happy, and I want to take my new skills and use them beyond Boka and BIÂN. I'm the same guy at the table and at my home these days. The avatar me has been retired.

If you struggled with your identity at a young age, like I did, there is a good chance you tinkered with creating an alternative you. The avatar I built over the years had a happy childhood, was mentally strong, was perpetually Zen, and always woke up ready to attack the day. I was like a method actor, so deep in my role that I didn't know the difference between the avatar and the real me. Dropping that character felt like losing a one-thousand-pound weight. I'm deeply imperfect, but I'm 100 percent me these days, and I'm 100 percent okay with that.

I'm so glad I hung on that night in Los Angeles. There is so much beauty in my kids, in my dining rooms, on the streets of Chicago, in the multicolored wonderland that is my life. My friend list is not as big as it used to be, but my curated group means so much more. They are the ones who understood the real me, even when I didn't.

The last thing I think about these days is more. The things I have in my life, the people, the projects, are beyond enough. For the first in my life, no refill is necessary.

In the end, I was wrong when I said, "I wasn't Kevin Boehm." I am a strange—but happy—mixture of Dee, Woody, and yes, even Larry. But also, and more importantly, I am the sum of everyone I have ever met, and at fifty-four years old, I realize that everyone was responsible, but no one is to blame.

ACKNOWLEDGMENTS

MOM: I WISH YOU COULD have gone on this journey with me and could have met the man I became through it. I got to know you all over again during this book journey, and what a gift that is. You are still my hero.

Missi Grubb and Ray Grubb: I love you both so much! Missi, my sweet sister. You are the kindest person I've ever met! You are the one true living witness to much of this book, and your warm heart was often a soft landing after tough times.

Larry and Woody: I know you both did the best you could. I forgive you both, and I'm sorry for my part in our fractured relationships. If your spiritual landing place features a window onto my current life, I hope it makes you proud.

Will Guidara: Thanks for the trampoline-toss commentary, laughs, brainstorming, feedback, and constant inspiration, but most of all thanks for the loyalty and friendship. I love you.

Ollie Petit: Thanks for thirty years of genuine friendship. You are my Belgian brother and emotional doppelgänger. If I had to pick one front-of-the-house guy to charm the pants off a table, it would always be you. I love you so much.

Joe Fisher: Our friendship picked up steam late in life, and what a joy it's been. "Are you losing this case, Mr. Fisher?" The answer is an emphatic no. To the future and BIÂN.

James Belletire: You are my oldest friend and have produced more laughs in my life than everyone else combined. You are the closest thing I have to an actual brother! You are a fine Irish boy!

Rob Katz: What a ride it's been! Through forty restaurants we have seen each other at the highest of highs and lowest of lows. I couldn't have picked a better partner. You are brilliant at so many things. Thanks for all the adventures, friendship, and memories.

Scott Alderson: You are a great man, a great chef, and a great friend with the largest of hearts. Your selfless drive to Springfield that night changed my life.

Dennis Ongkiko: I know you are on a similar journey to me, and you're walking uphill right now. I promise you that the trip down the other side is worth it. I hope more people hear your music; your talent cup runneth over.

Frank Galvin: Thanks for the phone calls, mentorship, edits, advice, work sessions, and brilliance. The fact that pop culture minutia occupies 72 percent of our brains sounds like an issue, but you and I both know it's a blessing. "There is no other case. This is the case."

Ben Weprin: You have the swagger of Jordan, the enthusiasm of Magic, the work ethic of Bird, and the small-town charm of Jimmy Chitwood. Thanks for all the laughs and deep conversations.

David Black, my literary agent: You told me four years ago that you believed in me, my story, and my writing, long before you had proper evidence of any of the three. I can't tell you how much that meant and still means.

Jamison Stoltz, editorial director, Abrams Press: Thank you for your belief in this project, your kindness, and your talent!

P.A.: You may never know or care how close your words came to nudging me off that ledge. I didn't know it at the time, but it was a gift. Fuck you and thank you.